Setting the Truth Free

First published in 2012 by
Liberties Press
Guinness Enterprise Centre | Taylor's Lane | Dublin 8
Tel: +353 (1) 415 1224
www.libertiespress.com | info@libertiespress.com

Trade enquiries to Gill & Macmillan Distribution
Hume Avenue | Park West | Dublin 12
T: +353 (1) 500 9534 | F: +353 (1) 500 9595 | E: sales@gillmacmillan.ie

Distributed in the UK by
Turnaround Publisher Services
Unit 3 | Olympia Trading Estate | Coburg Road | London N22 6TZ
T: +44 (0) 20 8829 3000 | E: orders@turnaround-uk.com

Distributed in the United States by
Dufour Editions | PO Box 7 | Chester Springs | Pennsylvania 19425

ISBN: 978-1-907593-37-6
2 4 6 8 10 9 7 5 3 1
A CIP record for this title is available from the British Library.

Cover design by Sin É Design
Internal design by Liberties Press
Printed by CPI Group (UK) Ltd, Croydon, CR0 4YY

JULIEANN CAMPBELL

Setting the Truth Free

The Inside Story of the
Bloody Sunday Justice Campaign

To all those who campaigned for truth and justice and to the memory of all those they fought for — the fallen and wounded of Bloody Sunday.

For my mum and hero, Susie Duddy . . .
A constant inspiration.

Contents

[acknowledgements]

This book would not have been possible without the generous assistance and support of many. Primarily, I wish to thank all those who lost someone on Bloody Sunday and all who survived and spoke with me at great length about these deeply personal experiences. Collectively, they helped me understand the true extent of the events of 30 January 1972 and the reasons why the Bloody Sunday Justice Campaign was so important. I only hope this book does your story justice.

Also to their fellow campaigners, supporters, lawyers and politicians who gave so freely of their time to speak with me about their involvement. This, too, is their story.

I am indebted to my colleagues in the Bloody Sunday Trust – who commissioned me to undertake this project. Thanks to them for their advice, faith and encouragement and for their contribution to this book. Also to Adrian Kerr and all at the Museum of Free Derry for their support and permitting me access to their invaluable archive of material relating to Bloody Sunday and the campaign.

I am deeply grateful to Conal McFeely, Joan and all at Creggan Enterprises and Ráth Mór for providing a quiet space in which to write and with the financial assistance to do so – thank you.

To Sean McLaughlin, who helped me delve into the vast *Derry Journal* archives and whose advice helped me shape both the style and the substance of the book; and to Eamonn McCann, Chair of the Bloody Sunday Trust, for consistent advice, passion, and his skilled proofreading of its final chapters.

To all my colleagues and friends at the *Derry Journal* who have supported me throughout this project and to my editors and management who gladly granted me leave to work on it and free reign of the *Derry Journal* archives. I appreciate it so much. Thanks also to An Cultúrlann for hosting the launch in Derry, and to Gareth Peirce for her insightful foreword.

For sound advice, my thanks to Paul Hippsley and all at Guildhall Press; the Irish Department of Foreign Affairs; all at Derry Scriptwriters Group and the University of Ulster CAIN website. I am also grateful to Deputy First Minister, Martin McGuinness and Dominic Doherty of the Derry Sinn Féin office and MP Mark Durkan and the Derry SDLP office.

To Christopher and our darling daughter, Saffron, who showed such overwhelming patience and love as the words consumed me. To my mum, Susie and my four brothers, Paul, Alan, Peter and David – thank you for everything. To the Duddys, especially my auntie Kay and uncle Gerry – who campaigned on behalf of the whole family and never gave up hope that the truth would be set free.

To Aisling Starrs, for her superb listening skills since this journey began, Mama Cass and all my friends for being there throughout. Thanks to all the photographers who permitted me to use their work in the book – Stanley Matchett, Hugh Gallagher, Robert White, Stephen Latimer of the *Derry Journal* for the author photo, Charlie McMenamin, the *Derry Journal* archives, Colman Doyle and the National Library of Ireland.

To Seán, Dan, Caroline and all at Liberties Press, Dublin – thank you for believing in an idea and seeing it through with foresight and passion. Lastly, to my daddy, Pat 'Soup' Campbell, and my granddad Johnny Campbell, from whom it seems I inherited a love of language and enough eloquence to express it.

[foreword]

In the same year that this record of an extraordinary campaign goes to press, the international community has mobilised to support protestors gunned down by ugly regimes in Libya, Egypt, Tunisia and Syria. In 1972 there was no such aid for the people of Derry; all they had was themselves. The very act of protest had been transformed into a crime. The engines of the British state pumped out an immediate false narrative, endorsed by the Lord Chief Justice of the day. There was no one, absolutely no one, to turn to. And yet not one sane individual of power or influence chose to comprehend the most basic proposition; that criminal state action would fuel reaction. The murders and the narrative that supported the murders, would fuel an armed conflict for decades.

The families of those who died achieved the impossible, compelling the state to pick up the mirror, to recognise itself and finally admit its guilt. The crimes that were committed against those who died were never meant to be exposed to any just scrutiny; there was only ever meant to be one narrative and in the absence of a root and branch revolution it would be thought impossible to shift a false state narrative. That is why what was accomplished by the Bloody Sunday families is so extraordinary and important for others; as the ship of the British state sails on, and continues to construct and perpetuate false narratives against other communities worldwide whom it deems suspect, they gain courage and inspiration from what finally happened in Derry, against all the odds.

At the end of the day the Saville Report itself will not be recognised as the most enduring achievement; that accolade must go to those who took thirty years to bring it about, and another twelve years to see it through. The inquiry itself established less than was comprehended within minutes by the targeted community in Derry. There was to be no moving forward for civil rights through peaceful protest. Bloody Sunday put paid to that and was intended to put paid to it. It is impossible not to see the trajectory. The same parachute regiment had shot down eleven innocent citizens in Ballymurphy the year before; senior police as well as army officers had protested in advance at the madness of deploying that regiment to police a civil rights march in Derry. And at the end of the day, the inquiry, acknowledging the innocence and integrity of the murdered protestors balked at tracing responsibility to the very top.

Although external events shook the fault lines of state complicity in Bloody Sunday from time to time, and although allies whose help had been sought over many years were finally persuaded which was the right side of history to be on, none of those external and accidental events would have ever progressed the possibility of an inquiry, had there not been at all times, for decades, the sustained, demanding moral integrity and stamina of the families. They were the soul, the heart, the iron and the steel. They are all our inspiration; to them the world owes its gratitude and respect.

Gareth Peirce
20 December 2011

Eminent human rights lawyer Gareth Peirce has worked on many high-profile cases, including the Guildford Four, the Birmingham Six, the family of Jean Charles de Menezes and many Guantanamo Bay detainees.

[introduction]

Jackie Duddy, the first person killed on Bloody Sunday, was my uncle. He was just seventeen when he was shot in the back as he ran across the car park of the Rossville Flats. A photograph of Father Edward Daly, later Bishop Daly, waving a white handkerchief as he helped carry Jackie's body away from the shooting has become the most enduring image of that day.

I wasn't yet born at the time. But like everyone else in Derry down the years since, I grew up in the shadow of Bloody Sunday. As children we were shielded from the shock of the event. It was considered unwise, or unnecessary, to tell us the truth. We knew only of our fallen uncle, who had died long before we'd come into the world. We were told that, back then, he had marched for peace and didn't come home, that soldiers had shot him. We could see from the photographs that he had our familiar cheeky smile. We knew from the trophies that were kept on display in the house and the pictures of him posing in his gloves that he had been a promising boxer with the world at his feet. 'My wee sparring partner,' my mother often calls him to this day.

Most of all, Jackie was the fabled family member whose photograph always seemed to be around, in newspapers, on gable walls, on television. I had never met him, but he was always there.

Our family knew little of politics. Having no time for boundaries or bigotry, my grandfather William Duddy had instilled a natural pride and sense of self in his offspring. 'We're cosmopolitans,' he would say, 'we fit in anywhere.' My mother says it, too. No doubt someday I will impart the same advice to my daughter, Saffron.

I was raised with a fear of demonstrations. We were forbidden from venturing near town if any marches or meetings were planned. To my mother, they represented an unknown danger; she wasn't willing to take the chance. I attended my first Bloody Sunday commemoration march when I was in my late twenties. I remember feeling anxious.

My auntie Kay Duddy lived next door to us, and I greatly admired her from the time I became aware of her involvement in the Bloody Sunday campaign. I remember telling friends proudly how she and my uncle Gerry were campaigning against the British government and had even delivered a petition to the Prime Minister at 10 Downing Street. As I learned more, I understood how horrifying – and how fascinating – the facts of Bloody Sunday were. I read all I could on the subject. I wanted to be involved. Kay and my uncle Gerry's determination on behalf of the wider family was amazing to me. They seemed so brave, taking on the might of the entire British establishment.

I have described Kay as a 'reluctant role model'. I recall promising her, during one of our many chats, that if she grew too old to carry on, I would step up and continue the fight. I am thankful that, because of her efforts and the efforts of so many like her, I will never need to do that now.

When I was asked in 2009 to become a member of the Bloody Sunday Trust – the organisation tasked with commemorating the massacre and preserving the memory of those killed – I jumped at the chance. As a result, I was to become much more deeply involved in the campaign. Then, the following year, while on maternity leave from the *Derry Journal*, I received a phone call from Eamonn McCann, Chair of the Trust. He spoke of the need for a focused media operation in the run-up to the publication of the Saville Report and asked if I would take the helm. The opportunity was too tantalising to turn down. Like so many others, I was hoping that truth and justice would prevail, and be proclaimed to the world. Now I could be part of preparing for the moment.

With my family's support, I left four-month-old Saffron in capable hands and joined Mickey McKinney, brother of victim Willie McKinney, in an office which the Trust opened at the Ráth Mór centre in Creggan. Mickey resumed the role he had filled at various times over the years, of family liaison worker. I was press officer. Together, we began cooking up ideas for furthering the cause.

Mickey and I often talked at length in our little office. He regularly regaled me with tales of the families' efforts over the years before I'd become involved, of the hostilities encountered every step of the way and how the families, even though there had been difficulties and disagreements, had always managed to get through by pulling together. It was during one of these conversations that the idea of this book emerged. 'Nobody has ever written about how we did it, how we got here,' he said one afternoon. I remember thinking at the time, I wish I could do that, I wonder if I could.

As press officer, I had to be a link between the families and the survivors on the one hand and the media on the other. I was struck by the way I was so warmly welcomed by the families, how normal and friendly they were. They could easily have resented my role.

I set up a series of intimate interviews with the families of the murdered and with the survivors, to remind the world, before the report was published and headlines and hype took over, just who the Bloody Sunday families were and why this mattered so much. Even though by that stage the families and myself were well used to one another, I found their courage awe-inspiring. Their natural warmth came through in their stories and human anxieties. They were full of amusing anecdotes and mischievous memories. When the report was finally published on 15 June 2010 and the families were called on to respond, they were as prepared as they could be.

On the day of publication, I had a team of volunteers backing me up at a temporary media centre, logging interview requests and liaising with literally hundreds of media outlets, meeting them with a steady gaze.

Lord Saville's report and the declarations of the victims' innocence made headline news all over the world. In persuading the British government to rectify the history books, the families and campaigners themselves had made history. The truth was set free.

At a Bloody Sunday Trust meeting some months later, a discussion developed about some kind of publication to mark the achievement of the families in winning truth and justice and to set down the story of the campaign. I spoke up for Mickey's idea that we should produce an account in the words of the campaigners themselves. By the end of the meeting, I found myself commissioned to research and write the book. Although I had wanted the job, I was now terrified to have it. All I could do was give it my all. This book is the result.

Julieann Campbell
October 2011

chapter one

'Day of Days'

15 June 2010 was a day like no other in Derry. As dawn broke, its deserted streets began to buzz with activity as contractors and Derry City Council employees readied Guildhall Square for imminent global attention.

Among them was Joe Mahon. Indistinguishable from the rest in his luminous work-jacket, he busied himself erecting safety fencing and mapping out exit and entrance points. Only a slight limp hinted at the fact that Joe had almost died during the 30 January 1972 massacre of Bloody Sunday. He had just turned sixteen. He still bore the scars and, thirty-eight years on, he still felt the gnawing guilt at having witnessed others murdered beside him.

That day, the long-awaited report of the Bloody Sunday Inquiry was to be published. Yet while fellow campaigners spent the morning fretting in the glare of the media, Joe Mahon shuffled by unnoticed. On one of the most important days of his life, he preferred to keep busy, apparently oblivious to his role in history.

'Of course it was defiance. They [the British authorities] took enough of my life without telling me what to do that day,' Joe Mahon recalled. 'I wasn't going to take a day off just because they said so. I have a life to lead and will do what I want.'

The press had been gathering since daybreak. A media circus set up camp in and around Guildhall Square. On the city walls were dozens of visiting news agencies. BBC, ITV, Channel 4 – all the major television networks had secured vantage points on the historic ramparts, their rigs and cameras aimed in the direction of the Guildhall. The media operation stretched far beyond the square, encompassing the area around Foyle Street, Shipquay Street and nearby Waterloo Place.

Just hours later, almost ten thousand people would pour onto the streets and squeeze into the square, intent on witnessing the verdict of Lord Saville's twelve-year-long inquiry. Families stood in huddled groups, talking excitedly. Blue skies and a blazing early sun added to the sense of occasion. An unfamiliar, indefinable feeling hung in the Derry air.

At around 7 AM – amid strict security and the flash of jostling news crews – legal teams representing the families of the murdered and wounded filed into the Guildhall to read the mammoth report. With just hours to digest the essence of ten colossal volumes, solicitors then had the task of relaying its findings to the families.

With his work complete and the morning fading, Joe Mahon grew uneasy, aware that he had somewhere else to be. Returning to his work van, he began a preoccupied drive back to his home on the outskirts of Derry. Within the hour, he was showered, neatly dressed and on his way back to the Bogside.

At 10.30 AM, a delegation of relatives – two per family as negotiated between the Bloody Sunday Trust and the Northern Ireland Office – gathered at the Bloody Sunday Memorial in Rossville Street for a silent procession to the Guildhall for the 'pre-read' of the report.

Among the gathering throng, Joe Mahon met Liam Wray. As a terrified sixteen-year-old, Joe had feigned death after witnessing the murder of Liam's brother, Jim, just a few feet from where he himself lay in Glenfada Park. Jim was shot twice in the back – the second time as he lay wounded – and in the intervening years, Joe had been consumed with an irrational guilt that he could have done more to help. In the midst of the media glare, Joe and Liam hugged one another tightly.

'I never shouted to Jim Wray to lie still and that's what really has been in the back of my mind all these years,' Joe recalls. 'I saw the para approaching and I didn't warn him and they murdered him. I felt like a coward. I should have spoken, told him to keep still.'

From the Memorial in Rossville Street, the relatives and injured, about a hundred in all, slowly made their way along Rossville Street – one of the main killing zones on Bloody Sunday – across William Street and into the heart of the city centre, accompanied by Derry's Mayor Colum Eastwood and a handful of politicians. Passers-by lowered their heads in respect and apprehension. Shopkeepers stood in doorways and traffic stopped as the procession passed. A phalanx of press photographers preceded the relatives, camera clicks slicing the eerie silence. The only other sound was the low murmur of a Sky News helicopter overhead.

It took only minutes to walk the short distance to the Guildhall. As they approached the entrance, some looked terrified; others waved cautiously to supporters wishing them well. One middle-aged woman shouted: 'Good on you! Good luck! You're nearly there.'

Once inside the Guildhall, the heavy oak doors were sealed and anxious relatives struggled to adjust to their strange situation. All mobile phones and cameras had been confiscated and labelled for collection after 3.30 PM. For five hours, they would remain on lockdown. Other family members would join them for the last hour.

As the designated relatives and the surviving wounded made their way upstairs to be briefed by their legal teams, Joe Mahon's stomach was a knot of nerves. He didn't need the report to say he was innocent – he knew that. More than anything, he wanted the Wray family to have it proclaimed that Jim was innocent and had been murdered in cold blood as he lay defenceless on the ground.

'All I was interested in from Saville was that the Wray family would hear that truth, that Jim wasn't throwing stones or armed, that he was on his stomach. They never checked him or turned him over to see if he had a gun, they just shot him in the back twice and left him there. They murdered him.'

A temporary media centre had been set up at the Tower Museum, just yards from Guildhall Square. Interest in Saville's report had been building for months. For the first time, the Bloody Sunday Trust, swamped with requests for interviews and information, had appointed a press officer. She was joined by an army of volunteers on the day.

In the early afternoon, the remaining family members, citizens of Derry and supporters from further afield gathered at the Rossville Street memorial before marching, this time in their thousands, to the Guildhall. En route, marchers ripped apart and trampled on a giant reproduction of the disgraced and soon-to-be repudiated Widgery Report. They poured in to pack out the square by three o'clock

Beneath the towering Guildhall, a huge television screen rested on the back of a lorry. Photographs of all the men and boys killed on Bloody Sunday intermittently flashed on the screen emblazoned with stark white lettering declaring each INNOCENT, the images lingering long enough to leave a powerful impression on the crowd. There was a minimal police presence, as if they too realised the sensitivity of the occasion.

All eyes were on the Guildhall clock, ticking towards 3.30 PM, when the findings were at last to be made public. The throng was united in rising anxiety and collective hope.

However, before the British government's appointed hour, defiant Derry got there first. With minutes to go, the crowd's attention was caught by a commotion behind the stained glass windows of the Guildhall as a hand thrust out a thumbs-up from within. The crowd erupted; vindication was at hand. Then other relatives waved copies of the report through the narrow window grills. The pre-emption of the government created one of the most thrilling and fulfilling moments in Derry's history. A sense of joyous relief spread across the crowd. Cameras on the walls swivelled, as if orchestrated by the simple thumbs-up gesture.

Moments later, British prime minister David Cameron stood up to address Parliament, the image projected on the giant screen. Announcing himself as 'deeply patriotic', Cameron told a solemn House of Commons, 'There is no doubt, there is nothing equivocal, there are no ambiguities. What happened on Bloody Sunday was both unjustified and unjustifiable. It was wrong.'

The Square exploded into cheering. With the city and the world listening, Cameron went on to reveal the detail of Saville's findings.

The Inquiry had found that none of the casualties of Bloody Sunday had posed any threat to British troops. Saville had ruled that some of the soldiers had lost 'their self-control' and that the first shots had come, without warning, from the military and not, as subsequently claimed by the army, from the IRA. He found that not one of the casualties was armed with a weapon when shot; some of the killed and injured had clearly been fleeing or going to the assistance of others who had been struck by paratroopers' bullets.

Cameron quoted Lord Saville in declaring that many soldiers had 'knowingly' put forward false accounts to justify their actions. Then came the proclamation that so many had longed to hear for all of thirty-nine years: 'On behalf of the government, indeed on behalf of our country, I am deeply sorry,' said Cameron.

As the implications of Cameron's words sank in, many in Guildhall Square looked stunned as they tried to digest the enormity of the moment – incredulous that the British government had at long last acknowledged the absolute innocence of those gunned down and publicly apologised for what Britain's army had inflicted upon them. To some, it seemed almost inconceivable that a British Tory prime minister could have made such a declaration.

Just a few minutes later, the families and wounded emerged shell-shocked and triumphant to a hurricane of acclamation. Lining up on the makeshift platform outside the building, they seemed overwhelmed. Joe Mahon stood to the back of the stage, his self-effacing smile tinged with sadness. It seemed like an age before the cheering subsided so the families could speak.

First was Mickey McKinney, brother of Willie, shot down in Glenfada Park. 'This is an historic day for Derry. We know as we stand here that that we stand among friends.' Tony Doherty, whose father Patrick had been shot dead as he crawled away from the shooting, spoke to the world on behalf of all the families. 'Unjustified and unjustifiable. Those are the words we have been waiting to hear since 30 January 1972,' he said with an audible lump in his throat. 'The victims of Bloody Sunday have been vindicated and the Parachute Regiment has been disgraced. Their medals of honour have to be removed. Widgery's great lie has been laid bare. The truth has been brought home at last. It can now be proclaimed to the world that the dead and the wounded of Bloody Sunday, civil rights marchers, were innocent one and all, gunned down in their own streets.'

One by one, representatives of each family came forward to publicly proclaim the acknowledged innocence of their loved ones. They were followed by the surviving wounded and the families of those who hadn't lived to see the day. In all, twenty-eight families bared their souls, the repeated cries of 'innocent' resonating across the city and the world.

In a final act of joyful liberation, relatives John Kelly and Jean Hegarty ripped apart an original copy of the Widgery whitewash, its insult left fluttering in the warm breeze across the euphoric Guildhall Square. Widgery was no more.

Stepping off the platform, campaigners found themselves swallowed up in a media frenzy. Though dazed by the day's events, Joe Mahon felt better than he had in many years, a massive weight lifted from his shoulders. Joe melted into the crowd. A short time later when the commotion had begun to die down, he donned his work-clothes again and set to dismantling of the safety barriers he had erected earlier. He ended the day as he had begun it – an ordinary man doing a day's work. But now something was different. Along with all the dead and the other wounded, he had been vindicated, found innocent in the eyes of the world.

Also exulting in the moment was Kay Duddy. Her teenage brother Jackie had been the first person to die on Bloody Sunday. When asked by a scrum of reporters how it had come to this, she said, 'Well, it all began in a room in West End Park, where we sat around drinking tea, wondering what we could do . . .'

[chapter two]

'We've waited long enough'

When evening fell, Kathleen Kelly would wrap herself in a winter coat and scarf and steal quietly out of her house in the Creggan estate. Within minutes, she was in the inky darkness of the City Cemetery and weaving through the shadowy rows of gravestones. Instinctively she knew where to go. When she reached Michael's grave, she would carefully lay a thick blanket over the wind-beaten plot to keep her darling son warm. It didn't matter that it was late. She would stay with him for a while.

Kathleen Kelly was never the same after the murder of her seventeen-year-old son on Bloody Sunday. Most nights she would spend time consumed in the lonely, moonlit cemetery. 'I thought she was going to die of a broken heart,' her son John Kelly confided. He, too, felt the anguish of Michael's death and longed for answers. It was a desire that would eventually propel him to the forefront of a campaign that led all the way to Westminster and the White House.

'We worried about my mother and her state of mind because she definitely wasn't well,' he recalled. 'She was just so heartbroken and almost in a different world. She had kept all Michael's clothing and belongings and requested that his things be buried with her, which they eventually were. She even kept a Mars bar that he had never eaten. We still have it now, almost forty years later.'

Mrs Kelly later acknowledged that those first years were a blur. In January

1992 she was to tell the *Sunday Tribune*: 'I knew nothing for four or five years after that,' she said. 'The daughters tell me things, but I never knew anything. I never even washed myself, I let myself go, and so the girls even had to wash me . . . I wasn't interested in the rest of my children when he died . . . I told the priest I will take my hatred to six feet under – and I will.'

When the families decided to challenge the British government in 1992, Mrs Kelly was fully behind the campaign and encouraged John to 'see it through'. When the Bloody Sunday Inquiry opened in 1998, a stronger, more resilient Mrs Kelly led the procession to the Guildhall.

But she would not live long enough to see Michael's innocence vindicated nor the truth of his murder explained. John revealed: 'Before she died in 2004, I lied and told her we'd won the case and that Michael and everyone else's name had been cleared. That had been so important to her. She passed away happy.' John and his siblings gathered up Michael's things. 'Everything went with her. She kept them in the knowledge that when she died, everything concerning Michael would go with her and it did.' Apart from the Mars bar, which remained with John, and a tiny bloodstained baby-gro used to stem the flow of blood from Michael. It is now on display in a glass case in the Museum of Free Derry – just yards from where he was shot dead.

The day after Bloody Sunday, a number of Catholic priests from Derry called a press conference in the City Hotel. All had been present the previous day. In an article in the *Derry Journal* following the publication of the Bloody Sunday Report, the retired Bishop of Derry Edward Daly – the priest forever linked to the tragedy – recalled his abhorrence during the press conference.

'There were seven of us in all. We were appalled and revolted by what we had witnessed. We shared in the heartbreak of the families. We were trying to cope with our own heartbreak and felt a duty to tell the world the truth,' Bishop Daly reflects. Press from around the world attended. The sight of seven priests lined up on a platform was an arresting one – their grave expression became an enduring and widely publicised image in the days and months to come. Along with Bishop (then Father) Daly, they were Frs. Anthony Mulvey,

George McLaughlin, Joseph Carolan, Denis Bradley, Michael McIvor and Tom O'Gara.

'We made three points in our statement,' Bishop Daly explains. 'We stated unequivocally that the army were guilty of wilful murder. We accused the army of shooting indiscriminately into a fleeing crowd, gloating over casualties and of preventing spiritual and medical attention reaching the wounded and dying.'

The unprecedented nature of the Bloody Sunday killings left an indelible stain on Derry and appalled the island as a whole. Anglo-Irish relations reached an all-time low as scores of the angry disenchanted flocked to join the IRA. 'Bloody Sunday was unique in that it was done by the state on its own citizens and in broad daylight,' journalist and political activist Eamonn McCann notes. 'There is no other atrocity with the same political resonance and impact. Stormont fell in March 1972, just weeks afterwards. Its ramifications have been critical for the political development of Northern Ireland. The Bloody Sunday issue runs right through the historical narrative of the Troubles. That tells you about its political significance.'

Since 1969, forty-five innocent civilians, both Catholic and Protestant, were killed in the North by the Parachute Regiment – more than the number attributable to any other regiment. Against this background, it's more than coincidence that a greater number died in the six months after Bloody Sunday (256), than during the previous three years (210). From February to December a staggering 445 people were killed in the conflict. The ripple effect shook Ireland hard. 1972 was to become the bloodiest year in a thirty-year struggle.

The Bloody Sunday families' campaign for justice did not begin immediately. It was to be twenty years before the Sunday Justice Campaign came into existence. It was to operate for just six years – from 1992 until 1998, when the British government broke with all precedent and parliamentary tradition and conceded a new inquiry.

In the intervening years, Bloody Sunday was rarely mentioned other than by those closely affected. Once a year on the anniversary, families, friends and fellow citizens would gather for annual commemorations in Derry. Impassioned speakers would call for truth and accountability but the world was no longer listening. Nevertheless, the annual march became for many an annual gesture of public remembrance.

The malice and contempt directed at the grieving and wounded was often hard to fathom. Ingrained bigotry and sectarian prejudice followed relatives and survivors wherever they went. The lies enshrined in the Widgery ensured their reputation as 'terrorist' families. The wounded faced years of persecution and vitriol, harassed at security checkpoints, picked out for special treatment at airports and so on.

The relatives of Jim Wray, murdered as he lay wounded in Glenfada Park, were still reeling from news of his death when they first felt the backlash. Just two days after the massacre, Jim's mother, Sarah and father, James received a letter from someone claiming to be the head of the loyalist paramilitary group the UVF (Ulster Volunteer Force). In other circumstances, the letter might have been dismissed as the ravings of a sectarian idiot. But in the circumstances of the time there was always a chance that it represented the views of a sizable number of people. The message read: '"May Sweet Jesus have mercy on his soul," Ha! Ha! What a laugh. That's what it says at your son's death in the *Irish News*. What you should have stated is this "May Hell Roast him" and the rest of his mates ... Your son was a fucking bastard and a fenian c***, he was full of hatred so he can say goodbye to glory. Your Rebel bastards are doomed ... "The Wray Family", get out of your home or be burned out. Ulster is British, God Save the Queen. No surrender.'

The stigma of being associated with Bloody Sunday and thereby with 'terrorism' persisted for many years. For some relatives, an enduring religious faith would see them through. Others would struggle to cope with the distain heaped upon them, retreating inwards or lashing out.

Lord Widgery's 1972 report did nothing to alleviate the suffering. Many had naively believed that an official investigation was bound to uncover the truth. But the report when it came was little better than a whitewash. The main blame was apportioned to the victims themselves.

A year after Bloody Sunday, the first commemoration march and rally was held, organised by the Northern Ireland Civil Rights Association. The second year also saw a NICRA commemoration. But belief in a civil rights strategy was waning. From 1975, Sinn Féin took control of the commemorations. The party would continue this association until the 1980s. At that point, some families were becoming frustrated, convinced that they could gain more support if they broadened the organisation. When families and friends began mobilising to address Bloody Sunday commemorative events themselves, Sinn Féin didn't hesitate to hand back the reins.

The group that then began to come together had no name at first. It was eventually to become the Bloody Sunday Initiative, tasked not to commemorate but to reopen the debate surrounding the January 1972 event.

Tony Doherty was a key organiser of the initial meetings. He was just ten when his father, Paddy was murdered as he tried to crawl away from the shooting. Tony and his five siblings, the youngest just seven months old, grew up in the shadow of the massacre which had taken his father. In his teens, Tony became involved in the republican movement and joined the IRA. 'Bloody Sunday would always have been there, but we were only children and I don't remember it being discussed in great detail,' he remembers. 'There was never any talk of a campaign or seeking justice. I think we just thought there was nothing we could do. That made anger build up underneath.

'I was eighteen when I went to prison on 1 March 1981, the day Bobby Sands went on hunger strike. I would have become involved in the republican movement two years earlier. Before Bloody Sunday our family wasn't republican, as such, but we became a republican family. Our house was often raided and we were generally targeted. Some of the family would have been arrested in their teens. I suppose the British army believed it had killed fourteen IRA people on Bloody Sunday and so, it would also have thought there were fourteen IRA families behind them, too. When I look back now, I can draw a direct line between my experience of losing a father to the British army and my decision to join the IRA.'

Tony remembers the night he and others were 'being processed' into the IRA. 'We were in the kitchen of this house and a man came in to suss the motivation of the people involved. We were all young men and I think I was asked first why I wanted to join the IRA. I told him I wanted to get revenge for my father and he said "that's not a good enough reason." He added that he had known my father. Then he moved to the next person.'

Afterwards, the man approached Tony again. '"This is not about revenge," he said. But I joined up anyway.'

It's a conversation that Tony has always remembered: 'I suppose it did reveal a certain motivation for revenge that I had at that time.'

Two months after his eighteenth birthday Tony was arrested and, along with five other people, charged with IRA membership, possession of a weapon and causing an explosion in Derry city centre. He went to jail in 1981, first to Crumlin Road Jail before moving to Long Kesh in 1982 in the aftermath of the hunger strike.

'I got to know the republican movement, and far more IRA men than I would have on the outside. So, in a way my schooling in the politics of the IRA was all done in jail. I spent just over four years in prison. I came out more educated and worldly, I suppose. I got out in April 1985. I was twenty-two and I thought I was old! I felt like I went in a teenager and came out a grown man. Safe to say, it didn't do me any harm – I used the benefit of all that time to read and become educated and politicised. I came out more sure of myself and the world around me.

'Back then there was no semblance of justice. Even the Birmingham Six and Guildford Four were looked on as hopeless cases. People accepted they were going to be in jail for a long time, if not forever. Everybody knew they were innocent but it didn't matter. Even in those days, I would have compared those two cases to Bloody Sunday, as huge miscarriages of justice.

'When I got out in 1985, I was quite rebellious and still a member of the IRA. It took a couple of years for me to find my feet. There was no talk of any peace process at that time. There was armed conflict and there was the development of the political struggle. I suppose I was involved in both. In 1992, I became a bit disenchanted with armed struggle. I became involved more in politics both within the movement and outside it. By 1989, we were talking about the Bloody Sunday Initiative and so I was starting to get a different type of consciousness about myself in relation to possibilities around Bloody Sunday.

'The first time I remember any discussion of doing something practical about Bloody Sunday was around 1987, with a friend of mine Gerry O'Hara. Gerry had been a great friend of Gerald Donaghey, had been with him on the march. He was very personally affected by Gerry Donaghey's death.

'We tried to gather together a group of families in the Sinn Féin centre in Cable Street but it didn't really amount to much. I'm not sure what focus it had. We had definite ideas of doing something but they didn't go anywhere. That was the first attempt to start a credible campaign.' It would be some years before the tentative plans grew to fruition.

In January 1988, while a handful of people debated the possibility of a new effort to seek justice for Bloody Sunday, across the city a woman called Peggy Deery died. She was just fifty-four. Her life had been difficult.

Peggy Deery was the only woman shot on Bloody Sunday. Her husband had died from cancer three months earlier, aged just thirty-seven, devastating Peggy and their fourteen children. The bullet that hit her caused terrible damage to her leg. Tony Deery remembers that the gunshot injury impacted on his mother for the rest of her life and put unbearable pressure on her family.

'She was shot in the thigh, a small hole in the front but the back of her leg was blew away and lying open. She couldn't walk after that and had to get a calliper.'

Peggy, thirty-eight at the time of Bloody Sunday, was hospitalised for six months and had frequent return stays. The severity of her injury meant that her children – the oldest sixteen, the youngest an infant of nine months – were left to rear each other. 'She was never the same again,' Tony says.

But it wasn't just families and friends who were traumatised by Bloody Sunday. Many prominent local people found themselves in perpetual angst and bitterly frustrated. One of those involved in the early discussions was political activist Eamonn McCann.

A journalist by trade, Eamonn McCann has never shied away from the sensitivities of Bloody Sunday. His reports and analyses have often courted controversy, but his writing achieved its overall objective – to keep Bloody

Sunday in the public eye. McCann was in the Bogside when the paras opened fire and witnessed the carnage unfolding. He was one of the first to discuss campaigning. 'I was born and grew up in Rossville Street where the killing took place and so it was somehow deeply personal to me. I knew some of the people personally too, and when you know people personally and know that they were not involved with arms, its gives you a certain strength and motivation to fight.'

The first indictment McCann penned about the atrocity was the pamphlet *What Happened in Derry?* published in February 1972. The pamphlet formed the basis for his 1992 book of the same title. 'A week after Widgery I also wrote an analysis of the report called 'The Widgery Whitewash'. It was based solely on the text, examining the way it handled evidence and its reasoning. If I do say so myself, nobody who read that little pamphlet could have been in any doubt that Widgery had deliberately lied about a case of mass killing. I remember the blatancy of the operation came as a shock. It wasn't at all subtle. The point is, if it was clear from the report itself that Widgery was lying, they all must have known it was lies. All the upper echelons of politics and military and the judiciary – they all knew it was lies and were relaxed about that. The arrogance and sheer cynicism was a big motivating factor for me.'

McCann recognises that the atrocity drove people away from constitutional politics and towards the IRA, but he believes Widgery's report was itself just as significant. 'If the highest judge in the land was involved in the conspiracy to hide the murder of people in Derry – how could you argue to Derry people that they should stay within the law in seeking redress? Widgery was an utter disaster for the British state and its relationship with Northern Ireland. Not as important as the killings in human terms, but in political terms.'

McCann further believes that the army's actions in Derry in 1972 ended the civil rights era. 'Bloody Sunday killed the Northern Ireland Civil Rights Association. It had organised the march and not one person on the speaking platform that day represented an armed threat to the state. In fact, NICRA represented an alternative strategy to armed struggle. But the NICRA leadership was literally shot off the stage on Bloody Sunday, they had to jump off the platform and throw themselves to the ground. NICRA never really recovered from that. Within a few weeks of Bloody Sunday, Stormont was abolished. After that, there really was no role for NICRA. After all, it had mainly been campaigning for the democratic reform of Stormont. McCann would soon join Tony Doherty and others in the establishment of a new group – the Bloody Sunday Initiative.

From around 1989, discussion concentrated on the idea of an organisation to refocus attention on Bloody Sunday. Tony Doherty remembers being spurred on by the case of the Guildford Four. 'The release of the Four in 1989 was an important event for me because you could see, for the first time, that there was a possibility of movement. That was part of my thinking in the setting up of the Bloody Sunday Initiative. But there was still no clear view of how to piece a credible campaign together.'

Robin Percival seems an unlikely campaigner on Bloody Sunday. Yet, he played a pivotal part in the early incarnations of the campaign and, in 1989, was the first person to draft a paper on the importance of addressing Bloody Sunday in a serious and organised way. Originally from Widnes outside Liverpool, Robin first visited Derry in the 1960s as part of the Fellowship of Reconciliation. He relocated to Derry in late 1972 and has remained there ever since. He is now an active member of both the Bloody Sunday Trust and the Parades Commission. As a former member of the party, Robin presented a paper entitled 'The Bloody Sunday Trust' to the ruling body of Derry Sinn Féin in August 1989. The paper, drafted with the help of Tony Doherty, discussed the need for a specific group aimed at addressing Bloody Sunday. 'We wanted to focus national and international attention on Bloody Sunday as a justice issue,' Tony Doherty says.

Robin adds: 'The paper I submitted spoke of a Bloody Sunday Trust but in the end we decided to call it the Bloody Sunday Initiative. This was an attempt to create a broad-based organisation containing members of Sinn Féin, but also others, who were not members. If you look at the checklist in that paper, pretty much everything on it has since happened. It even mentioned setting up a museum to house all the archival material being collected, although it was described back then as an interpretive centre.'

Robin's ideas laid the foundations for both the Initiative and the subsequent Justice Campaign, as Tony Doherty suggests. 'I think Robin saw things a bit differently than your average Derry person. Robin was English, from outside, and so had a different perspective. We grew up with Bloody Sunday and felt bad about it, but got used to it. I think Derry had got used to it. But Robin hadn't.'

The Bloody Sunday Initiative was formally established in August 1989, setting up office in a room at 1 West End Park, a grand mock-Tudor property overlooking the Bogside. Tony Doherty remembers the initial meetings. 'I suppose the primary purpose was to focus national and international attention on Bloody Sunday as a justice issue, although I have to say there was no clarity on how exactly to go about it. We needed to get organised and get people motivated. We were very conscious of the need for a global perspective and spent two years planning to use the twentieth anniversary in 1992 to really begin that.'

One of the first things the BSI did was commission Eamonn McCann to write *Bloody Sunday – What Happened in Derry*. McCann enlisted the support of Maureen Collins (née Shiels), Bridie Hannigan and Tony Doherty and the team set to work interviewing friends and relatives of the dead and wounded. 'It was a great piece of work because for the first time we were interviewing families for our own sake,' says Tony. 'This wasn't journalists coming and leaving again, it was self-generated.'

But while activity around the establishment of the BSI proceeded, numbers attending the annual commemorations dwindled. By the end of the 1980s, outside the organising group, the issue was slipping down most people's priorities. Many in Derry and beyond viewed the commemorations as essentially republican. Eventually, those involved in the BSI concluded that the political associations remained detrimental. Robin Percival explains: 'As the march was in terminal decline, the decision was made basically to hand over responsibility for the whole issue to the new BSI.'

The 1990s were to prove eventful as far as human rights issues in the North were concerned. With the Guildford Four released, attention turned to the Birmingham Six. In August 1975, six Irish men living in Birmingham, including Derry man Johnny Walker, were accused and later convicted of detonating IRA bombs in two Birmingham pubs, killing 21 people and injuring over 160 more. They had, by this time, served almost sixteen years.

In planning the 1990 anniversary weekend, the BSI set out to present a human rights weekend focusing on miscarriages of justice and, in particular, the case of the Birmingham Six. Paul Hill and Gerry Conlon from the Guildford Four were invited to address the 1990 anniversary rally. 'It may seem a bit opportunistic, but we decided to focus on the Birmingham Six because by that time it was pretty clear to everyone that they were innocent. We wanted to make that connection by supporting them and encouraging as many others as we could to support them too.'

A five-thousand-strong crowd marched to the rally at Free Derry Corner as Johnny Walker's daughter Joanne joined the two Guildford men on the platform to read out the names of the dead and wounded of Bloody Sunday, as well as the names of the Six. It was the first major event organised by the BSI. But its optimism was shattered by sudden tragedy and controversy.

As the main body of the march moved up Westland Street, an IRA bomb, aimed at British army patrols high on the City Walls, exploded, showering the crowd below with debris and unintentionally killing an innocent marcher, Charles Love. 'It was a total, unmitigated disaster,' says Robin Percival.

'People wonder about the key events that led the IRA to end their campaign. I think this was one of them, in fact that it was absolutely critical. To be fair to Sinn Féin, they had put a lot of effort into attracting people from all over the country to possibly the biggest Bloody Sunday parade since the first anniversary. Then the IRA chose to use the occasion to carry out one of their most spectacular botched operations. It was unbelievable. People had marched in good faith and look what happened.'

The OC of the Derry brigade of the IRA attended a subsequent Sinn Féin meeting to explain. 'They were quite open about it. They had seen an opportunity and they hadn't thought of the bigger picture,' Robin recalls. 'But the families and city were shocked. I believe that was one of the seminal events that led to the first ceasefire.

'Obviously the Bloody Sunday Initiative had to comment on it and debated what we would say. It gives you an insight into IRA thinking at the time in that they went bananas at the thought that we were going to use the word "condemn". We ended up describing it as a "gross error of judgement", which I think was at least as strong. "Condemn" is used with such abandon now it has lost much of its power.'

Despite the setback and the widespread distress at the death of Charles Love, 1991 saw the project broaden out with a full weekend of events setting the scene for the forthcoming campaign. The theme was 'Towards Justice'. The BSI organised a number of events, including discussions on shoot to kill/death squads, women and inequality, Christians and oppression, and censorship. A dramatisation and subsequent discussion on knowing your rights when arrested or harassed on the street also drew crowds. The rally after the march was addressed by British Labour MP Jeremy Corbyn, who had been to the forefront of the campaign to release the Birmingham Six. The BSI invited the family of Charles Love to unveil a plaque in his memory. In the programme listing commemoration events, the Initiative described the Love family's acceptance of the invite as 'an inspiration to us and to all who campaign for justice and human rights.' Marchers applauded as Mr Patrick Love uncovered a marble plaque erected on the wall of Glenfada Park, close to where his son had been killed by falling debris.

Jubilant scenes outside the Old Bailey flashed from TV screens all over the world on 14 March 1991, as the Birmingham Six finally walked free. Relentless campaigning and a surge in public support saw their convictions quashed; they emerged triumphant to cheers from thousands thronging the London streets outside.

Many family members cite the public vindication of the Birmingham Six as a primary catalyst for them becoming active over Bloody Sunday. It seemed clear that campaigning, when conducted on a large scale, could get results. Mickey McKinney, brother of Willie, recalls: 'I remember watching the news and I was thrilled for them, but I got angry too. I thought "That's brilliant for them, but what about Bloody Sunday?" It made me realise I needed to do something.' Mickey would soon become one of the key players in the campaign.

Some months after the release of the Birmingham Six, Channel 4 broadcast a programme about Bloody Sunday as part of its 'Secret History' documentary series, which challenged the Widgery findings and fuelling renewed debate around the issue. Bloody Sunday was making its way back into the mainstream, back into the public's consciousness.

Over the next few years, public attitudes towards Bloody Sunday began to shift. Perhaps, after all, the British army had lied. Could it be that those Derry folk seen as IRA stooges had, like the Birmingham Six, been telling the truth after all?

[chapter three]

'Are these people dead?
Am I dead?'

The twentieth anniversary saw the biggest march of the campaign since 1973, and the weekend events continued with the previous year's international theme, under the general heading, 'One World, One Struggle', focusing on human rights across the globe. The campaigners attempted to internationalise their efforts to gain recognition. Speakers from Central and Southern America, as well as from the South African ANC were invited to attend, while Christy Moore performed with bands from Ecuador and Peru. Tentative relationships were forged.

Coinciding with the twentieth anniversary was the launch of Eamonn McCann's book, *Bloody Sunday: What Happened in Derry*, commissioned by the Bloody Sunday Initiative (BSI) and published by Brandon Books. Regarded as one of the seminal books on the issue, McCann's book helped to renew interest in Bloody Sunday and contained a background analysis of the events leading up to the killings. Most remarkable was the series of interviews with relatives and friends, conducted by Maureen Shiels and Bridie Hannigan of the local Women's Living History Circle. In these, family members talked candidly about the lives of the killed and wounded men and boys, painting a personal portrait of each and giving an identity to names.

Eamonn McCann's book generated much needed interest in the subject and, more importantly, brought the families together and ignited the embers of defiance. The launch in Bookworm Community Bookshop in the city centre was one of the key commemoration events that year. A large number of families gathered together – a rare occurrence up until that point.

'People find it hard to believe, but we didn't really know each other very well in those days,' Tony Doherty says. 'Those of us who attended marches would have met up briefly once a year, but until Eamonn's book was launched, we were essentially strangers. For the first time since the early 1970s, that launch brought us all together in one place. We just got talking about the book and that led on to talking about the possibilities in front of us.'

Twentieth anniversary commemorations were not confined to Derry. A huge march was held in London, calling for British withdrawal from Ireland. Labour MP Ken Livingstone said 'Still, no-one has paid a penny fine or served a day in prison. Bloody Sunday was a crime for which its main organiser was decorated by the state, giving a knighthood to a supervisor of death squads.'

Rock star Peter Gabriel voiced support for the demonstration, alongside MPs Peter Hain, Jeremy Corbyn and Tony Benn, filmmaker Ken Loach, journalist John Pilger, poet Adrian Mitchell and Gerry Hunter and Billy Power of the Birmingham Six.

Eamonn McCann remembers the Dublin launch of the book: 'We invited every TD and senator and we held the launch in a hotel directly across the road from Leinster House so they literally had only to cross the road. But of the dozens invited, only one turned up – Tony Gregory, Independent TD for Dublin Central. Now, that tells you something. The thought was persisting that to be associated with the campaign was to be associated with something dangerous. The same thing happened with the Birmingham Six. It was many years before we were able to get any action in the South.'

The possibility of sustained campaigning about Bloody Sunday came up repeatedly during the 1992 commemorations. The seeds of the campaign were sown. 'Over the course of that weekend, we decided that the time was right.' Tony Doherty says.

A public meeting was called in early February 1992. 'I had the success of the Birmingham Six case very much in mind,' Tony says. 'The BSI was the only group in Derry which had actively campaigned for the Birmingham Six's release. That highlighted what might be possible in our own case. We had organised the homecoming for Johnny Walker after sixteen years in jail. We brought him from the airport to a huge reception at Free Derry Corner. People began to sense possibilities in the air.'

The initial meeting took place in the Pilot's Row Centre, built upon the killing ground of Bloody Sunday. Gerry Duddy recalls his oldest sister, Ann, telling him about it. 'I told her, "Well, if I am going down there tonight, I am going to give it everything." She told me, "You go for it, you go for it." So I did.'

Forty to fifty people attended the meeting, the majority of them relatives. Thirty-three people – interestingly enough, including four English men – signed up. They became the first members of the Bloody Sunday Justice Campaign.

Mary Doherty, sister of Gerald Donaghey, came with her daughter, Geraldine. Tony Doherty and his brother Paul represented their father, Paddy. Kay and Gerry Duddy were there for Jackie. John Kelly for Michael, Margaret and Liam Wray for Jim, John and Linda Nash for their brother William, shot dead, and their father Alexander, shot and injured going to his son's aid. Mickey, John and Joe McKinney attended too, seeking justice for their brother Willie. Others in attendance included BSI members Robin Percival, Martin Finucane, as well as George Downey and John Walker of the Birmingham Six.

'The meeting only attracted seven or eight families and we needed more,' Mickey McKinney recalls. 'So I suggested that we should go round the rest of the families and try to convince them to become involved.' John McKinney agreed: 'I had to try. I was the youngest of the family and it ate me up seeing what it did to my mother and father. My mother took it to the grave.'

As campaign plans began to take shape, many relatives felt more at ease for being able welcomed to distance themselves from any political alliance.

Liam Wray appreciates the effort Sinn Féin put into organising the annual commemorations, but welcomed the family-led campaign. 'Over the years, the annual event had come to be seen as a Sinn Féin occasion. Admittedly, nobody else had come forward to take on the task, so I'm grateful to Sinn Féin for that. But we were being criticised for being IRA families and because of that many families would have nothing to do with the commemorations and I wouldn't criticise them for that.' The campaign still had its work cut out convincing the wider world of its honourable intentions. It would take many years to garner support from across the political spectrum.

After a lot of brainstorming at the initial Pilot's Row meeting, several relatives were tasked with approaching all remaining families. It was also agreed that the campaign would need clear, simple demands. Eventually, a three-point platform was agreed and Robin Percival was asked to write it up in time for publication.

Although heavily involved from the beginning, Eamonn McCann didn't think at that point that the campaign would succeed. 'I couldn't see any constitutional way that the British elite would be able to have another inquiry, even if they wanted one,' Eamonn said. 'After all, Widgery was the Lord Chief Justice, the ultimate custodian of British law and constitution. If he set out the supposedly definitive truth after a formal inquiry established by parliament and parliament had then accepted it, in my secret heart I couldn't see any mechanism whereby that could be overthrown. Indeed, I'm still puzzled about that. I suspect that by the late 1990s the campaign had put on so much pressure that without a second inquiry, the whole peace process might have been stymied. So they just ignored their own constitution.

'My aim at the time was to expose the fact that these people were liars, not just about Bloody Sunday but in relation to a wide range of issues that could be brought under the heading of State security.' He believes that the then political and judicial establishment, as evidenced by the 1972 Widgery report, were involved in a conspiracy to cover up the use of lethal force by the paras against unarmed civilians on Bloody Sunday.

In the days after the Pilot's Row meeting, Mickey McKinney, John Kelly and others began systematically contacting survivors and the families of the dead to explain what the new campaign was about. 'The only way we were going to succeed was if we were united,' Mickey McKinney recalls. 'It took a long time to get everybody on board. There were party political problems within the families. We had to be very clear to everyone that this would be a family-owned affair.' Some families still didn't see the benefit of a campaign but nevertheless now gave their blessing for the campaign to go ahead.

For a while, the Bloody Sunday Justice Campaign (BSJC) and the Bloody Sunday Initiative co-existed. Then the Initiative branched out to champion wider human rights issues, leaving the BSJC with its specific remit. On 15 April 1992, the newly established BSJC was officially launched in Pilot's Row. 'The room was packed and there were news crews from BBC and ITV, as well as all the local press. It was brilliant to see so much interest.' Mickey McKinney says. At the launch Johnny Walker, who often acted as spokesperson for the group, said that the people of Derry deserved justice – and that he knew from personal experience what it was like to be denied justice for sixteen and a half years.

The three demands made by the BSJC were: the repudiation of Widgery and institution of a new inquiry; a formal acknowledgement of the innocence of all the victims; and the prosecution of those responsible for the deaths and injuries. The campaign stressed that these were its only demands. A statement went out: 'We welcome into membership anyone who supports our objectives irrespective of religion or political persuasion.'

Eamonn McCann revealed plans for relatives to travel to Westminster the following month, at the invitation of Labour MP Jeremy Corbyn, to lobby parliamentarians, and to Leinster House in Dublin to lobby TDs. The group also announced its intention to write to all local councils throughout Ireland asking them to raise the continued injustice of Bloody Sunday with both the London and Dublin governments. The general public was urged to write to the British government and declare support for the campaign. 'Twenty years is long enough,' Eamonn McCann told reporters. 'We intend to see to it that the people don't have to suffer another year without the British government admitting that what happened here was murder and without acknowledging that those killed and injured were totally innocent.'

The campaign launch was a big success, Tony Doherty recalls. 'I'm sure some people were a bit cynical, thinking that Bloody Sunday was too far back in history, that we'd never get anywhere. But most of the people around us wished us well. The launch drew a fair bit of community support and a lot of newspaper coverage locally. It was to take a couple more years before we broke through into the mainstream press in England.'

At this point in 1992, some family members who had previously been uninvolved began to throw their weight behind the campaign. But the three demands were to cause some consternation. Bishop of Derry, Dr Edward Daly – the priest whose image waving a bloodstained hankie would become synonymous with Bloody Sunday – felt that he could not endorse all three demands.

Bishop Daly explained in a letter to John Kelly that many men from Derry involved in the early conflict had fled the city to avoid arrest. Some of these were now desperate to return home. Over the years, Bishop Daly had appealed on behalf of quite a number of men in this position and, for this reason, felt that he couldn't endorse the third demand. 'While the cases are not exactly the same, I believe that, if I were to take a different position in the case of those who murdered members of your families, it would appear to be inconsistent and might weaken the case I have made on (the local men's) behalf,' the Bishop wrote.

But John remained resolute. 'The decision had already been made. The demands had been set in stone and we weren't going to alter them.' Notwithstanding his reservations, Bishop Daly gave the campaign a substantial donation. 'That was a good sign' says John. 'Bishop Daly has been a huge supporter all the years since.'

It was only now that the campaign began in earnest. All involved were novices, but quickly embraced their roles. After decades of comparative silence, previously disheartened relatives had the opportunity and the impetus to speak up, to share their grief and argue their case. Collectively, they were to prove an unstoppable force.

Kay and Gerry Duddy played prominent roles. They were focused on pursuing justice for their brother Jackie. He'd been one of fifteen children and a promising amateur boxer who had, against his father's orders, attended the march with friends 'for the craic'. He was running alongside Father Daly when shot in the back in the car park of the Rossville Flats. He was seventeen, the first fatality of Bloody Sunday. The harrowing image of his lifeless body being carried to safety, flanked by Fr Edward Daly waving his white hankie, has become the most recognisable image of the atrocity. The Duddy family cannot escape it. Widgery ruled that Jackie was most likely a nail-bomber.

Gerry Duddy was fourteen on Bloody Sunday. Like many others, the Duddy boys had been forbidden to go on the march. Nevertheless, Gerry, Patrick and Jackie joined the thousands congregating at Bishop's Field. When the army began using water cannon in William Street, Gerry knew to keep back. The cannon sprayed a purple dye to help identify rioters, so his father would know he had been marching. Gerry remembers talking to Jackie minutes before he was shot. 'We were actually hiding on our older brother Billy. I don't know if Billy was on the march, but he was in the Bogside somewhere and had warned me to get home because there was going to be trouble. So, when I bumped into Jackie, I warned him "you better watch out, Billy's looking for you and he'll send you home." "I'm alright" he said, "I'm a big boy".

'That was the last time I saw him alive,' Gerry says.

Kay Duddy went to the morgue to identify Jackie's body but she remembers little of the hours and days afterwards. 'I don't remember Jackie's remains being in our house or any of the funerals. That time passed in a blur. None of it has ever come back, and I'm not sure I would want it to.'

Jackie's murder devastated his fourteen siblings and recently widowed father, William. 'My father was so naïve he thought the truth would come out through Widgery,' says Gerry. Widgery's report and the allegations that Jackie had been carrying nail-bombs came as a second devastating blow. 'That's why the campaign was necessary,' says Kay. 'Jackie was just a seventeen-year-old boy who loved his boxing and his girlfriends, just one of our gang and a member of our family. He was buried with his name blackened and that lie just had to be lifted.'

Twenty-six-year-old Willie McKinney was the eldest of ten children. He was a keen amateur photographer, often spotted around the town with his treasured 8mm cine camera, particularly at times of trouble. He recorded confrontations and civil rights marches, as well as local man Sammy Devenney's funeral after he was beaten to death by the RUC in April 1969. Willie always tried to get as close to events as possible, to capture them for posterity. Willie worked as a compositor for the *Derry Journal* newspaper and prided himself on arranging the text and pictures neatly on the pages he put together. He was quiet and reserved by nature and nicknamed 'the professor' by his family. He also had a penchant for the music of Jim Reeves.

Until moments before the shooting began, Willie was filming. The footage captures dramatic scenes of the confrontation on William Street/Aggro Corner and the spray of the water cannon soaking the marchers. It ends abruptly as the tape runs out. Minutes later, Willie was shot in the back by a paratrooper. He collapsed in Glenfada Park alongside Jim Wray and Joe Mahon. He suffered two gunshot wounds. One bullet entered through the back, ripping through his lung and severing his stomach, liver, spleen and colon, before exiting his chest. Another bullet tore a gaping wound in his left arm. He died moments later, his camera lying by his side where it fell. It was never used again.

Mickey McKinney remembers his last glimpses of his big brother. 'He was up a tree in Southway with his camera, getting a good angle of the march. I said to my mates "there's our Willie up there!" That was the last time I ever saw him alive. I was going steady with Goretti, my wife-to-be, at the time and it was only around her that I ever cried about it afterwards. We were concerned about how it affected my mother and father, so there was almost an avoidance of the subject at home. It was rarely talked about.'

John McKinney was the youngest in the house. 'I was only eight but seeing what this did to my mother and father was terrible. The number one reason I got involved was for my mother – I wanted justice for Willie too, but seeing my mother going through hell was the real driving force.' Nancy 'Anne' McKinney died in July 2005 just as the hearings of the second inquiry finished. 'She never saw the end of it,' says Mickey.

John Kelly was always intent on clearing his younger brother's name. Michael was seventeen and the seventh child in a family of thirteen when he was shot dead behind a rubble barricade in Rossville Street. He had no interest in politics; the march on 30 January 1972 was the first he had ever attended. He was training to be a sewing machine mechanic and was a keen pigeon fancier in his spare time. 'My mother helped him build a pigeon loft in the back yard. Sometimes he would take a couple of pigeons to work and let them loose to find their way back home, where my mother would've been watching out for them,' John remembers. 'She enjoyed that.'

Having persuaded his mother to allow him to go, Michael went on the march with friends. 'All his pals were going and there was supposed to be plenty of good-looking girls.'

Just before the march, John told Michael, 'Just be careful, Michael. If anything happens, get off sides.' Michael was standing among a group of people at the barricade in Rossville Street when Soldier F fired a shot into the crowd and Michael was hit. John was close by, taking cover. 'I didn't know where it was coming from, but I knew it was army fire. Then there were people crowded around somebody who'd been shot and I realised it was our Michael.'

Michael and others were spirited to Altnagelvin Hospital in an ambulance. There were two bodies in the vehicle. Michael was pronounced dead upon arrival. John was deeply traumatised, but managed to make a phone call to a friend who relayed the news that Michael was in Altnagelvin to their father at home. Presently, Mr Kelly turned up and, when told that Michael was dead, slid down the wall in shock and wept.

John remembers seeing paras at the hospital, 'wandering around laughing'. He and his father had to go to the mortuary to identify the body formally. The room resembled a horror scene with bodies and blood everywhere. They had to look at each person individually before recognising Michael in the distinctive suit that he'd worn.

Later, as they waited outside the mortuary for a lift home, an army Saracen pulled up and soldiers started dragging bodies out by the hands and feet into the mortuary. 'We couldn't believe what we were seeing,' says John. But there was a more distressing experience to come. Michael's mother was waiting at home for news. 'She was totally devastated. I remember Michael was beautiful, lying in his wee coffin, not a mark on his face. I remember my mother coming running into the room, running to the coffin and lifting his body out shouting and crying "Michael! Son! Michael! Son!" We had to restrain her and try and place him back in the coffin'.

Liam Wray's brother Jim was shot while lying injured on the ground in Glenfada Park. Lord Widgery would later conclude that he had been handling a weapon. Liam speaks fondly of his murdered brother: 'Jim was quite a tall, thin fella and, at 6'1", he was taller than the average Derry man and played basketball at St Joseph's Boys School. He was older than me, but I still refer to him as a young fella. I'm fifty-eight now, Jim died at twenty-two and that's the age I still see him at.'

The Wray family, five brothers and four sisters, were a close-knit, Derry family. Their parents were often back and forth to England for work. 'Jim was a very happy person, full of love and very close to my mother. When my father was in England, Jim became the authority in the house – a role he was quite happy with. Most of the money he earned was put back into the house apart from the odd Saturday night spent in the Castle Bar. He was a big brother you could depend on.'

Liam remembers that Jim was socialist in his views and definitely non-sectarian. He had had Protestant girlfriends and had fallen in love with a Jewish girl, Miriam. They became engaged just weeks before Bloody Sunday. 'Jim brought

Miriam home the Christmas before he was murdered to meet the family. I believe they both had to seek special dispensation to marry.'

The Wray family attended every commemoration march and seized every opportunity to debate Bloody Sunday. Jim's father, James Senior, became one of the more vocal parents, regularly airing his feelings in local papers. 'My father wasn't intimidated by speaking publicly and was interviewed in the run-up to every anniversary,' Liam remembers. 'He seized every opportunity to get his own word out.'

Liam has always been comforted by the idea that his big brother died with his youthful ideals intact. 'I have four children and ten grandchildren now . . . Jim died young and there are times I think to myself, "You didn't live long enough to let life tarnish you." There's a certain beauty in that. So many people in this town develop a sense of hatred, anger and, partisanship, because of their experiences in those years. When Jim died, he was still full of that exuberance, love, and positive attitudes and that is something I cherish.'

Mickey Bradley survived Bloody Sunday. He had been just twenty-two when he witnessed the murder of Jackie Duddy. Seconds later, he too was hit – the bullet ripping through his right arm, penetrating his chest right through to his other arm. The injury left Mickey permanently disabled and he was to spend the rest of his life in pain.

Bloody Sunday changed Mickey's life forever. He spent years immersed in research and investigation – often to the detriment of his family life – and was one of the first survivors to sign up to the campaign. He would die before hearing the truth or seeing justice. His step-daughter Jackie Bradley knows only too well how important the issue had become for him.

Mickey needed no persuasion to join the campaign. Jackie remembers: 'They were called survivors, but he wasn't really a survivor. It took him over. Every single day he talked about Bloody Sunday and it really affected the family. He had an office upstairs filled with papers and he was always reading or researching something. He talked about it to everybody – even the dogs in the street knew Mickey had been shot on Bloody Sunday . . . He wanted to prove himself innocent from the day and hour that it happened. That was his whole life. Widgery named him as a nail-bomber and gunman and he could never accept that.'

The shooting left Mickey with the use of only his left hand and he was never able to work again. 'That really affected the whole house,' Jackie says. 'I know every family have their own story to tell, but within this house our life was torn apart with mood swings and depression…When he went outside he was a clown – putting on a happy face. Nobody knew what went on in this household. The physical side of it was always there – the wound and the paralysis, there every day. We had to help him with all the things people take for granted, like putting on his shoes and socks in the morning. All these years, he had to depend on other people. Mickey was never the same person after Bloody Sunday, never.'

Alana Burke was horrified when initially approached about a campaign. Although badly wounded, Alana had not been not struck by a bullet, but crushed by one of the armoured army vehicles advancing towards the Bogside. Alana says that when someone phoned her to ask about joining the campaign. She said, 'I remember screaming, "How dare you phone me, bringing that back to my mind." I wanted nothing to do with Bloody Sunday after trying to suppress it for so many years. It was too much.'

Alana was eighteen when, she went on the march. She remembers being delighted at the chance to show off a stylish new coat. Less than two hours later, she was hit by an army Saracen as she and hundreds of others fled the paratroopers. A naturally vibrant, bubbly woman, she sustained such injuries to her pelvis that, forty years later, she remains in near-constant pain.

'No matter how many times you tell the story or how much therapy you have, it makes no difference. Bloody Sunday changed everything. It will never, ever go away.'

Alana's most terrible memory was not the armoured vehicle that hit her but of the ambulance that carried her away. 'I was semi-conscious on the floor and there were dead bodies on either side of me. I just remember thinking: are these people dead? Am I dead?'

The teenager returned to her mother and eight siblings in a wheelchair, with crushed pelvis and vertebrae. After months of rehabilitation, she slowly learned to walk again, but the damage didn't go away. 'Doctors told me it was a miracle that I conceived my son Gareth as my pelvis and insides were so badly damaged – they don't know how he survived. They told me to be thankful that my body was so messed up, so I would never have any more. A few years later, I had to have a hysterectomy. Bloody Sunday dictated the way my life was going to go. I dreamed of having a couple of children but it just wasn't to be. I went on to adopt another boy.'

Although terrified of reliving the trauma, Alana listened when fellow survivors Mickey Bridge and Mickey Bradley urged her involvement. Eventually she agreed to give the meetings a chance. It was a personal milestone.

'It was so hard reliving it all over again, but I knew what they were doing was right,' After a few meetings I became more comfortable talking about it. It gradually became easier. We gathered strength from each other. Sharing and listening helped us come to terms with what had happened. I think it made us stronger.'

At the second campaign meeting, the group found a name. 'It was Robin Percival who suggested we call ourselves the Bloody Sunday Justice Campaign, and that was agreed,' Mickey McKinney recalls. 'We tried to organise ourselves properly. John (Kelly) became Chair, I was Vice-Chair, Gerry (Duddy) was Treasurer and Geraldine (Doherty) was the minute-taker.'

'I had never chaired anything in my life and hadn't a clue what a chairman did,' John Kelly laughs. 'But I thought it a privilege that anyone would think I was capable of it. I had never been a secretary, or a treasurer. In fact, I had never been in any organisation before. I think the majority of the people involved at the beginning had no idea what they were going to do, but once the dust settled, there were a few of us really into it, and would never miss meetings. Some people attended occasionally. There was a lot of family dynamics at play. It wasn't always easy.'

Now the hard work began. With Widgery's whitewash deemed the official version of events, it was not going to be easy to convince the world that what had happened was a state-sanctioned massacre. Campaigners were often hurt and frustrated at having to justify themselves and their motives to the wider population, particularly those in their own town.

'People presumed there was a Sinn Féin agenda, that we were being used in some way, but it was nothing like that,' says Gerry Duddy. 'The families themselves had decided to do something about it. It was a rule from the first meeting to the last – no matter what your personal politics, you left them at the door. There may have been different opinions but we all had one thing in common, that this was all about Bloody Sunday.'

[chapter four]

'He died in their hands, not mine'

'How many brothers do you have?' an aggressive RUC detective asked Leo Young in the interrogation cells the morning after Bloody Sunday. Sleep-deprived and still bewildered by the traumatic events of the previous day, Leo replied that he had two brothers. 'You've only one now,' the detective spat back. Hours later, Leo realised that the detective was telling the truth.

Leo had been on the civil rights march. But instead of searching for his brother when the shooting started, he found himself desperately struggling to save a seventeen-year-old stranger from bleeding to death.

Gerald Donaghey was shot and grievously wounded as he tried to escape the troops in Glenfada Park alongside Gerard McKinney. In the following days, while Derry waked its dead, army photographs emerged showing Gerald's lifeless body slumped across the back seat of a car with a sizable nail-bomb bulging from the pocket of his tight denim jeans. A soldier claimed to have found a total of four bombs in his possession. They had been planted. Testimony from civilians including a doctor, a soldier and an army medical officer who had examined Gerald at a checkpoint, contradicted the soldiers' evidence.

Despite all the civilian evidence to the contrary, Lord Saville would later rule that Gerald 'probably' had nail-bombs on his person when he was shot. Campaigners were incredulous: the evidence showed, too, that the fatal bullet had pierced the pocket supposedly packed with a nail-bomb.

Leo Young was among the terrified civilians who had helped carry the dying Gerald to a nearby house. 'When we undid his shirt and saw the open gunshot wound, my head was really spinning, and then a doctor appeared and said we had to get him to hospital,' he recalls. He definitely had nothing in his pockets. I searched his pockets myself when I was looking for ID because nobody knew who he was. He didn't have any on him. He was just a fresh young boy that we had to get to hospital.' Leo had no idea of the tragedy ahead of him.

John Young, the youngest of a family of six, had also been on the march. Leo had promised their mother that he would keep an eye on him. John was seventeen and full of exuberance. He split his time working at John Temple's menswear shop and as a roadie for a popular showband of the day, The Scene. He adored showbands. Although worried sick about his brother, Leo found himself caught up in the mayhem and agreed to help Raymond Rogan – whose house Gerry Donaghey had been carried into – get the nameless boy to hospital. Both men knew the army would probably stop the car in search of rioters. Their fears were realised before they were clear of the Bogside. They were halted at a checkpoint near the Long Tower Chapel, less than a mile from where the boy had been shot.

Leo remembers that he and Raymond Rogan were 'dragged out by the scruff of the neck'. 'I pleaded with the soldiers about the young fella in the back of the car. He was still alive, I had held him and looked into his eyes. He was dying and needed help. But his body did not arrive at Altnagelvin hospital until over two hours later, around 6.30pm. He died in their hands, not in mine.'

Gerald Donaghey's big sister Mary Doherty campaigned for many years to clear his name. She became one of the strongest voices advocating the victims' cause. They had been particularly close. Mary was older and married and had taken Gerald in to live with her when he was eleven after both their parents died within four weeks of each other. She became the mother figure in young Gerald's life.

Mary Doherty succumbed to cancer just months after the publication of the Saville Report. Her death dealt a crushing blow to fellow campaigners. Her role was taken over by her daughter Geraldine. 'I was born the year after Bloody Sunday so I never knew Gerald,' Geraldine explains. 'But my mother would have done anything for him.'

Regardless of all her campaigning, Mary had gone to her grave dissatisfied. Lord Saville did not concede that the military had planted weapons on her brother; the terrorist slur remained. All other families could rejoice in the declarations of innocence, but Gerald Donaghey's family couldn't.

Leo Young remains entirely convinced of Gerald's innocence. Four decades later, he still regrets the turn of events that led to the trio separating at the checkpoint and Gerald being, presumably, left to bleed to death alone. He insists that Lord Saville's ruling on the matter was simply wrong.

Leo's ordeal did not end when he and Raymond Rogan were forced to abandon the blood-soaked youngster. Even worse was to come. Leo was arrested at the checkpoint and his clothes seized for forensic tests. He was taken to Strand Road RUC barracks and then onto Ballykelly where he was interrogated throughout the night.

'I had no idea so many people were dead, that John was dead – they never told me. I lost all track of time. They questioned me about how many nail-bombs the young boy had on him. I told them that if he had been contaminated then I would have been contaminated too as he had been lying over my chest.'

The following afternoon Leo was told of his brother's death. 'Back at Strand Road barracks, a detective came in and asked if "Young" was here. He glanced at a folder before looking me straight in the face. That's when he asked, "How many brothers do you have?" and I said two, and he said "You've only one now".'

Leo didn't fully grasp what the detective was implying. 'It didn't hit me until I was halfway home. When I reached the corner of Inishowen Gardens, I could see our house on Westway and people gathered outside and thought "Jesus no . . ."'

'They were waiting at the door. I felt so guilty facing my mother but she just said "You better go up and see him" as John was already laid out upstairs. It was terrible. He was shot near the eye and the bullet travelled down and broke his spine on the way out.'

'I was twenty-five years old at the time and our John was only seventeen. If he was living today, he would be in his fifties and might have had a family, but he never got that chance. He was always so full of ideas of what he was going to do, but then like everyone else, he was in the wrong place at the wrong time. And look what happened.'

Floyd Gilmour was another family member to come on board in the first year of the campaign. His brother Hugh had been murdered just yards away from the safety of the Rossville Flats. A terrified marcher, Geraldine Richmond, saw Hugh fall and cradled him in her arms, whispering an Act of Contrition in his ear as his life ebbed away. Before he died, Hugh cried out, 'I want my mammy, go get me mammy.'

Hugh Gilmour was seventeen in 1972 and lived with his family of eight in the high-rise Rossville Flats. He was an ardent Liverpool supporter and had just bought his first car, determined to pass his driving test.

Floyd played an integral role in the campaign and travelled far and wide to spread the word. When Floyd died at the beginning of the millennium, his sister Olive stepped into the breach: 'I was really close to Floyd . . . I had never really thought about Bloody Sunday much and it was only when Floyd, God have mercy on him, got involved that I began considering the possibility that we might get somewhere. When he died, I had already retired, so I decided to take over where he left off. The world needed to know it was murder.'

'I often asked myself why – when we knew they weren't gunmen or bombers – we needed proof. When I thought about it seriously, though, I realised that what it was that the rest of the world needed to know.'

Olive remembers her baby brother with great fondness. 'There was no badness in our Hugh. He left school and worked in the tyre factory in William Street. He was an apprentice motor mechanic when he died. He went to the pictures every Friday night and always brought my mother home a quarter of dolly mixtures!'

Living in Rossville Flats, Hugh Gilmour had found himself at the forefront of the civil unrest sweeping the North in 1969. 'Hugh never missed his work, but when the Troubles really began he would come home from work, have his dinner, get a wash and head straight out to Rossville Street for a bit of rioting,' Olive says. 'There was nothing unusual in a wee bit of rioting back then – all the young ones were at it! It was just a bit of a laugh I suppose, a sign of the times.'

Although unaware of her brother's fatal shooting, Olive witnessed many other horrors from her vantage point in the flats overlooking the killing ground. 'I watched everything unfold from the veranda and saw some terrible things,' she says. She was determined to testify before the Widgery Tribunal in Coleraine and was one of the few civilians witnesses called. 'I saw Jackie Duddy getting shot, Mickey Bridge getting shot, I saw Paddy Doherty lying on the ground . . . People were saying that Widgery was a waste of time, but I knew I had to go there for Jackie Duddy – I watched him die. I just needed to tell them all that he had nothing in his hands when they shot him and I just presumed Widgery would give us a fair trial.'

Giving evidence was an ordeal for all involved. Genuine eyewitnesses were berated, their claims of murder ignored. When Lord Widgery subsequently published his findings, Olive, Floyd and the rest of the family were furious. 'I went ballistic,' Olive admits. 'I think my mother and father just blanked it out. My mother knew that Hugh wasn't a gun man or bomber and so she just didn't care what anyone thought. She knew the truth and Derry knew the truth. She kept it all locked in. Hugh was her baby, he had that innocence about him.'

Early campaign meetings were something of a ritual for many. Although the campaign had the backing of all the families, only seven or eight families regularly attended meetings in West End Park.

Geraldine Doherty remembers: 'Every Tuesday night without fail, Mickey McKinney would collect me, my mother and Kay Duddy to go to the meetings. We would all be huddled around a wee heater in West End Park. At the beginning, nobody really knew where we were going, but we met up and talked anyway. I was the minute-taker at that time.' Initial campaign meetings proved difficult while people got to know each other, but the process gradually became easier.

'We shared ideas, no matter how ridiculous they seemed,' says Kay. 'At that stage, we hadn't even a pen or pencil or a writing pad to take notes on, so all that basic stuff was needed and we realised we were going to have to do a lot of fundraising.'

Tony Doherty remembers some of the intricacies of establishing the campaign. 'We did the typical things that a campaign is supposed to do. We got headed paper drawn up and we started writing to anyone we could think of. At the time, I was volunteering full time for the Bloody Sunday Initiative and I would have taken on a lot of the initial spadework, contacting people, writing letters and drawing up campaign statements.'

With little concept or experience in campaigning, they relied on instinct and group discussion. 'It was a huge learning process,' Kay Duddy admits.

'Looking back, it was almost like a support group too because we suddenly had a chance to talk about it all. It was very emotional, very highly strung at times. It was frustrating, and there were nights where we just hadn't a clue what we were talking about or what we were doing.

'Although we had waited twenty years, the timing seemed right. Personally, I always imagined someone would have come clean about Bloody Sunday years ago. I always thought someone somewhere would say "hang on – this is wrong". But they didn't – so me and Gerry got involved with the family's blessing. For a while it carried on like that, just reporting back to the family how things were going.'

The Bloody Sunday Justice Campaign began to seek funding. In May 1992, Derry City Council announced that while supporting 'in principle' plans to heighten pressure on the British government, it was reserving judgement on funding the group until the legal implications were examined. Campaign chairperson John Kelly attended the monthly meeting of the Council's Policy and Resources Committee where he outlined the group's aims and asked for support, 'financially and morally'. He estimated the campaign would need a total grant of more than £16,000 to set up a campaign office, pay administration, salary and electricity costs. John explained to the committee: 'Such a massive exercise needs a physical and financial base in Derry and it is in relation to establishing such a base that we hope Derry City Council can be of practical assistance.'

The request met with a mixed response. SDLP councillor Pat Devine reasoned that, before making any decision, the Council would have to receive both legal and financial advice. Sinn Féin's Mitchel McLaughlin, later a Northern Ireland MLA, voiced his support. He spoke of the 'general acknowledgment in Derry that Bloody Sunday was a great injustice and that the subsequent Widgery Report was no more than an intricately planned whitewash.'

The SDLP's Tony Carlin agreed: 'We are duty bound to support this campaign. Bloody Sunday has been a contributing factor to the violence we are currently experiencing. It should be made clear to all in the public limelight that Derry City Council is behind this group and their aims.'

In contrast, DUP Deputy Mayor, councillor William Hay, was not so supportive. 'We all have our own personal beliefs of what happened on Bloody Sunday. The DUP's stance is that the IRA manipulated the march for their own selfish ends . . . when the unionist tradition in this city stand back and view the individuals associated with this group and those who support it, they are reluctant to lend it their support.'

As the campaign strove to convey its message and motivation to as wide a spectrum as possible, Tony Doherty travelled to London to speak at a high-profile human rights convention in spring 1992. Tony travelled with fellow campaigner Martin Finucane. Both hoped they could present the case to an unfamiliar but sympathetic audience.

'I was really sick beforehand in the toilets with nerves,' Tony admits. 'It meant that we were beginning to get into the mainstream human rights arena in Britain, which is exactly where we needed to go. But I was really nervous about presenting the case, and even more so about talking personally about my own father's case.'

Despite his apprehensions, Tony delivered a blazing speech that all present agreed did his fellow campaigners proud. Exponents on many human rights issues were taking part, including speakers from the plastic bullets campaign and collusion campaign. The event attracted considerable media attention. For the fledgling Bloody Sunday campaigners, it marked the first of many presentations in England.

On Saturday 20 June 1992, the Bloody Sunday Justice Campaign launched a new postcard campaign urging British prime minister John Major to reopen the case. Family members set up a stall outside the old Ulster Bank on Waterloo Place in Derry where they sat, often huddled under umbrellas, speaking to local people and handing out the postcards. Each of the pre-addressed cards carried the campaign logo and listed the three demands.

'By signing your card, you can register your anger or discontent to the British government which still refuses to admit to its crimes in Ireland even after twenty years,' they told the press.

The postcards and public lobbying generated much needed publicity and had the added benefit of helping local people put a face to those behind the campaign. Mickey McKinney says the postcard initiative was one of the campaign's early successes. 'The public responded very well and sent the postcards off to Downing Street. We felt we were really beginning to spread the word, that people were beginning to listen.'

John Kelly wrote to Prime Minister John Major on 2 July 1992 to express the campaign's 'widely held dissatisfaction as to the government's continued inaction' over Bloody Sunday. Referring to a letter from Major in March in which he said the victims 'should be regarded' as innocent, he urged Major to 'publicly and unambiguously' acknowledge the innocence of victims, 'publicly repudiate the Widgery report in its entirety' and press for prosecutions of those responsible.

'The lack of will shown by successive British governments to arrive at the truth and administer justice in the case of Bloody Sunday has seriously undermined our faith in and respect for the law. I despair that we have not progressed in our search for justice after all this time.'

The campaign was already gaining attention in the USA. In August 1992, relatives of the fourteen people shot dead received commemorative parchments issued by the City Council of Chicago following the passing of a resolution by remembering the Derry dead. As John Kelly observed at the time, this resolution was an indication of the group's efforts to keep the injustices of Bloody Sunday at the fore both at home and abroad.

Within a month of their latest correspondence, the families received a response from 10 Downing Street. The letter from the Prime Minister's private secretary on 29 August said nothing new: 'The government is conscious of the depth of feeling to which "Bloody Sunday" still gives rise,' it read. 'As far as the events of that day itself are concerned, the Prime Minister has already explained in the correspondence to which you refer why the government does not think it would be right to review or reopen the Tribunal of Inquiry established in 1972.'

Although the campaign lobbied relentlessly, their requests were often met with distain and indifference. Mary Robinson, President of Ireland at the time, refused to meet family members or lay a wreath at the Bloody Sunday memorial during a visit to Derry on Sunday 6 September 1992. Ironically, the President had been in town to open a conference entitled 'Beyond Hate'. The Bloody Sunday Justice Campaign described Robinson's 'blatant snub' as both 'insensitive and inexcusable', particularly as she has just laid a wreath in Enniskillen, Fermanagh, and met with relatives of those killed in an IRA bomb attack there on Remembrance Sunday in 1989.

John Kelly said at the time: 'While we welcome the President's visit to Enniskillen and endorse the laying of the floral tribute at the cenotaph, we find it very surprising she did not pay such a tribute to the dead of Bloody Sunday . . . Her insensitivity is inexcusable.'

'This was a human rights issue and we were trying to put it right,' he reflects. 'Murder had happened on the streets of Derry and we were trying to engage with people and gain support for the campaign. We weren't looking for money or anything like that, we just wanted to explain what we were trying to do and hopefully get their support."

Campaigners also found that the Protestant church leaders, while generally sympathetic, wouldn't openly say this or couldn't publically support them. Still, the families refused to give up. They knew that genuine cross-community support was important to the foundations of the campaign and its wider acceptance. It would be worth the perseverance.

In October 1992, six months into the campaign, the Bloody Sunday Justice Campaign announced it was to seek legal advice on prosecuting both military and government personnel involved in the decision to open fire. A spokesperson said at the time: 'The campaign has set up a research unit which shall study and – with professional advice from both here and Britain – help prepare the case of murder against those responsible. We are now in regular contact with civil liberties groups in Ireland, Britain and Europe.'

The families gradually felt more at ease speaking to reporters and became adept at using the press to their advantage. 'We had to learn to use the press rather than letting them use us,' Kay Duddy says. 'Usually, if it's not bad news, it doesn't sell papers, but I think eventually the press realised we were on to something.'

The families realised that they would benefit greatly from legal support. The group had strong connections with Martin Finucane, brother of murdered Belfast solicitor, Pat Finucane, so they contacted Madden & Finucane Solicitors in Belfast, initiating what was to become a long relationship with the firm.

Initial meetings between campaigners and legal advisors were held in Peter Madden's office in Belfast with solicitor Seamus Treacy, a specialist in human rights cases. Treacy later represented families during the Bloody Sunday Inquiry and, in 2007, was appointed a high court judge. 'That was the first time we had ever met legal advisors,' Tony Doherty says. 'These people would have been close personal friends of Pat Finucane and were quite friendly towards us and towards any notion of us doing something legally.'

There was no clear outcome from the initial meeting at Madden & Finucane, but the group discussed the possibility of taking their case to the European

Court of Human Rights. 'Seamus Treacy told us that because Bloody Sunday had been subject to an inquiry in 1972 that was effectively the end of the possible remedies under domestic law. That was unbelievable considering there had never been a murder investigation. But we were advised we could start looking at the European Commission.'

The Nashs, a close-knit family of thirteen, immersed themselves in the early campaign and remained to the forefront throughout.

In January 1972, the family had been celebrating the success of son Charlie following a triumph at the National Boxing Championships in Dublin. They were also jubilant about the marriage of another son, John. State-sanctioned murder was the last thing on their mind.

On 30 January, the day after the family wedding, nineteen-year-old William was gunned down at the rubble barricade on Rossville Street. Seconds later, his father Alex was shot and wounded as he ran to his dying son's side from the shelter of adjacent houses.

Bloody Sunday transformed the Nash family forever. Neither William nor his father, Alex were particularly political. Neither was posing any threat of any kind when the advancing paratroopers opened fire. William had worked alongside his father on the Derry docks; he loved country and western music. He died wearing his best suit, having toasted his brother's wedding the previous day and not yet been home to change. As author Don Mullan notes in *Eyewitness Bloody Sunday*, the smart suit was 'hardly the regalia of a "terrorist"'.

Confined to Altnagelvin Hospital, Alexander Nash had to watch his son's funeral on television, his sobs and the wailing of other survivors swirling through the crowded ward.

The rubble barricade in Rossville Street lay directly in the paratroopers' line of fire as they advanced into the Bogside. Five young men were killed there, amid the bricks and detritus: William Nash, Michael Kelly, John Young, Kevin McElhinney and Michael McDaid. While scores of marchers sheltered from the hail of bullets, they paid the price for being caught in open ground, paid with their lives.

Michael McDaid, the second youngest of a family of twelve and a barman in Derry's Celtic Bar, was killed instantly by a single gunshot to the face. He was twenty. After Bloody Sunday, a photograph emerged showing a crowd gathered around the mortally wounded Michael Kelly behind the barricade. In the background, Michael McDaid is clearly visible walking away from the gunfight, his back to the soldiers, presumably escaping the affray and heading towards the safety of Free Derry Corner. The photograph captures Michael's final steps.

Michael always prided himself on being immaculately dressed, his trousers neatly ironed, his shoes always shined. When gunned down, he was wearing his very best clothes and a particularly smart suit jacket – dressed to impress.

Like many of the mothers of the Bloody Sunday dead, Michael's mother was never the same. The McDaids' home was a loving household filled with frequent singing and much happiness. After Michael was murdered, the family never heard their mother sing again. The wider McDaid family were involved from the earliest incarnations of the campaign, as Michael's brother Kevin recalls: 'At the start, myself and my mother and brother John went to a meeting in Pilot's Row. It was mainly families and anyone else who was interested in starting a campaign. After the whitewash of the first inquiry, that had been it for me. I thought we just had to accept it.

'When the campaign got into full swing, I didn't do much. I wasn't the best of speakers. But I was always there and always willing if they needed me. To be honest, I never really thought the tables would turn, but people did eventually begin to take notice.

'I was seventeen when Michael died. As we grew up, we didn't exactly grow apart but we did our own thing. We still got along great. Michael ended up getting a Ford Cortina, it was his pride and joy. He would take me and my mother and father to Buncrana or Galway. They were the first holidays we ever took.'

The Bloody Sunday families, as they had collectively become known, continued to campaign strongly. But financial support was proving elusive. Efforts to fundraise at a local level were largely unsuccessful. There was frustration at times as the group tried to find its feet, and the members were at pains to stress that the BSJC was a family-led campaign, a fact that was not always accepted by the Catholic Church, the Irish government or Derry City Council at the time. There was no apparent support for the families' efforts.

On 17 October 1992, the families sought the support of Ireland's Catholic Cardinal, Cathal Daly. Having written His Eminence a respectful letter, they were shocked when he declined to meet them. The Cardinal's initial response was just a few lines long: 'I am exceedingly busy for many weeks ahead and cannot see an early free date. I have read your literature carefully and I offer good wishes for the campaign.'

John Kelly recalls: 'We were very, very angry. We couldn't believe that the head of the Catholic Church in this country refused to meet his own people. It was a major snub.'

The campaign replied, assuring the Cardinal that they would be willing to wait for his convenience, since the campaign was a long-term affair. That too received a negative response – this time from the Diocesan Secretary – saying that His Eminence was too busy to reply personally. Campaigners were stunned, naturally expecting more of a Cardinal of All Ireland.

Tony recalls with some resentment the early refusal of Derry's local authority to provide funding for the group. 'They said that had been advised that funding the campaign would have been contrary to the rules of local government because there would have been no clear benefit to the population of the city – which is just unbelievable.'

In time, the Council's attitude changed. But its financial support was never guaranteed. 'It was, in my opinion disgraceful that a nationalist council wasn't prepared to support the families – particularly when you look at the events of 15 June 2010 when the Saville Report was finally published, and you see the benefits that that brought for the city,' Tony said.

He believes that sheer perseverance was responsible for the Council's change of heart. 'Eventually it became clear that we weren't going to go away and that the campaign was very much family-led. But we should never have had to go out of our way to prove that – it should have been easily understood within the context of Derry.'

Patrick Campbell was among thirteen marchers wounded. The experience so horrified him that he never spoke a word about Bloody Sunday again. A Creggan man and father of six, Patrick went to his grave in January 1985, aged sixty-six, never having seen justice done.

Patrick's son Johnny became involved in the campaign in the early 1990s. 'My father literally never mentioned it, never went on another march or watched anything about it on TV.' Johnny was twenty-two when his father was shot and he remembers the trauma. When the campaign was established he was eager to help: 'I jumped in with two feet and started attending meetings. John, Mickey and the others did the bulk of the work and just kept us informed – they deserve all the credit. When the campaign really kicked off, it was exciting. There were many highs. But there was plenty of knock-backs and downers too. It was very frustrating at times.'

Intent on seeking support outside Derry and, particularly in Britain, relatives contacted the London-based human rights group, British Irish Rights Watch. The relationship they forged with BIRW director Jane Winter was to last through the campaign and the inquiry and well into the new millennium.

'Jane Winter was a massive help to us over the years,' Mickey McKinney says. 'She was there to give advice and was involved in the search for documents – a major player. She really opened doors for us.'

'It was the beginnings of the campaign in 1992 when I got a letter saying that it was the twentieth anniversary of Bloody Sunday and they needed some outside help and advice on how to broaden the issue,' said Jane. She was aware of Bloody Sunday and vividly recalls being 'very, very shocked' at the time. 'I was a twenty-one year old university student and I thought it was an outrage. But I wasn't involved in anything to do with Northern Ireland then, and most people in England weren't interested in Northern Ireland. Bloody Sunday seemed to become yesterday's news very quickly and there was no obvious campaign that ever reached London. But when they got in touch, it was obvious to me that this was a significant human rights issue.'

As a result, Jane then contacted the Bloody Sunday Initiative in Derry and spoke with Martin Finucane. Persuaded to help, she agreed to travel to the North to meet with families and campaigners.

The meeting was by no means crowded, with just a small number of core campaigners present. 'Listening to them speak, I realised that they had been banging their heads against a brick wall for twenty years and were really at a loss,' Jane says.

'My immediate thought was that it would be difficult to take the case to the European Court of Human Rights, as you have to apply within six months of having exhausted all domestic remedies. They hadn't taken any domestic remedies but all the time limits meant it would have been very difficult to move in that direction and so I suggested that I begin to write a report to submit to the United Nations.'

Jane returned to London to begin researching and drafting the UN report. In Derry, the work continued unabated, with campaigners thinking up increasingly novel ways to fund their endeavours.

'To begin with, we ran functions in the Delacroix Bar,' Mickey McKinney remembers. 'We didn't make a lot of money early on, and so Gerry Duddy came up with the idea of the 200 Club – each one of us would take twenty tickets a month for prizes donated by local people and businessmen and had to sell them by the end of the next month. The winner got £100 and we made money from the ticket sales. We also held draws coming up to Christmas too. Once we had Tommy Burn play in The Wolfe Tones. That was our biggest fundraiser ever. I think we raised £4,000 in one night.'

Tony Doherty remembers campaigners distributing BSJC collection boxes into shops all over the city to encourage public donations. 'Everything cost money, getting the postcards and campaign leaflets drawn up and printed, sending campaign representatives to various places – we needed the finances to do these things.'

One major source of funding was the Catholic, Irish-American organisation, the Ancient Order of Hibernians (AOH), which had particularly strong connections to the North. Their contribution and encouragement proved invaluable. Mickey McKinney has been a member of the AOH since 1975. Willie had been a member in the 1960s. Mickey coordinated with the organisation and kept them abreast of developments.

'I made contact with the president of the local AOH Club, Jimbo Crossan. I would meet Jimbo on a Saturday night and he'd come up with ideas on how to secure funding from the AOH here in Ireland, as well as in Scotland and America. Over the years since, the AOH has been the campaign's best funder and they deserve a lot of credit.'

The campaign organised public meetings and provided speakers to events in Derry, Belfast and Dublin. For many, it was a full-time job; there was always work to be done, people to lobby.

Tony Doherty acknowledged the wide support the campaign was beginning to attract. 'People held benefits in various parts of the country to help fund it. I remember Pearce Doherty, who is now a TD in Donegal, ran events for us in the early 1990s.'

But there was still a residual suspicion of the campaign, particularly in some circles in the South. 'We were continuing to do a lot of letter writing to the likes of Taoiseach Charlie Haughey and other politicians both in Ireland and England. Charlie Haughey was an absolute disgrace. He refused to meet us and refused to do anything for us. But we got publicity out of that, so the effort wasn't entirely wasted.'

The press south of the border was not particularly interested, Tony recalls. 'There was a lot of apathy in the Southern media with regard to Northern issues. Most of them were tired of hearing about the conflict . . . I think that at that point our campaign was generally viewed as some sort of republican-front organisation. But I was always genuine in the view that this shouldn't be a republican campaign because, if it was, it wouldn't get anywhere. There were also families who weren't republicans and the campaign had to be representative of all. But that's not how other people saw it, obviously.'

Widely held beliefs would prove difficult to change, and it remained an up-hill struggle to alter perceptions.

Survivor Alana Burke revisited traumatic memories to join others in pursuit of truth, but it was never easy. 'There were so many obstacles and it was difficult at times because of the names we were called and people's general perception of us. At the time of Bloody Sunday I got hate mail to my home and there were so many articles in newspapers over the years that stripped you of your reputation. People tried to discredit the families at every opportunity. But in the end, we would achieve vindication.'

[chapter five]

'Breaking down barriers'

Some of the campaign's key players were neither relatives nor survivors. A succession of lawyers, authors, professors and human rights activists played fundamental roles. Solicitor Patricia Coyle was a key player, having been deeply involved in the early stages of the campaign. John Kelly acknowledges her huge contribution: 'Patricia played a major role in the final outcome of the campaign. I think the fact that she is from Derry was important. The case really mattered to her.'

Patricia was a fledgling solicitor at Madden and Finucane in Belfast when she first became involved in the Bloody Sunday case.

'Initially Kevin Winters, a partner in the firm, together with Martin Finucane, brother of Pat Finucane, met with the families in Derry in early 1992,' she recalls.

Madden's late partner, Pat Finucane, was a Belfast-based defence lawyer murdered in 1989 for defending prominent republicans. Loyalist paramilitaries burst into his home and shot him fourteen times as he ate Sunday dinner with his wife and children. The UDA later admitted responsibility. It remains widely believed that the group acted in collusion with security forces. To this day, the full truth of this killing has yet to come out.

Kevin Winters commissioned a report from Keith Borer, a forensic scientist based in Durham, England, dealing with the unreliability of the paraffin test used to test for lead on the victims of Bloody Sunday. Patricia didn't need to think twice when Kevin then asked her if she was interested in dealing with the case.

'As a native of Derry and a child of the 1970s, I grew up well aware of the impact of Bloody Sunday and the stench and notoriety of the Widgery Inquiry . . . My parents and members of our extended family were on the NICRA march in 1972. The fact that Widgery remained as the official record of what happened was reprehensible.'

In the summer of 1992, Patricia received a slim blue file from Kevin Winters, which, at that stage, contained instructions from the families, minutes of meetings with the families, the Keith Borer report and correspondence with government and the families.

Patricia says it was clear they only had a very limited amount of material and that intensive research would be needed. She says that the Borer Report was an important starting point in that it confirmed that the paraffin test was 'crude in the extreme' and susceptible to false positives from everyday items such as leaded paint and petrol fumes. It also dealt with the high possibility of secondary transfer and contamination from lead particles from soldiers who had fired shots and then manhandled those killed when transferring them to vehicles.

Patricia says of the Widgery report. 'The first injustice of the Widgery Report was the effective exoneration of the soldiers who had killed and wounded. The second injustice was the "official" stain left on the victims. That is why commissioning a forensic report was important from a legal perspective. The third injustice was to the Derry people, to all the civilian witnesses who were never called to give evidence at the Widgery Tribunal. Widgery's report cites the alleged late arrival of the civilian statements as reason to discount them entirely. This artifice was contrived by Widgery so he could ignore the civilian evidence.'

The sheer number of potential eyewitnesses is one of the reasons the subsequent Saville Inquiry was to become so complex and lengthy. Patricia believes that in 1972, the absence of civilian evidence from the body of evidence 'created a natural bias in itself.'

After reviewing the file, Patricia arranged to meet with the clients in Derry. It was a meeting that was to have a profound effect on her both personally and professionally.

'I will never forget that first meeting with the families and the wounded. We gathered at the Pat Finucane Centre in West End Park. The room was packed and there were not enough chairs for everyone. I had not been in practice very long. I was nervous. I had a basic understanding of the history and evidence of the case and of the obvious evidential problems with the Widgery Inquiry and Report.

'Even at that stage, being from Derry left me with an acute sense of responsibility towards the clients. Ironically, they had little expectation of any real results from lawyers so the bar was set low from the start.'

What was required was either new or previously undiscovered evidence, which would significantly change the pattern of evidence given to the Widgery Inquiry or demonstrate bias. Material of that sort could have opened the way to an international application to the European Court of Human Rights.

At that first meeting in 1992, it was agreed that the first step was to collect all available documentary evidence. 'In any case, a lawyer requires core materials,' Patricia says. 'In this case we did not have any documents other than the Borer Report, background instructions from the clients and correspondence. 1992 was just before the age of online Internet searches so documents had to be physically tracked down. What took three years to find then would probably take three hours with today's technology.'

Several basic documents were needed: the Widgery Report, the full transcript of the Widgery Inquiry proceedings, and a copy of the Tribunals of Inquiry (Evidence) Act 1921. 'John Kelly provided me with an original version of the Widgery Report. I got a copy of the 1921 Tribunal of Inquiry Act at Queens' Law Library. An initial comparative analysis of just those two documents alone was very telling. It shows the degree to which Widgery deliberately failed in what he was tasked to do. The purpose of a public inquiry under the 1921 Act is to restore public confidence – the reverse of which occurred with the publication of Widgery's report in April 1972.'

Tony Doherty welcomed Patricia Coyle's intervention. 'Patricia was great to work with. She was terrific with people and passionate about the campaign. She would often say how proud she was to represent us and I think she genuinely meant it.'

While Patricia busied herself examining the intricacies of the case, the families and survivors continued to meet regularly. The gatherings were often fraught affairs but campaigners persevered, focusing on the bigger picture.

'The meetings created a new sense of solidarity,' affirmed Liam Wray. 'There were many arguments and many different views but there was a real sense of family, too. They talk about the Bloody Sunday families, but it would be more accurate to say the Bloody Sunday family.

'In general terms, we were all individuals carrying this hurt and this anger and it became, for good or bad, a large family. At times, that was a really special thing to be a part of – at other times it was hard going.

'There was great innovation at times, opportunities that were realised and used to make the campaign better. On refection, some of the meetings were rough and people nearly came to blows.

'Whoever thinks the Bloody Sunday families are a solid unit is crazy. We were all very different people with different views. But we had one goal that kept everybody together. We always gave the face to the public that we were completely solid. But any family has its natural ups and downs. In the end, we worked well together and we supported each other fine.'

There were difficulties ensuring that the campaign remained politically neutral and family led – particularly while seeking all-round support from Sinn Féin and the SDLP, as well as Derry City Council.

'Sinn Féin was ready to support us, but we had to work at the SDLP. We spent some time chasing after John Hume. He was busy, hard to pin down, we often had to be patient and just wait. We needed him.'

John Hume, leader of the SDLP at the time, became a strong advocate of the Bloody Sunday Justice Campaign. He would later become the only person to receive the world's three most prestigious peace awards – the 1998 Nobel Peace Prize, the Gandhi Peace Prize and the Martin Luther King Award.

On 20 January 1993, John Major responded to another letter from John Hume supporting the families with an assurance that he was 'well aware of the depth of feeling that remains in Londonderry about "Bloody Sunday". It would not be right for me to seek to cast judgement on the events of "Bloody Sunday" at this distance in time; nor would it be right for me, retrospectively, to comment on the actions of the soldiers on that day, or on the guilt or innocence of any individual or individuals involved in those events.

'The government made clear in 1974 that those who were killed on "Bloody Sunday" should be regarded as innocent of any allegations that they were shot whilst handling firearms or explosives. I hope that the families of those who died will accept that assurance.'

Hume welcomed the fact that relatives had been able to take some encouragement from the letter. However, he added: 'If, as the Prime Minister admits, the victims were innocent of handling weapons or explosives when they were shot, there could be no justification for shooting them. That fundamental reality should be acknowledged by the authorities.'

The families gave a guarded welcome to the long overdue admission. But it wasn't enough. They issued a statement: 'We view Mr. Major's partial admission of innocence as our first significant success after almost a year of solid campaigning. However, now that we have established some degree of innocence of the victims of Bloody Sunday, we shall continue in our quest for justice . . . Those responsible for the murders of innocent people on Bloody Sunday are still at large; no attempt has been made to bring them to justice. Prosecutions of these people remains the ultimate objective of the BSJC which we shall pursue with renewed vigour in 1993.'

Rather than pacify the citizens of Derry, Major's letter had quite the opposite effect.

'The admission of innocence only sharpened the case for the campaign,' activist Eamonn McCann agrees. 'Some people, including John Hume, welcomed the admission of innocence from Major, saying, "well, that's it then, it's over." But we had to disagree – to say they were innocent only raises the question of why they were shot.'

Jane Winter, of British Irish Rights Watch, described Major's admission as 'a big step forward.'

'It was progress, however small. It was the first time there had ever been a chink of recognition from the government.'

However, the limits of the British government's willingness to move towards the truth came through the day after Major's letter when NI Secretary of State, Sir Patrick Mayhew told the Commons that, while he appreciated that Bloody Sunday had been a 'great tragedy', he felt it 'unwise' to re-open a matter which had already been the subject of a judicial inquiry. In Derry, family members publicly vowed to step up their campaign.

And another storm was brewing. A week after Major's letter, the Bloody Sunday Justice Campaign called for the resignation of NI Security Minister, Michael Mates for remarks he'd made on RTÉ television's *Prime Time* programme. 'There would have been no murder if it hadn't been for the bloody riot organised by those very nationalists and I think that has to be said . . . It was a very violent riot. They [soldiers] were very frightened. It was out of hand. The police were in no way able to cope and the army had no means of defending themselves other than bullets . . . I think the army was very unfairly blamed for it,' Mates insisted.

The campaign described Mates's attempt to blame victims for their own deaths as 'shocking and disconcerting' and branded his remarks 'an insult to the victims'.

'We say directly to Michael Mates: this is the most pathetic justification for murder that we have heard in twenty-three years of violence. You have insulted the memory of the dead of Bloody Sunday. Apologies are not enough. You are unfit for office, you should resign and leave this country.'

Derry City Council also called for Mates' resignation, while, from

Washington, Congressman Joseph Kennedy – son of assassinated presidential hopeful Bobby Kennedy – hit out at the security minister's remarks. 'More than adding insult to injury for the families and the memory of the victims, his attitude only sends a message from the British government to the nationalist community that their most basic human and civil right – the right to life – does not count,' the Congressman said.

On Sunday 31 January 1993, a crowd of around 7,000 gathered at the Creggan Shops for the annual commemoration march, the surge in attendance no doubt due to the well-publicised campaign launch and widespread media coverage over the previous months. The concerted effort to depoliticise commemorations also had a big impact on attendance numbers, attracting many more to walk the route alongside the families.

Former Birmingham Six prisoner Paddy Hill was among those invited to speak at the 1993 rally. Addressing the crowd, he described the British army as 'filth and scum' and said the only way to deal with them was to 'send them back . . . in boxes because that's what they do to us.'

The outburst sparked a storm of protest. Several unionist politicians called for Hill's prosecution. The march organisers were forced to reiterate: 'We have consistently stated that we do not support violence and are committed to working non-violently. We do not support the shooting of British soldiers or anyone else.'

A few days later, Paddy Hill admitted that personal stress combined with the emotion he felt when confronted with the legacy of Bloody Sunday and the recent comments of Michael Mates, had left him 'quite overcome' and led him to say a number of things 'I did not intend or mean to say and which I now deeply regret.

'I can only apologise to all those who were justifiably offended and distressed by what I said, especially those who supported myself and my fellow prisoners over the years and who were, and are, completely opposed to violence. I hope this statement will undo some of the damage that has been done,' he added.

Weeks later, in late February 1993, the British prime minister rejected another call for a new inquiry, this time from the British Labour Party's NI spokesperson, Kevin McNamara. The refusal compounded the anger of campaigners and led to more press coverage. Tony Doherty's brother Paul called on church leaders and political parties in Britain to add their voices to the demands for action.

'There is now a rising tide of opinion both in Britain and Ireland demanding that the British government moves on Bloody Sunday and John Major is struggling to swim against it . . . It must now be evident to all that Bloody Sunday is not going to disappear. We who are campaigning to clear the names of the deceased and to bring to justice those responsible for their murders will continue to challenge the Majors and the Mates of this world.'

Campaigning was tough for many relatives, survivors and activists. Eamonn McCann attests to the constant workload. 'In my experience, many campaigns begin to falter because there is simply nothing for people to do and no new initiatives to take. But in the Bloody Sunday campaign, there was always something to do every day, always a flurry of activity from somewhere. Once you were in, you had no option to keep at it.'

Another regular issue was the need for funding to keep the campaign afloat. The campaign looked to Derry City Council for help. After a heated debate at the beginning of March 1993, the Council voted to grant £16,000 to the campaign. The decision, by 15 votes to 10, came despite the possibility of the Auditor General imposing a surcharge on councillors if he decided that the cause was political. All ten unionist councillors opposed the move.

On 16 March, the Auditor General served a prohibition order on the Council preventing it from paying the £16,000 grant on the grounds that the aims of the BSJC were not attainable and, anyway, would not benefit the entire community.

Tony Doherty urged councillors to challenge the order. 'In essence, the Auditor General is saying that Bloody Sunday is not important to the people of Derry and that the just resolution of the murders of fourteen Derry men and boys by the British army will not be of tangible benefit to us.'

However, councillors chose not to challenge the prohibition order.

In March 1993, Kathleen Kelly wrote a personal letter to John Major explaining her continuing heartbreak over the death of her son and stressing the importance of truth. In reply, Mr. Major said that while he was moved by her story, he could not agree to reopen an investigation. Mrs Kelly said that the 'glimmer of hope' she had felt in January at Major's letter to John Hume had been snuffed out.

Confusion was arising between the BSI and BSJC. On this account, the Initiative decided in May 1993 to change its name to the Pat Finucane Centre for Human Rights and Social Change, with a remit to champion wider human rights issues. The centre – now widely known as, simply, the PFC – continues to operate advice centres in Derry and Armagh. One of its core activities is researching and documenting the many controversial deaths during the Northern Ireland conflict.

Despite her having refused three times to meet with the campaign, in June 1993 the BSJC again asked President Mary Robinson to receive a delegation.

Once again, the President was to decline the families' invitation – this time pointing to 'constitutional parameters' of her office. In a letter to John Kelly, the President's secretary wrote: 'She very much regrets that the constitutional parameters of her office preclude her involvement in issues of policy and it is not open to her to endorse or be associated with any campaign which involves such issues. She regrets that it would not be possible for her to meet members of the Campaign and continue to operate within those parameters.'

Again, campaigners were furious and frustrated that their case was still being viewed as a political rather than as a human rights issue. John Kelly said: 'We had anticipated hostility and suspicion from the British government and its supporters who have most to lose from the truth regarding Bloody Sunday. However, we were unprepared for the attitude among officialdom in the Republic, exemplified by the snub we received from the President.'

Throughout this period, Patricia Coyle continued to search out relevant material, including archives and photographic libraries. Many Northern editors proved helpful. 'Without a hint of bureaucracy, the editors of the *Derry Journal*, *Belfast Telegraph*, *Irish News*, and the *Newsletter* opened their newspaper and photograph archives. I visited their offices across Northern Ireland and copied all contemporaneous newspaper footage and photographs available. The *Sunday Times* archivists provided copies of their original Insight Team's report from 1972 and related documents.'

But more was needed. Patricia took the bus to the Northern Ireland Public Records Office (PRONI) on Belfast's Balmoral Avenue. 'Again, these were the days before online searches so physical checks were required,' she recalls. 'I checked the paper catalogue index and it turned out that the solicitor who had acted for the families in 1972 had lodged his papers from the Widgery Inquiry there.'

Patricia found that the PRONI papers contained nothing she did not already have, apart from post-mortem reports from the original inquests. The inquests on 21 August 1973 had been chaired by Derry Coroner Major Hubert O'Neill. 'The jury recorded open verdicts in every case,' Patricia recalls. 'The coroner, however, had no difficulty stating publicly that "the soldiers ran amok" and that what happened had been "sheer unadulterated murder".' However, his damning indictment had had little effect on official thinking over the years since.

Patricia asked for copies of the inquest papers lodged with the PRONI, which, in turn, sought permission from the solicitor who had lodged the papers after the Widgery Inquiry. Initially, he refused and withdrew the papers from the Public Records Office. It was only when the families and wounded wrote directly to the solicitor that he re-lodged the papers and gave permission for Patricia to copy them. The Bloody Sunday archive was continuing to grow.

The transcript of the original Widgery proceedings was still proving elusive. Patricia Coyle checked local councils in Belfast, Derry and elsewhere, university colleges, Derry City Council, council and independent libraries, etc. All to no avail. The Widgery Tribunal had convened at Coleraine County

Hall, thirty miles from Derry. Patricia phoned Coleraine Library and discovered it had a 'special collection' housed in a portable cabin outside the County Hall. A librarian agreed to check for the transcript and phoned Patricia back the same day to confirm they had it.

'The next day I drove to Coleraine County Hall where I was led to a small back room in a portable cabin at the rear of the building,' Patricia remembers. 'Sitting in the room was a large old-fashioned black travel trunk with heavy hinges, a large lock on the front and a handle on each side. The black trunk contained twenty-one volumes of transcripts, one for each of the days of the Widgery Tribunal. They were bound to the left hand side with ribbon and typed in old-fashioned typewriter transcript. The transcript had been lying undisturbed for twenty years.'

Patricia persuaded the librarian to allow her to borrow and copy the transcript for further scrutiny. Back at Madden & Finucane, they copied everything.

'A comparative analysis between the original Widgery transcript and the Widgery Report provided three simple conclusions,' Patricia says.

'First, the Widgery Inquiry was stage-managed in terms of geography and time in order to facilitate an outcome favourable to the military. Second, the Inquiry did not hear from other than a fraction of the civilian eyewitnesses who were available and, third, notwithstanding the extent of the stage management, the report still did not deal with the innate conflicts and discrepancies in the soldiers' evidence, such as the evidence in relation to the shootings in Glenfada Park.

'These conclusions were neither new nor rocket science. A number of independent reports published shortly after Bloody Sunday had already laid this ground but the original transcript provided a very useful comparative tool.'

Meanwhile, Jane Winter had been working on a report on Bloody Sunday for submission to the United Nations: 'We were all volunteers, so I worked on the report in my spare time for about six months. Up until then, there had been no reports from the point of view of the victims and what happened to them. So that's what I tried to research and encapsulate, the human rights angle, the fact that these people had been wilfully deprived of their lives.'

The paper was completed in January 1994 and sent to the United Nations Special Rapporteur on Summary or Arbitrary Executions, which dealt with non-sanctioned state killings. But once again, the families faced a rebuff. They would eventually reject the report.

Jane Winter describes the UN response as 'very disappointing'. 'Unfortunately, there were massive genocides going on at time in places like Rwanda, and the UN made up a rule which hadn't existed before, that they wouldn't look at anything more than two years old. It was very disappointing,' Jane said. 'Perhaps, from their point of view, fourteen deaths and fourteen injuries in Northern Ireland was a relatively small event – though obviously not for the people of Derry.'

With the Widgery transcript now a compelling comparative tool, Patricia Coyle wrote to the British prime minister on the 24 January 1994 requesting a new public inquiry based upon the 'innate problems within the transcript.'

Despite all this progress, campaigners still faced difficulties back home in Derry. John Kelly remembers: 'When we hit the streets to build support, people thought we were republicans. We had to break down a lot of barriers and get people to accept who we were. That took a long time. At the beginning, as far as I was concerned, we were just trying to get the case reopened. Under what format or in what way, I didn't know. None of us knew. The campaign became 24/7. Some of us lived and breathed it. You couldn't get away from it. I was always thinking about it, always working on it.'

On 27 January 1994, a group of relatives travelled to Downing Street to hand over the public petition. They also delivered Jane Winter's thirty-six page British Irish Rights Watch report, which defined the events of 30 January 1972 as 'summary and arbitrary execution of unarmed civilians.'

John Hume had arranged the relatives' admission to Downing Street to present the documents. Bloody Sunday had rarely merited little mention in London, so the occasion generated considerable press interest. High profile supporters like Labour MPs Jeremy Corbyn and Tony Benn accompanied the Derry group.

'When John Hume arranged for the families to visit Number 10 and the Houses of Parliament – that was great publicity for us,' Mickey McKinney remembers. 'When we walked into Downing Street with Hume, I saw that as our first big PR event.'

Hume spoke at an impromptu press conference in Downing Street calling on the government to overturn the findings of the Widgery report and establish a new independent inquiry. The delegation then walked the short distance to the Houses of Parliament where they held a meeting attended by MPs from all main political parties. Copies of Jane Winter's report were distributed. Despite the initial reservations some families had had, they had been warmly received and left Westminster buoyed with promises of all-party support.

'They listened to us, which was all you could expect at that stage,' says Mickey McKinney. 'Here we were talking about something horrible in the distant past. It wasn't going to be easy.'

That year's commemoration fell on the actual anniversary of Bloody Sunday, 30 January. Thousands braved a bitter frost to congregate in Creggan and wind their way downhill towards the Bogside. As always, an air of cheery optimism prevailed.

'By this stage we had started to travel all over,' Mickey McKinney remembers. 'Me, John, Gerry and others. It could be daunting.'

Shy by nature, Gerry Duddy did not adapt easily to the art of public speaking. 'At first it wasn't easy, but, like most things in life, you adapt and learn how to get your message across and then you grow in confidence.'

He laughs when remembering the first time he took the campaign on the road, to speak at the university in Athlone. 'I needed money to get there so I went to the Telstar Bar in Creggan and got a half bottle of Vodka and – this is gospel – I raffled off the bottle to pay for my bus fare! There weren't very many at the talk, thank God, and me standing with my wee bit of paper. I did okay, considering. That was my first time speaking, and probably one of the first times anyone from the campaign went to speak anywhere.'

On his first trip to England, Gerry spoke at a rally in Birmingham then travelled on to London to speak there. It was to become a regular occurrence. In London, marches were organised by stalwart supporter Jim Redmond.

Birmingham Troops Out organiser Mary Pearson also forged a firm friendship with Gerry. 'Mary was great,' he says, 'She organised everything in Birmingham, brought people over from Derry to speak at the rallies and held demonstrations. She's a one-woman campaign!'

Gerry took the responsibility of representing the campaign very seriously but also enjoyed charming audiences with an irreverent approach. A touch of humour was often welcome and lifted the atmosphere. Bloody Sunday was always a difficult conversation piece. The campaign was generally gruelling and sometimes fatiguing, both physically and mentally.

'On one occasion,' Gerry recalls, 'I was invited to speak at a few different events and commemorations at once, so I travelled to Birmingham, then to London, and then on to Chicago. It was tiring but it was worth it. People listened, and then they wanted to help.'

Less than a month after the families were welcomed into Westminster, Downing Street yet again rejected their appeals. A letter dated 17 February 1994 from NI Security Minister, Sir John Wheeler declared: 'The government continues to believe that it would not be right, after a Tribunal of Inquiry has reported, to set up a further inquiry into events that took place twenty-two years ago.'

Tony Doherty was scathing: 'It's obvious, given the short space of time involved, that the British government didn't give any serious consideration to the British-Irish Rights Watch report. The Bloody Sunday issue was being treated in an off-hand manner by both John Major and John Wheeler.'

Tony was also critical of the assertion that it 'would not be right' to reinvestigate events of twenty-two years ago. 'At what stage does it stop being right to investigate crimes?' he asked.

However, the campaigners found that they could at least rely on Major's latest letter to strengthen their application to the European Court of Human

Rights at Strasbourg. The case was based on a contention that there was an on-going breach of Article Two of the Convention, the right to life. As Patricia Coyle saw it, the letter illustrated the British government's continuing refusal to conform to the Article Two requirement for an adequate investigation of the deaths. The only effective remedy was a fresh public inquiry. Now Europe would have to consider this case.

In the summer of 1994, protests and chaotic scenes greeted Prince Charles, Colonel-in-Chief of the Parachute Regiment, when he visited the city in which his soldiers had massacred unarmed civilians two decades earlier.

The main protest took place inside the Craft Village in the city centre on 7 July. Amid a cacophony of booing and chanting, campaigners called on the heir to the British throne to remember the dead of 1972. It proved an embarrassing episode for the prince and his entourage. A planned walkabout of the city centre was abandoned.

Speaking for the campaign, Tony Doherty described Bloody Sunday as 'a day of shame and infamy for the Parachute Regiment . . . For this man, the Colonel-in-Chief of the Parachute Regiment, to be invited here as some sort of honoured guest is an insult to the memory of those who died that day. Bloody Sunday is still an open sore for the people who lost their loved ones. This visit only serves to add insult to that injury.'

In August 1994, Madden & Finucane submitted its application to the European Court of Human Rights, which included a comparative analysis of the evidence based upon the Widgery transcript and the Borer Report on the forensics. Patricia Coyle is clear that the case only reached this stage with the assistance of many supporters, including in particular, barrister Seamus Treacy.

'On every occasion, without hesitation, without funding and for almost six years from 1992 to 1997, Seamus drafted correspondence, assembled the application to the European Court of Human Rights, examined evidence as it came to hand and assisted at every stage . He lent his intellect, strategic thinking, objectivity and experience to the case. He was invaluable.'

Years were to pass before the European Courts would respond. Ultimately, the application would be rejected – a decision Patricia Coyle describes as 'somewhat ironic' in that the European Court stated that 'to reopen an inquiry twenty-two years after an event would not be an effective remedy.'

On the 31 August 1994, the IRA announced a 'complete' ceasefire after a quarter of a century of armed conflict. British PM John Major responded that: 'We are beyond the beginning but we are not yet in sight of the end.'

Jane Winter believes the IRA ceasefire had an effect on the campaign. 'It was beginning to dawn on the British government that they had to do something about Northern Ireland and, if they addressed Northern Ireland, they had to address Bloody Sunday too.'

In Derry, the campaign continued unabated. Letters were still dispatched daily, relatives travelled to raise the campaign's profile in other cities and countries and Derry people generally rallied around. But there was still a long journey ahead. Despite all, no concrete evidence had yet emerged to challenge the official verdict of Widgery's tribunal and the British government remained stubbornly opposed to the campaign's appeals.

New faces joined the campaign every week. Some felt energised by the campaign's relentlessness and regular newspaper coverage. Others gathered from within themselves the courage to face a reality they had chosen to forget.

Father of six Daniel McGowan had not even been on the civil rights march in January 1972 when he was wounded by army gunfire as he helped carry the wounded Patrick Campbell to safety. Daniel died in 2004. His widow, Teresa speaks of him with great affection: 'At the start, I managed to talk Danny into coming to campaign meetings with me, but when he saw the crowd he made an excuse to go downstairs for something and never came back. My husband was far too emotional for those meetings. He wanted no talk about Bloody Sunday and even got emotional when he saw anything about it on TV. You wouldn't have thought it to look at him – but he was a sensitive kind of man.'

After Daniel's death, Teresa vowed to continue her involvement with campaign and, with the backing of their children, support the families' fight.

'I was six months pregnant when Danny was shot on Bloody Sunday,' she says. 'He came back a changed person – it affected him terribly. But I know it could have been so much worse. . . .'

chapter six

'Securing the south'

If the President of Ireland refused to come to the campaign, then the campaign would have to go to the President: the families decided to stage a demonstration outside Mary Robinson's official residence in Dublin's Phoenix Park.

Tony Doherty recalls: 'We decided to hold a picket at Áras an Uachtaráin. It was a small group – myself, Baldy McKinney, Robin Percival, my brother Paul and Gerry Duddy – just one carload. When we got there, Gardaí and armed plain clothes "taskies" were waiting and they took our names and addresses.'

John McKinney recalls the tense security during the Áras an Uachtaráin protest. 'The Gardaí had stopped us in Monaghan that morning. Later on, when they were giving us hassle outside the Phoenix Park, a guard asked us, "What were you lot doing in Monaghan this morning?" I just said "How else do you drive to Dublin?" I think they were letting us know that they were watching us – more than we realised.

'They told us the quicker we got back up north the better. It was really bitter – scary too. It was the first time I had ever heard a Garda saying, "get back up to the black north." They followed us everywhere that day.

'It shows how unaware people in the south were about the campaign in those days. When we were standing outside the Phoenix Park, somebody passed us in a car and roared out the window, "Are you still killing children?" That was bad

. . . they must have thought we were involved with the IRA or something.' They received a police 'escort' all the way back to Derry. 'The guards practically drove behind us right back to the border to make sure we had gone. Apparently, this was the only time that the Phoenix Park was picketed – and it was us who did it!'

It was now 1995 and the campaign was continuing to gather momentum. Both at home and abroad, there seemed to be a distinct shift in attitudes. Improved political relations on all sides bolstered the campaign's credibility. Taoiseach John Bruton designated one of his own civil servants to act as liaison between the Irish government and the families. The tides were turning.

In January 1995, Tony Doherty received an invitation to speak on Bloody Sunday at the public hearings of the Irish Forum for Peace and Reconciliation. The high-profile event, televised by both the BBC and RTÉ, took place over several days at Dublin Castle with representatives of all Irish political parties in attendance.

'I was asked to make a submission along with a man whose daughter was killed in the Enniskillen bombing,' Tony recalls. 'He spoke from his perspective and I spoke from mine but we also had a bit of an interchange which was really interesting. I think the event sent out the signal that we were a serious campaign. Besides, I had made it clear in my submission that we were not just out for revenge.

'From that year on, the Irish government took us much more seriously. That was clearly signalled by John Bruton appointing a civil servant to work with us.'

The 1995 commemoration weekend, themed 'A Time for Justice', included a public debate on 'Changing Southern perspectives on the North', a People's Forum on 'Visions of a New Ireland' and a series of workshops, including one for eight-year-olds and upwards on 'Dismantling Prejudice'. Gerry Duddy addressed the commemoration rally alongside Sinn Féin president, Gerry Adams. Adams's presence on the platform caused some concern but the campaign reiterated that he was there as an ex-internee, pointing out that the original Bloody Sunday march had been an anti-internment demonstration.

In February 1995, SDLP members of Derry City Council called directly on the British prime minister to acknowledge that the Widgery Tribunal had been a 'black stain' on the history of British involvement with Ireland. The party said: 'Having met on a number of times with relatives of the innocent victims of Bloody Sunday, the SDLP grouping on Derry City Council wish to be associated with the efforts of the BSJC to exonerate the names of the thirteen people who died so tragically on Bloody Sunday.'

Acknowledging the lack of financial support, but also the important role played in the campaign by John Hume, the SDLP added that, while 'restricted in council from giving financial support to this campaign, [they] have none the less played a part in projecting the campaign forward on a political front.'

Meanwhile, one campaigner took it upon himself to try again with Mary Robinson. Having learned that various campaigns against state violence had been invited to the presidential residence, John McKinney decided to join them.

'I wanted to make a point of asking her face to face to lay a wreath at the monument,' he says. 'I wanted to see what she would say to me in person. So the campaign eventually agreed and I went down myself with the other campaigns. 'She shook hands with members of the various campaigns and, when she came to me, I introduced myself and said I had a brother killed on Bloody Sunday. I told her I wanted her to lay a wreath at the BS monument in Derry. I still remember the language that she used, saying she couldn't be seen to be political and that her constitutional position wouldn't permit her to get involved in campaigns. I said, "But you laid a wreath in Enniskillen. We are not a political group – we are a human rights group – innocent people who died just like those who died in Enniskillen. I felt she dismissed it.'

Kevin McElhinney adored music – especially the flamboyant vibes of Marc Bolan and T-Rex – it was his passion. He loved going to dances. He didn't smoke, didn't drink and hadn't missed a day's work in Lipton's Supermarket. Kevin was shot dead by a British paratrooper as he sought shelter at the rubble barricade on Rossville Street. He was seventeen.

The McElhinney family had always supported the campaign in principle, becoming more active in the late 1990s. Jean Hegarty (née McElhinney) would later represent the family in negotiations.

As a young woman, Jean had emigrated to Canada where she remained until 1995. Having just returned to Derry, she reflected on her brother's death.

'I have a certain amount of guilt about walking away after Bloody Sunday. Going back to Canada, and only phoning my mother on Kevin's birthday and on the anniversaries, I should have done more. When I came back, I started going to meetings with my sister Roslyn and gradually got more involved.'

Jean says her family rarely discussed Kevin's murder. 'It was a subject that we didn't talk about. We sometimes talked about Kevin, of course, but never about Bloody Sunday. We were always quite a non-political family and preferred to keep to ourselves. But, when the commemorations became more family-led, we really came on board.'

Nowadays, Jean is administrator for the Bloody Sunday Trust and one of the two Bloody Sunday relatives employed in the Museum of Free Derry in Glenfada Park.

On 16 February 1995, three years after she had first refused to meet them, the Bloody Sunday relatives were finally granted an audience with Mary Robinson. They were received by her as part of a 'Relatives for Justice' delegation. On meeting her, they asked her yet again for support for their campaign and invited her to lay a wreath at the Bloody Sunday memorial the next time she was in Derry. 'When she finally met them, Mary Robinson was really quite gracious,' Jane Winter remembers.

On 28 April 1995, the campaign condemned a planned visit to Dublin by Prince Charles. His visit to Derry a year earlier had caused chaos. 'By his silence alone, even after being confronted in Derry last year, Prince Charles implicitly supports the glorification of the shameful deeds of this highly trained death squad,' a campaign statement read. 'Bloody Sunday, in particular, is still considered a military success by the twisted minds of the British military establishment.'

When Prince Charles landed in Dublin in May 1995, campaigners seized the opportunity and travelled south. Planning to camp overnight outside the Mansion House, home to the Mayor of Dublin, family members and campaigners waited patiently for the heir to the British throne to appear.

'We took a busload down. We were going to sleep outside the Mansion House the night before to make sure we saw him. It was all quite exciting. There was a rally outside the GPO the day before,' John McKinney recalls.

John laughs remembering that Mary Nelis, a local Sinn Féin councillor, also made the trip to Dublin with the families. 'I remember her writing her speech on the bus on the way down, it was one of the best speeches I ever heard. I remember she actually code-named the weekend "Operation Big Ears"! I don't know why, but I've always remembered that!'

Addressing the Dublin rally, Linda Roddy hit out: 'Twenty-three years after Bloody Sunday the Commander-in-Chief of the Parachute Regiment is being celebrated by Irish people on Irish soil . . . If he is truly interested in buildings friendships with Irish people, then he should meet with us and not hide behind royal protocol or self-imposed constitutional restraints.'

'We slept outside the Mansion House because we were scared the guards wouldn't let us near the place in the morning,' John McKinney remembers. 'It was dry weather but freezing and there were only a couple of sleeping bags. Our Mickey and John Kelly complained the whole time because, every time they moved to find a loo, we stole their sleeping bags!'

John Kelly recalls the sleeping bag incident well, 'They slept like babies, and we had to stay awake all night!'

'The guards told us we could stay as long as we weren't disorderly,' John McKinney continued. 'We assured them we would only raise our voices and, so, when Charles arrived, we were only about twenty feet away from him and he got a lot of verbal about Bloody Sunday. We held up the pictures of the fourteen men and he did look in our direction and make eye contact but nothing more.' Although they'd recorded no tangible progress, the families left Dublin satisfied that at least they'd made their presence felt.

While the campaign continued unabated in Derry, Patricia Coyle was still engrossed in the search for evidence. Having already discovered the original Coroner's Report in Belfast, Patricia knew the next step was to gain access to the Public Records Office in Kew Gardens where the national and government archives are kept. The existence of Bloody Sunday material at Kew had already been confirmed by Dessie Baker, an independent researcher from Derry who had come across many files relating to Bloody Sunday and the Widgery Report while conducting his own, unrelated research at Kew. He penned two articles about the potential archive for both the *Derry Journal* and *Fingerpost* magazine: 'I just wanted to make sure the information was out there for anyone interested.'

Patricia explains, 'I wrote to the Public Record Office at Kew Gardens in the middle of 1995 and was surprised when they wrote back and confirmed that the Home Office had lodged the papers from the Widgery Inquiry papers there. Attached to the letter from the National Archives was a catalogue list.

'That catalogue showed almost thirty categories of materials lodged by the original Inquiry, seventeen of which were open to the public but thirteen of which were subject to a closure restriction for periods of either thirty or seventy-five years. The hunt for documents suddenly became interesting.

Each of the open categories had a reference number. Against each reference number was a narrative describing the contents of that category. The open categories contained volumes of the Inquiry's transcripts, a large number of photographs, inquest documents, statements of evidence (including the largely ignored civilian eye-witness evidence) and other materials. One of the open categories also contained the army helicopter footage which was listed as stored at the British Film Institute in central London.

'Of much greater interest were the restricted categories. The thirteen closed categories had a reference number but no descriptive narrative whatsoever. I was hungry to know what materials were in the closed categories, the extent of the materials, and why restrictions were imposed on the closed categories, some for up to seventy-five years. What did Widgery or the government want to hide for seventy-five years?'

From 1992 to 1997, the legal aspects of the case were conducted on a pro-bono basis. There was no money for travel to London, for example, to review what was available in the Public Records Office in Kew Gardens. Patricia and Peter Madden were happy that Jane Winter agreed to take this task on.

Jane went to look at the open categories in August 1995. In the meantime, Patricia wrote to the Home Office attaching the PRO list, asking that they open the thirteen closed categories in advance of the thirty or seventy-five years restriction. It took the Home Office a number of months to reply.

'I was later told by a Derry woman who worked there, Mary Conaghan, originally from Creggan, that after our request was received the contents of the thirteen closed categories were removed by staff from the Home Office who arrived one day and loaded them into the boots of their cars. I presume that the thirteen closed categories had to be checked before permission to open was given. I have often wondered however if anything was removed from those thirteen categories at that stage.'

During a visit to the Public Records Office in August 1995, Jane Winter unearthed the infamous Heath-Widgery memo. This was a record of a meeting between Prime Minister Edward Heath, Lord Chief Justice Widgery and Lord Chancellor Hailsham in Downing Street the day after Bloody Sunday. In it, the Prime Minister suggests that the recommendations on procedure for inquiries made by Lord Salmon in the 1921 Act 'might not necessarily be relevant in this case.' He also advised Widgery to remember that 'we are in Northern Ireland fighting not only a military war but a propaganda war', while the Lord Chancellor suggested that the Treasury Solicitor would need to 'brief counsel for the army.'

Jane Winter takes up the story: 'I was very surprised that there were so few papers and documents. This was a public inquiry – I expected to find the whole transcript of the inquiry, all kinds of papers and notes but there were just scraps and a lot of photos. The photos proved that all the victims were unarmed. But there were also twenty-eight series of files that were closed from public view for seventy-five years. I think the idea was that anyone who was alive on Bloody Sunday would either be too old or be dead so no one would be around to look at these files.'

Jane spent two days at Kew Gardens, sifting through papers and documents. It was a very solitary process. 'At first I found nothing we didn't already know, but then, on 4 August 1996, I came across a document headed 'secret' at the back of one of the files – which made me immediately wake up and take interest.' This was the Heath-Widgery memo. Jane couldn't believe her luck.

'I thought, well, this changes everything. This was meant to be an independent inquiry by the Lord Chief Justice – who chose to sit on his own with no other judges – and here is the Prime Minister trying to influence him! That cannot be right. He was also giving Widgery a very political message – that this was not just a military war but a propaganda war. That was interesting in itself as the UK government was always very resistant to describing what was happening in Northern Ireland as a war; they always wanted to downplay it and describe it as a low level kind of conflict.

'I thought this is a highly significant document and I wondered how it got into the file. It obviously shouldn't have been there, but it was. I wondered if someone had put it there deliberately. I'd like to think someone put it there because they knew that what had happened on Bloody Sunday was wrong and wanted the world to know. Somebody wanted the whole thing to unravel maybe. It was well worth having spent two whole days at the Public Records Office and, of course, I wondered, if that was in the open files, what's in all the closed files?'

When news of the memo filtered through to the families in Derry, a press conference was quickly called for 10 November 1995 at the Pat Finucane Centre. Jane Winter had travelled from London for the press conference to discuss her find and copies of the memo were distributed to the media. The revelations generated a flurry of press interest and a statement released by the Bloody Sunday Justice Campaign described the memo as 'only the tip of the iceberg.'

The BSJC statement read: 'The British government have at their disposal reams of information which they intend to keep closed for at least seventy-five years . . . It simply proves what many have instinctively suspected for many years; that the British government and judiciary actively colluded, at the highest levels, to prevent any vestige of truth from emerging from this so-called fair and balanced tribunal.'

That week's *Derry Journal* ran with a front-page banner headline 'Widgery memo damns British' and claimed that the discovery of the confidential minutes would 'send shockwaves through the British establishment.'

'This was absolute dynamite, everything we had ever known but had no source for – and now it was on paper,' Tony says. 'It demonstrates that there had been a conspiracy from start to finish. It became as clear as the nose on your face that, not only were the soldiers coached on what to say at the original tribunal, but also that Widgery had been told by Heath himself to keep the propaganda needs of the British army in mind. It was gold dust to us, the first major breakthrough in terms of incriminating the British government since 1972.'

'We started to feel a glimmer of hope then,' says Kay Duddy. 'It was a frustrating time, a sad time and an exciting time because we realised people were beginning to listen.'

Said Dr Edward Daly: 'I have always said that Bloody Sunday was the first atrocity and the Widgery Tribunal was the second atrocity. Clearly this document shows that there was never any intention to try to find out what happened.'

Teresa McGowan spoke of the effect this new evidence had on the families. 'Everything was going for the better, you could see the change and people had lighter hearts.'

In the course of the campaign, the families had come across a bag of eyewitness statements taken in 1972. Rummaging through them one morning 'just out of curiosity', Tony Doherty found a statement by fifteen-year-old Don Mullan.

'I had been introduced to Don Mullan once before and happened to meet him again on William Street one day afterwards and we got talking,' Tony remembers. 'I told him I had read his statement after Bloody Sunday. He had completely forgotten that he had ever made a statement and wanted to see it. When he went and looked through them all, he realised how important they were.

The statements had been lying under the stairs in civil rights activist Brigid Bond's house for many years. A remarkable figure, Mrs Bond had been to the forefront of the Derry Civil Rights Association and had helped co-ordinate the taking of the statements in the days following Bloody Sunday. After she died, her husband had found the papers and passed them on to the families. He had also found the original Bloody Sunday civil rights banner still stained with Bernard McGuigan's blood. The banner is now on display in the Museum of Free Derry.

Don Mullan remembers: 'I had completely forgotten ever making a statement about Bloody Sunday and I was curious as to what I had written, so Tony arranged for me to meet with Mickey McKinney and John Kelly the following week at the Pat Finucane Centre in West End Park. There was an old battered filing cabinet and they brought out a well-worn plastic supermarket bag full of old papers and said, "yours is in there somewhere".'

Don took the bag to a table at the corner of the room and began looking through it. 'I realised when reading them that these were very, very important. I'm sure no-one realised at the time, but in taking these statements they had created primary source documents of one of the seminal events of modern Irish history. I just knew I had to do something with them.'

Don was only fifteen when he attended his first-ever civil rights march on 30 January 1972. Caught up in the commotion near Glenfada Park, he witnessed horror, including the fatal shooting of Michael Kelly at the rubble barricade on Rossville Street.

Don made arrangements to have the statements copied. Reading through them, he was forced to think about his own experiences. 'The most vivid memory I have from Bloody Sunday is a sound – the sound of Michael Kelly a few feet away from me. It sounded like he was winded by a knock-out punch. I remember him clutching his stomach and collapsing into the foetal position.

'I remembered that my best friend Shauny McLaughlin and I had returned to the Bogside the day after and retraced my steps around the rubble barricade. Not far from there, we found the blue and white civil rights banner on the ground, now heavily bloodstained. I vividly remember that on top of the banner was a brick and, on top of the brick was a little Bo-Peep matchbox and in the matchbox was a human eyelid and eyelashes. That was really shocking to me.'

The day after the 1972 killings, a team of volunteers had assembled in Holy Child Primary School in Creggan to take the statements from eyewitnesses. Don decided to go along. 'Whoever came up with the idea of taking civilian statements was a genius, because in the end that's what brought Widgery down. All these statements were collected, typed out and submitted to the original tribunal but Widgery chose to ignore them on the basis that they had arrived too late.'

Determined to make something of the documents, Don contacted old friend, Seamus Cashman, founder of the Wolfhound Press in Dublin. Cashman agreed that the wealth of statements should be published.

'Seamus was a fantastic support and remains a great mentor to me. When I told him, he said "we'll do it, Don". He just had an instinct that these were important documents that needed to be seen. The powerful thing about these statements is that they all say the same thing and you cannot get a community to agree on a collective lie, that's the power of it. The consistency was extraordinary.

'I also found that one in ten of these statements were saying that, in addition to the paratroopers on ground level, that there were also soldiers shooting from the walls, and that sparked my curiosity – what were these guys shooting at from the walls? Then, in one of the appendices at the back of Dr Raymond McClean's book *The Road to Bloody Sunday*, were details of post mortems that he had attended and he had recorded that three of the Bloody Sunday dead had 45 degree downward trajectory wounds so I thought, wow, that was interesting. That was the beginning of it all.'

Propelled by his theory of shooting from the walls, Don spoke to family members to gauge their opinion. Mickey McKinney recalls: 'Don wanted to do a book based on the statements and discussed the idea with Gerry, John and myself. We all agreed it would be a powerful way of getting the truth of what really happened out there.'

With campaign support, Don Mullan threw himself into researching the book, which was to be called *Eyewitness Bloody Sunday* and would go on to be a bestseller. 'I had never done anything like this in my life. This was the first real investigation I ever did.'

From hundreds of eyewitness accounts, Don Mullan selected eighty to one hundred for inclusion in the book. Mickey McKinney and John Kelly and others were tasked with tracking down the various eyewitnesses to ask permission that their 1972 statements could be published.

'Tracking everyone down took some time, and, on Tuesday nights, at meetings, we would discuss who lived where, and at the next meeting, we would fill each other in on progress. Most people agreed to let their statements be used in the book, but not everyone. I went to the door of one person, who witnessed the killings in Glenfada Park, and his wife answered. She wouldn't even mention the old statement to him because he had never got over what he had seen on Bloody Sunday.'

Some eyewitnesses didn't even remember making a statement. John Kelly remembers one woman: 'I spoke to her on the phone. I said, "You were there on Bloody Sunday?" and she agreed. I said "You made a statement?" and she said "No, I didn't." I read her statement to her over the phone to see if she'd remember. She said "You're right!" She just couldn't remember. The phone call had brought it all back to her. That woman went on to give evidence to Saville.'

John recalls another occasion when he tracked down a man to ask about his 1972 statement. 'I started explaining about the campaign and the book. He shot back, 'Ah, it's a waste of time' and put the phone down. And that was that.'

Back in Dublin, Don Mullan threw himself into writing his book. It became something of a catharsis. 'The chapter I found most difficult to write was the one on Glenfada Park. I stayed up late writing, as often that's the best time to write without interruptions, and that night I went through a night of terror. It took a lot of work that night but, at the end of it, I found great peace, it was very cathartic and remarkable considering earlier that year I had discovered I was dyslexic. If I hadn't found that out then I wouldn't have had the confidence to take on a serious subject matter like this.'

Delving deeper into his theory about soldiers shooting from the walls, Don enlisted the help of Italian-born independent ballistics expert, Robert Breglio. The autopsy results appeared to indicate that Michael McDaid, William Nash and John Young had been shot from an elevated trajectory.

'I was in New York and Breglio agreed to meet me in a Greek restaurant on Staten Island. I brought all the documents with me, explained everything, and he told me, "I will call it as I see it." I said that's fine, that's exactly what I want. After examining all the papers, Breglio wrote me a statement saying he believed that these three people were, indeed, shot by snipers from the vicinity of the Derry Walls. That was very compelling.'

While Don was in New York, he got a call from Lena Ferguson of Channel 4 News, who had heard about his theory of soldiers shooting from the walls. She grilled him on every detail.

'I told her that I couldn't explain why this theory had never come out before, especially considering the whole body of statements mentioning firing from the walls and the new ballistic evidence supporting it. On this basis, Channel 4 decided to do the first of their Bloody Sunday reports. They really championed it and the theory of the shooting from the walls was a sensation at the time. There's no doubt that it helped the campaign build momentum.

'Channel 4 News cannot be underestimated in terms of their contribution to this entire campaign.'

The families' optimism as they awaited the outcome of their application to the European Courts was dealt a heavy blow when, on 29 April 1996, they were told that their case had been turned down. The court held that to reopen an inquiry into an event twenty-two years after it happened could not be an effective remedy.

Tony Doherty believes that the Court might have feared 'opening the floodgates' to dozens of other cases from Northern Ireland if they took on Bloody

Sunday. Jane Winter adds: 'I think Europe was afraid that it would set a precedent. They were quite right too, as we already had a list of cases, which, if Bloody Sunday succeeded, we were going to take to Europe. So that was another blow to the campaign.'

Relatives were 'profoundly disappointed' at the decision but vowed to continue the fight. Speaking years later, Tony Doherty believes that even major setbacks like this strengthened the campaign's resolve: 'Although the European application failed, it still got us a lot of publicity,' he says. 'We were still novices in terms of publicity but we did our best and still had our successes.'

The campaign also kept up the pressure through constant correspondence. On 29 June 1996, they wrote another letter to Prince Charles asking him to condemn his soldier's actions in Derry on Bloody Sunday. This time they received a curt reply from his private secretary suggesting it was 'necessary to move on'.

The Bloody Sunday Trust played an increasingly vital role in the campaign. Conal McFeely, vice-chair of the BST, became particularly active. His involvement with Bloody Sunday actually went back to the day itself when he went on the march with his brother Donnacha and Gerald Donaghey. Their friend's murder hit them hard: 'I was only eighteen years old at the time and, so, Bloody Sunday had a profound effect on me and my family,' he says.

'I became formally involved when approached by Mickey McKinney in 1995 when he needed my help with a funding application. Mickey was concerned with how the trauma was affecting the families and out of that discussion, the campaign, which was continually evolving, agreed that it was time to establish a new structure.'

Conal believes there were four key people moving things forward at that time: Mickey McKinney, Gerry Duddy, Tony Doherty and John Kelly. 'At that stage, they wanted to reactivate the issue and move things to another level. They really wanted to engage wider society and so approached me because of my work with Creggan Enterprises and, more specifically, within the social economy. Out of that dialogue a decision was made to establish the Bloody Sunday Trust in 1996.'

The Bloody Sunday Trust was officially launched some months later.

As discussions continued on setting up a Trust, and Don Mullan marvelled over the recently unearthed eyewitness statements for his book, Patricia Coyle, working independently, waited for news from the Home Office about releasing their classified files.

Several weeks after the request was made, the Home Office granted permission for twelve of the thirteen categories to be opened. The refusal to open the thirteenth category was based on the fact that it contained medical reports relating to those killed and wounded. Patricia arranged to travel to London to examine the files.

[chapter seven]

'You will *not* believe this . . . '

'I arrived on the early morning flight,' Patricia Coyle remembers. 'There was no money for London accommodation so it was there and back the same day. When I got to Kew and told reception what I was there for, Mary Conaghan, the Derry woman working there, came downstairs to speak to me. She told me about the men from the Home Office taking away the documents we had requested.'

Kew was busy that day. The open-plan viewing area was monitored from every angle by internal surveillance cameras and subject to tight controls. Patricia requested the twelve newly-opened categories and sat down at her assigned seat to await their arrival.

The new evidence Patricia was to find in the dusty files would alter the course of the campaign. Essentially, it was what the families had been hoping for to advance the campaign and put it on a new and more solid footing.

The previously unseen evidence comprised:

1. Original statements of evidence, given by the soldiers who had fired, made to the Military Police on the night of Bloody Sunday.

2. Further statements, made by some of the same soldiers, weeks after their first statements to the Military Police.

3. Further formal statements by the same soldiers to the Treasury Solicitor's

Office acting as the legal team for the Widgery Inquiry.

4. A Schedule confirming the disclosure of documents at the time of the 1972 inquiry.

5. Memos from the Tribunal Secretary to Lord Widgery commenting on issues and arguments that had arisen during the Inquiry hearings.

6. Strategic documents relating to evidence before the inquiry and potential witnesses.

7. Early drafts of sections of the tribunal's report with hand-written notations.

8. Summaries of Widgery's responses to some of these comments and notations.

'That first reading of those documents will remain with me forever,' Patricia says. 'It was clear that the soldiers' statements taken by the Military Police on the evening of Bloody Sunday, the first statements of evidence provided by the shooters, had never seen the light of day.

'There were two other sets of statements from the same soldiers taken a few weeks after Bloody Sunday, essentially a second version, followed by the third version given to the tribunal's legal team. The evidence differed with each version. The final version, ultimately given to the Widgery Inquiry, was, without doubt in my opinion, the result of a tailoring process.'

The first question arising was whether the lawyers for the families and the wounded had received all versions of the soldiers' statements in 1972. Patricia was convinced this wasn't the case. 'It was already clear to me, from my knowledge of the transcript, that the legal teams could not have had access to the first and second versions of the statements by the soldiers.'

A carefully handwritten disclosure list confirmed this was the case. 'This faded list itemised each document provided to all the legal teams at the Inquiry in 1972 and confirmed that the lawyers for the families and the wounded were given almost nothing. They received just a fraction of the information and only the final tailored versions of the shooters' statements.'

Patricia then discovered an untidy note written on one of the pages of the draft versions of the Widgery Report. 'I was stunned when I saw a black hand-written scribble on the right hand side of a page. It read: "The LCJ will pile up the forensic evidence against the deceased." LCJ is short for Lord Chief Justice – Widgery.

'I will never forget that moment. From a legal perspective, that one hand-written scrawl was enough to undermine the Widgery Tribunal and Report. In campaign terms, what we now had was a newly-discovered body of evidence that had been wilfully withheld from lawyers for the families and wounded in 1972. It was shocking.'

Patricia remained in the viewing area until late afternoon reviewing all the documents. She took notes using a pencil as pens were forbidden. She approached staff to inquire about copying and was advised that Crown copyright ruled and that permission would have to be sought by the PRO from the Home Office. She lodged a request for copies of all twelve newly opened categories.

Before leaving Kew, Patricia phoned Peter Madden from the public telephone on the ground floor of the PRO: 'You will not believe this', she began . . .

She left to go to the British Film Institute in Central London where, according to the PRO catalogue listing, the helicopter footage from Bloody Sunday referred to at the Widgery Inquiry was stored. She showed a copy of the Kew catalogue to the librarian at the British Film Institute. 'After making enquiries she advised me that the helicopter footage had recently been removed from the British Film Institute. I asked by whom and to where. She told me the Home Office and that it had been relocated outside London.'

Patricia left London that evening thinking that the release of the documents she'd discovered at Kew had been 'odd in the extreme'. 'On the flight back, I wondered how those who had vetted the documents had not appreciated their significance. I have two schools of thought on this: either the opening of the categories was an act of gross incompetence by those who did not, in fact, appreciate their immense significance, or it was a deliberate action on their part on political direction. I subscribe to the gross incompetence theory.'

Back in Belfast, Peter Madden sent a cheque to Kew for the copies.

As soon as the copies arrived in the winter of 1996, pristinely packaged in brown paper, Patricia and Peter Madden drove to Derry to meet with the families and share the good news. 'There was shock and delight,' Patricia remembers. 'The significance was clear to them and they relished the now very real prospect of a fresh inquiry. It was a very upbeat, optimistic meeting.' Strengthened by the magnitude of the new evidence, the Bloody Sunday Justice Campaign moved up a new level.

'Everyone agreed that the new materials needed to be assessed by an independent legal expert,' said Patricia. 'It was agreed that the brief should go to Professor Dermot Walsh, Chair of Law at Limerick University, who had particular expertise in emergency law.'

Gerry Duddy recalls the excitement of the moment. 'It was like being given a million pounds when Patricia came back and told us what she had found. The first feeling was that we could start believing seriously there now was a chance of a new inquiry.'

'Patricia Coyle has to be applauded for what she did in unearthing all that evidence,' Alana Burke says. 'In a way, that's what kicked everything off and made us realise that the campaign was working.'

Eamonn McCann believes that, in its early stages, the campaign had the character of a 'moral crusade'. 'It was right and proper and certainly necessary for the families' peace of mind that Widgery be overturned. But it was the discovery of the new evidence that alerted people to the fact that the story was advancing. It wasn't just the contents of this new evidence, it was the realisation that the campaign was reaching new, firmer ground, that it would be possible to make more decisive progress. The fresh evidence didn't change the moral case, but it certainly strengthened the legal case.

'The revelations injected momentum into the campaign and gave people a confidence, not just an inner confidence, but a confidence based on material things that were actually happening.

'As the campaign's credibility increased, the campaigners were learning how to use the media. At times, a real head of enthusiasm would build up to get publicity for some detail that, as a journalist, I thought didn't deserve half a column inch. Then it would appear somewhere over two columns. The thing was to keep the ongoing issue of Bloody Sunday in the public eye, and that worked.'

Having lobbied so hard on behalf of his late father Patrick, John Campbell was elated. 'We knew of all the lies and twists and turns over the years but now, suddenly we had the proof. It was black and white in front of us. It felt like, at last, we had something to grip.'

In autumn 1996, Patricia Coyle contacted Professor Dermot Walsh in Limerick on behalf of the Bloody Sunday Trust. They hoped he might assess the relevance of the new material and the significance it might have on the findings of the Widgery Tribunal.

'What had started as a thin blue file in the summer of 1992 was now a large archive in the firm,' Patricia remembers. 'In the summer of 1996, I loaded up the relevant portions of the archive into my car and drove to Limerick.'

'Patricia did not have to waste time on persuasion,' Professor Walsh recalls. He still remembers the feelings of anguish and rage he had felt, aged fifteen, watching the events unfold on the news in 1972. 'She opened the boot of her car and, to my amazement, it was crammed full of boxes upon boxes of files. There were even some on the back seat. My amazement turned to despair when she told me that they would need a report on my findings in time for the twenty-fifth anniversary – just three months away.'

So voluminous was the material, that Professor Walsh feared he wouldn't have enough time to read it, let alone make sense of it and write a coherent and meaningful report. But, despite having just taken up a Chair in Law at the University of Limerick, he agreed.

'Patricia had taken the trouble to come all the way down to Limerick in the expectation that I would do it, and time was running out.' Professor Walsh immersed himself in the report. 'I worked every night, usually into the early hours, and weekends. I even worked Christmas Day.'

And, yet, he found the work neither exhausting nor a chore. He was sustained by a sense of being able to play 'a vital role in undoing a fundamental wrong.' As he ploughed slowly though the mountain of material, he became increasingly aware that his conclusions called into question the very essence of all he had been led to believe in – the rule of law and the ethical basis of the legal system.

The most expansive commemoration programme to date was being planned for the twenty-fifth anniversary. The aim was to turn the Bloody Sunday weekend into an international event.

The campaign had broken into the mainstream British media. On 17 January 1997, Channel Four News broadcast the first of an explosive series of reports on Bloody Sunday, featuring an interview with an anonymous paratrooper who had served on Bloody Sunday. Filmed in silhouette, the soldier admitted that unarmed civilians had been targeted and murdered. Citing the new ballistic evidence and scores of eyewitness testimony, the report also claimed that British soldiers had fired at civilians from the vicinity of the Derry Walls, possibly killing John Young, William Nash and Michael McDaid.

The following week, on Tuesday 21 January 1997, author Don Mullan launched his book, *Eyewitness Bloody Sunday* at the community centre on Fanad Drive in Creggan – in the very heart of the community most affected by the massacre. Almost 700 people turned up for an evening of shared recollection and reconciliation.

The author himself was nervous. 'It was the fiftieth anniversary of Creggan, and they had asked me to launch the book in the community centre as part of the events. Of course, I was delighted to do so and I left my mother's sick bed to attend the launch.

'It was an amazing night. Hundreds turned up. It was a sign that people felt we had turned a corner. All the families were there. As I stood to speak, I could see Bishop Daly and Bishop Hegarty to my left, and Sinn Féin's Martin McGuinness and Mitchel McLaughlin to my right. The most humbling part of the evening, for me, was that I was given a standing ovation from my own people – it was really very emotional, very special.'

'All the great and the good attended Don's launch,' Mickey McKinney recalls. 'I wasn't exactly sure where the book was going to take us, but we all knew it would help raise the profile of the campaign. I think the conspiracy revealed in the new evidence, the theory that soldiers were shooting from the walls, helped propel the need for a new inquiry.'

Damian 'Bubbles' Donaghy, the youngest person shot on Bloody Sunday, praised the author's contribution. 'Don and I were at school together and I've known him all my life. His book had a massive effect on the campaign, and got us great publicity. The support we had grew and grew.'

'A lot of work went into the book and it had a major impact,' John Kelly agrees. 'It was all part of the process of bringing the issue to the forefront; taking it from under the carpet and thrusting it into the limelight.'

Although immensely proud of his work, Don Mullan refuses to take the credit for its contents. '*Eyewitness Bloody Sunday* was very much a community book. The real heroes are those who came up with the idea of getting people to commit their stories to paper immediately after Bloody Sunday – the Northern Ireland Civil Rights Association and the National Council for Civil Liberties. It was absolutely brilliant, and, having rediscovered those statements, I had the privilege of being the editor and pulling it all together.'

Eamonn McCann is in no doubt about the powerful impact of Don Mullan's book. 'The fact that there had been shooting by soldiers from the Walls and that Widgery had ignored it was a major development. The fact that, as it turned out, none of the casualties had been hit by any of the bullets from the Walls was neither here nor there. Don showed, without a shadow of a doubt, that Widgery had turned a blind eye to a large number of shots fired by soldiers at the time of the massacre. That was a huge legitimate story in itself. It pointed to the dishonesty and deliberate political blindness of Widgery. It said something fundamental about the way the law worked when the reputation of the army was at stake. Truth and justice didn't register.'

The same day as the book launch, the *Derry Journal* broke the story of how the soldiers' statements had been changed – and changed again – back in 1972. 'Paras' Sunday stories were fixed – the proof' read the headline emblazoned across the paper's front page. The piece detailed discrepancies, such as Soldier S claiming at Widgery that he came under fire when he 'debussed from his pig'

– something never mentioned in his original statements. Or Soldier F, who shot at least three people, 'forgetting' to mention in his first statement that he had killed a 'gunman' at Rossville Street.

The news confirmed decades of suspicion in Derry. Mickey McKinney spoke for a majority of the population when he said that the statements had been altered 'to let the soldiers away with murder'.

At the invitation of family members and Don Mullan, respected US ballistics expert Robert Breglio arrived in Derry on 25 January 1997. During his brief visit, Breglio conducted interviews with survivors and key witnesses and examined the locations of the shootings, including the Derry Walls.

Days later, another *Journal* front page splashed the headline 'Bloody Sunday cover-up exposed', detailing yet more critical new evidence. Military radio messages recorded on Bloody Sunday by local amateur radio 'ham' Jimmy Porter had come to light after twenty-five years. The recordings included hours of army radio messages.

The tapes had been buried in the garden of a friend of Jimmy Porter's across the border in County Donegal. Now they added further weight to the argument that soldiers were not only stationed on, but had fired from the Derry Walls. They also confirmed that troops disobeyed orders by stopping a dying victim from being transported to hospital.

Porter's tapes had been rejected by the 1972 Widgery Tribunal on the grounds that they had been obtained illegally – another example of the Lord Chief Justice waving away evidence which might not suit the soldiers' case.

The same week saw more than a dozen Conservative and Labour MPs lodge early day motions at Westminster calling for a new independent, international inquiry into Bloody Sunday. Eleven Labour backbenchers, led by Tony Benn and Jeremy Corbyn, said the twenty-fifth anniversary should be marked by a fresh investigation.

Bloody Sunday again made front-page news on 28 January when the Northern Ireland Office made public its refusal to release the medical records of the dead and injured until 2047. The records and the seventy-five year rule governing their release had emerged during Don Mullan's research.

Condemning the NIO decision, John Kelly said it was a 'strange decision' given that the campaign had already sourced the autopsy reports and, as a result, the families would have no concerns about releasing their loved ones' medical files, too. 'What are they hiding? This refusal is in keeping with all the other attempts of the British government to prevent truth and culpability being established,' said John.

The 1997 commemorative events attracted thousands more supporters than usual. Among the items on the programme was a presentation in St Mary's Church in Creggan where fourteen coffins had lined the altar twenty-five years earlier. 'The Way of the Cross: The Road to Bloody Sunday' was a collaboration between family members, survivors and local clergy, including Bishop Daly. Harrowing sounds recorded on the day echoed through the church interspersed with music, providing an emotive aural backdrop to a powerful visual exhibition.

The photographs of the murders were the last things to arrive for the 'Way of the Cross' presentation. 'I can remember walking into the parochial house with the photographs and handing them to the priest and he started to cry. People came from everywhere to view that exhibition,' remembers John Kelly.

Ahead of the march in Derry, Gerry Duddy travelled to London to speak at a march from Highbury Fields. The main speakers were Martin McGuinness, Tony Benn MP, and Irish Labour Party TD Declan Bree. The march drew the biggest London turn-out so far. Here, too, support was significantly growing.

The milestone anniversary culminated in two key events – the launch of the newly established Bloody Sunday Trust and the publication of Professor Walsh's analysis of the new evidence unearthed by Patricia Coyle. The two events took place together at the Ráth Mór Centre in Creggan and drew a considerable crowd.

The Bloody Sunday Trust was to consist of family members, lawyers, academics and other concerned citizens from Derry and elsewhere. Its aims were pronounced as promoting conflict resolution, peace and reconciliation by learning the lessons of Bloody Sunday. The Trust's key proposition was that the whole of society, not just the relatives of the dead, had a part to play in the process of reconciliation and healing in relation to Bloody Sunday.

At the launch, the BST's first chairman, Robin Percival, said: 'We would hope to examine the history of Derry and to promote respect for human life, human rights, tolerance and diversity within the city as a means of conflict resolution and peace and reconciliation.'

The BST brought new people to the table: law lecturer Angela Hegarty, Dr Raymond McClean, who had attended the dying on Bloody Sunday and written the first book on the subject, *The Road to Bloody Sunday*, social economy campaigner Conal McFeely, Patricia Coyle, Jane Winter and a range of others.

'The Trust brought a new dynamic,' Conal McFeely says. 'These people brought new experience and skills with them.' The campaign was girding itself for its decisive phase.

The Trust planned to submit Professor Walsh's *The Bloody Sunday Tribunal of Inquiry – A Resounding Defeat for Truth, Justice and the Rule of Law* to the British and Irish governments as part of a renewed bid for a fresh inquiry.

Professor Walsh describes the launch as 'one of those few events in life that you never forget.'

'As I sat on the podium listening to the other speakers and waiting my turn, I got a very real sense that, after many frustrating years, the ground was moving decisively in favour of the victims.

'The families were there. Their support groups were there. The local, national and world press were there. Key observers were there. And the evidence was there to establish, once and for all, that the truth about Bloody Sunday had been buried by a flawed inquiry for twenty-five years.'

Bishop Edward Daly, patron of the new Trust, welcomed Professor Walsh's report. It was now 'solidly established', he said, that Widgery had 'found the innocent guilty and the guilty innocent'.

While the campaign flourished in Derry, Gerry Duddy took it further afield. 'We had always talked about taking the campaign to America – we had contacts there but never actually sent anybody over. I was the first to go.'

Gerry's first trip to the USA resulted from the toss of a coin with John Kelly.

Chris Fogarty, of The Friends of Irish Freedom, had phoned, inquiring what he could do to help. 'I was standing behind John and I said, "Tell him we need to bring one or two family members over." Within half an hour, he had phoned back and agreed – but stressed they could only afford one person to travel. So I said to John "let's toss for it".'

In America, Gerry spoke at a number of Irish-American centres and high schools. Ordinarily, he had no visual aids and spoke from memory. 'That trip was the first time we actually had pictures of Bloody Sunday to show people. These were really powerful photographs and, so, anywhere I spoke, I put them out so, when I was telling the story, they could see it all too.'

On 30 January 1997, Gerry found himself invited to a session of the Illinois State Senate, along with Chris Fogarty and Mary O'Sullivan, also from Friends of Irish Freedom. 'I must have met scores and scores of senators and politicians on that trip and tried to talk to them all. It was important to get the story around in America and this was the platform.'

Transcripts of the occasion show Senator Patrick O'Malley introducing his guest: 'Ladies and gentlemen of the Senate, we have the unique opportunity here today to remember something that occurred in a land away from ours that represented the great fight for freedom that exists in another part of the world...'

By the time the twenty-fifth anniversary arrived, public support for the campaign was at its highest point. On a crisp, cold Sunday afternoon, more than 40,000 people took to the streets and marched along the original 1972 route, winding their way down from Creggan's vantage point to the rally at Free Derry Corner.

Mickey McKinney knew that the campaign had moved up a gear. 'I think it was our biggest march ever. There was real international interest, and we really got the feeling that people were sitting up and taking notice.'

Tony Doherty believes that uncovering the PRO documents was

instrumental in the surge of public support and had created a 'snowball effect'. 'The twenty-fifth anniversary was absolutely massive. It seemed to be an escalating phenomenon and I think it had become clear that our issue wasn't going to go away.'

John Kelly believes the events helped solidify people around the campaign. 'There was an awful lot of pressure in organising everything and making sure it all ran smoothly. But, then, when you looked at 40,000 people marching through the city along the route that led to the Bloody Sunday killing ground, you got the feeling that now we couldn't be ignored.'

The occasion overwhelmed Kay Duddy, too, but for different reasons. Twenty-five years on, this was the first commemoration march she'd been part of. She had never dared attend before, secretly terrified there would be another bloodbath.

'I went on my first march that year with Reverend Terence McCaughey and his son Kevin. I put them up in my house for the weekend. I was still fearful to go on the march, but I went with them. I am proud that I did.'

Meanwhile, the BST was engaging a wide range of people, in academia, trades unions, the private sector, community sector and ordinary citizens, insisting that the issue of Bloody Sunday should not be left just to the families. 'We argued that this was something you had to join in if you believed in truth and justice,' Conal McFeely says. 'Then we employed our first paid Trust workers, Colm Barton, as an archivist, Patricia McBride, now a Victims Commissioner, and, then, Mickey and John as family liaison workers.'

On 14 February, newly buoyed up relatives and campaigners, along with John Hume, met with Northern Ireland Secretary of State, Patrick Mayhew. 'We put all the new evidence in front of him and asked him to look at it and respond to our call for a new inquiry,' says John Kelly.

The dossier they handed over was crammed with eyewitness testimonies, soldiers' statements, post-mortem notes and the transcripts of army radio recordings. 'We have presented a substantial volume of material which the families know is new evidence,' John Hume told the media.

One day later, the families' hopes were dashed again when Mayhew dismissed any prospects of a government apology during an interview on BBC Radio Ulster.

'He told us he'd examine the material we gave him and get back to us,' John Kelly recalls. 'Yet, here he was, a couple of hours later. On the TV, saying there would be no new inquiry.' An apology, Mayhew told the interviewer, would only be necessary 'for criminal wrongdoing, and there was nothing in the Widgery Report to support that.'

The families were 'appalled' by the remarks and accused Mayhew of continuing a British 'whitewash'. They asked for immediate talks with the Irish government. At the time, John Kelly said: 'We feel it is now of enormous importance to have the Irish government as a friend and ally in our quest for justice.'

On Wednesday, 19 February, a delegation of relatives held talks with John Bruton in Dublin. They urged the Taoiseach to use his influence with the Clinton administration in the US to raise the issue of a new inquiry and they left Dublin assured of full support.

Campaigners described the meetings as an 'unprecedented display of Irish political solidarity for the twenty-five year plight of the Bloody Sunday families.'

John Kelly told a Belfast press conference the same week: 'We are not campaigning for apologies – the time for apologies has come and gone. No one should ask for one on our behalf . . . The new evidence condemns the Paras outright.'

[chapter eight]

'The Derry ones are coming!'

The impact of Don Mullan's book helped the families solidify their contacts with the Irish government. Don, himself, observes that until that point, Bloody Sunday had been seen as connected 'in some way to violent Republicanism and, so, the Irish establishment was afraid of it.'

However, he adds, 'The Irish government realised that I had no political or paramilitary ties, that my background was obviously in human rights. So, I was contacted by the Taoiseach's department when the book came out. For the next two years, I suppose I was the conduit between the Irish government and the families.'

'After Don's book came out we took the whole gang down to Dublin and made it a big PR stunt – "the Bloody Sunday families are coming!"' – remembers Mickey McKinney. 'By then, cross-party support for the campaign was really beginning to emerge.'

On 20 February 1997, a busload of optimistic campaigners, lawyers and family members set off for Dublin. A packed itinerary would see the families having tea with US Ambassador Jean Kennedy Smith at the Ambassador's Residence in the Phoenix Park at 4.45 PM; then on to Government Buildings for a 6.15 PM meeting with Taoiseach John Bruton, Tànaiste (deputy Prime Minister) and Foreign Affairs Minister Dick Spring, and Minister for Social Welfare Proinsias de Rossa. John Hume was also present. After this, they were to attend a meeting with Progressive Democrat leaders Des O'Malley, Bobby Molloy and Brendan Malone at Leinster House at 7 PM; and finally to the press room at Dublin Airport an hour later to meet Fianna Fáil leader Bertie Ahern and front bencher Ray Burke TD, the minute they touched down from a trip abroad.

The change in attitude from previous visits was astounding. Previously, the families had received a frosty reception and found themselves protesting outside the President's residence. That visit had ended with a police 'escort' out of the city by police. Now they were being treated like dignitaries.

Jane Winter recalls: 'Don had somehow organised a police escort to help us get from the Ambassador's residence in Phoenix Park to the Taoiseach's office during the afternoon rush hour. We were in a coach, and our driver had been instructed by a police officer on an out-rider motorbike to follow their blue lights and not to stop for any red ones. So there we were, hurtling down the quays through every red light at rush hour, all other traffic at a standstill. The families were all feeling very elated, all waving out of the windows shouting, "the Derry ones are coming!" It took just ten minutes to get across Dublin at rush hour. I remember the young Derry driver turning to me with a big smile and saying, "I've never had so much fun in my life!" It was great.'

'That day was incredible,' John Kelly agrees. 'We met so many people, the delegation sat down and we chatted. Everybody was relaxed. Anybody that wanted to speak could speak and I really believe we were listened to.'

'It was a pretty weird experience,' Tony Doherty admits. 'Travelling at full speed from the Ambassador's residence at the Áras all the way across Dublin to the Taoiseach's office in a small bus with the Gardaí stopping the traffic at intersections for us. . . .'

Don Mullan adds: 'It was hilarious. We felt like royalty! Despite all the sadness, there were moments like that in the campaign – moments that were uplifting, incredible and unforgettable.'

The visit was an outstanding success in its key objective. The Irish government, swayed by the mountain of new evidence, agreed to do all it could to help.

'With the Irish government now quite keen to get involved,' Tony Doherty

The Victims of Bloody Sunday

Barney McGuigan

Gerald Donaghey (left)

Jim Wray (far right)

John Young (centre)

Hugh Gilmour

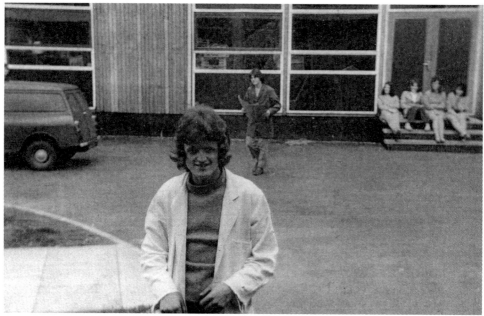

Michael Kelly

Kevin McElhinney

Gerard McKinney

John Johnston

Patrick Doherty

Michael McDaid

Jackie Duddy

William Nash

William McKinney

Taken on 30 January 1972, the civil rights march reaches the top of Westland Street and among the crowd of thousands a carnival atmosphere prevails.

Marchers plead for calm as some of the procession reaches the British army barricade in William Street.

Michael Kelly (17) lies mortally wounded at the rubble barricade on Rossville Street after British paratroopers open fire on marchers. In the background, Michael McDaid can be seen wearing a light-coloured checked jacket. Seconds later, he too was shot dead.

Photo courtesy of Robert White

As marchers flee the Bogside, local photographer Robert White captures the moment when Hugh Gilmour (17) clutches his stomach, hit by a paratrooper's bullet. He died within minutes.

Photo © Gilles Peress

Rioting erupts as the marchers are confronted by the British army and refused entry to the city centre. To the front left of the photograph, Jim Wray (22) can be seen sitting on the road, staging a peaceful demonstration. Minutes later, he would be shot twice in the back.

A halo of blood surrounds father-of-six Barney McGuigan (41), shot in the head as he waved a white hankie while going to the aid of the dying Patrick Doherty (31). Hugh Gilmour's body lies to the far left of the scene.

Photo © Gilles Peress

Father-of-six Patrick Doherty (31) is on the left side, unarmed and attempting to cover his face from the effects of CS gas. He is pictured crawling away from the gunfire towards the shelter of Joseph Place in the Bogside. Moments later he was shot in the buttock, the bullet travelling upwards through his body and exiting his chest. His cries attracted the attention of a nearby crowd, one of whom, Barney McGuigan, was shot dead as he tried to reach him.

Photo © William Ruckseyer

A devastated crowd gathers around a crimson pool of blood and Barney McGuigan's shoes, which were removed upon death as a matter of courtesy.

Children pray by the bloodied civil rights banner, which is now displayed in the
Museum of Free Derry.

Photo courtesy of the *Derry Journal*

The launch of the Bloody Sunday Justice Campaign in April 1992. From left to right: Johnny Walker, Birmingham Six; Eamonn McCann, activist; John Kelly, brother of Bloody Sunday victim Michael Kelly.

Photo courtesy of the *Derry Journal*

In July 1994, protests and chaotic scenes greeted Prince Charles, Colonel-in-Chief of the Parachute Regiment, when he visited the city in which his soldiers had massacred unarmed civilians two decades earlier.

A Bloody Sunday Commemoration March winds its way through the Brandywell and towards the Bogside in the early 1990s.

Photo courtesy of the *Derry Journal*

Photo courtesy of the *Derry Journal*

Families involved in the Bloody Sunday Justice Campaign prepare for their first trip to the USA for St Patrick's Day 1997. Pictured standing, from left: Margaret Wray, John Duddy, Eileen Green, Charlie McGuigan and his sisters, John Kelly, Connor Duddy, Margaret Kelly, Kevin Green, Goretti and Mickey McKinney. Kneeling at front: Kay Duddy, Geraldine Doherty.

Photo courtesy of the *Derry Journal*

Derry's Bogside Artists helped create huge banners depicting the faces of those killed on Bloody Sunday for the twenty-fifth anniversary commemorations in January 1997.

Photo courtesy of Hugh Gallagher

Bloody Sunday portraits are held aloft along the Derry Walls. As many as 40,000 marchers congregated in the Bogside below for the twenty-fifth anniversary rally.

The Bloody Sunday Trust is launched at the Ráth Mór centre on 30 January 1997. Pictured standing, from left, is Linda Roddy, solicitor Patricia Coyle, John Kelly, Mickey McKinney, Conal McFeely, Robin Percival, Tony Doherty, Caoimhin O'Murchadha, Denis Mullan, Paddy McDermott and Colm Barton. Seated, from left, are Professor Dermott Walsh, BIRW human rights activist Jane Winter, Lecturer in Law Angela Hegarty and Bishop of Derry, Seamus Hegarty.

Don Mullan, author of *Eyewitness Bloody Sunday*, and US ballistics expert Robert Breglio pictured on Derry's walls overlooking the Bogside at the end of January 1997. During his brief visit, Breglio conducted interviews with survivors and key witnesses and examined key locations to further his theory of soldiers shooting from the walls.

Linda Roddy, whose brother William was murdered on Bloody Sunday, pictured with one of the Bloody Sunday petitions in March 1997. Linda's father, Alex was also shot and injured while going to his son's aid.

The Bloody Sunday families and survivors meet with American Ambassador, Jean Kennedy Smith, sister of assassinated US president, John F. Kennedy, at her residence in Dublin's Phoenix Park in February 1997.

The families present a 40,000 signature petition calling for action on Bloody Sunday to 10 Downing Street on 3 July 1997 alongside Derry MP John Hume and MPs Tony Benn and Jeremy Corbyn.

Taoiseach Bertie Ahern lays a wreath at the Bloody Sunday Memorial in January 1998.

Photo courtesy of the *Derry Journal*

Derry MP John Hume and US Senator Edward 'Ted' Kennedy say a prayer at the Bloody Sunday Memorial on Rossville Street, January 1998.

Photo courtesy of the *Derry Journal*

The Bloody Sunday families hold a press conference in Derry's Guildhall on Thursday 29 January 1998 following the announcement of the Bloody Sunday Inquiry by British prime minister Tony Blair earlier that day.

Two of the surviving mothers of Bloody Sunday lead relatives through the city centre towards the Guildhall for Lord Saville's first appearance in Derry on Friday 3 April 1998. Front row, from left: Eileen Green, Nancy 'Anne' McKinney, Kay Duddy, Kathleen Kelly, Helen Young.

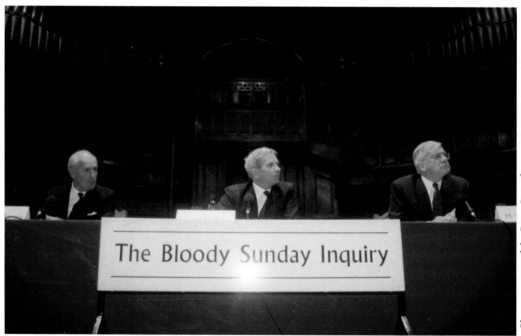

Lord Saville opens proceedings of the Bloody Sunday Inquiry in Derry on Friday 3 April 1998 alongside Honourable William L. Hoyt, former Chief Justice of New Brunswick, Canada, and the Right Honourable Sir Edward Somers from New Zealand.

Lord Saville and his colleagues visit the Bogside during their first day in the city on
3 April 1998.

Relatives hold a press conference at Pilot's Row Community Centre following Saville's first
day of proceedings on 3 April 1998. From left: John Kelly, Mickey McKinney, solicitor Peter
Madden, author Don Mullan.

The winter sun illuminates a row of relatives carrying crosses at the front of the annual Bloody Sunday commemoration march in January 1999.

Mickey McKinney and John Kelly open the Bloody Sunday Centre on Shipquay Street in 1999, just yards from proceedings at the Guildhall.

John Kelly and Mickey McKinney give U2's the Edge a tour of the Bloody Sunday Centre during a visit to the city in 1999.

A huge crowd of the Bloody Sunday families and wounded pictured in Westminister after the Bloody Sunday Inquiry relocated to London to hear military evidence in 2003.

Mickey McKinney (left) and John Kelly lead the Bloody Sunday march from the Creggan shops for the 2006 commemorations.

Relatives lead the Bloody Sunday commemoration march in 2008.

Photo courtesy of the *Derry Journal*

Relatives and local politicians highlight the 'Set the Truth Free' campaign on 1 March 2010 with a countdown to Lord Saville's estimated date of publication. The eyes pictured above the slogan and used on the campaign material are those of seventeen-year-old Gerald Donaghey, who died on Bloody Sunday.

Photo courtesy of Charlie McMenamin

The 'Set the Truth Free' campaign takes its message to Buckingham Palace, London, for St Patrick's Day 2010.

The families and survivors affected by the Bloody Sunday massacre pictured outside the Ráth Mór centre on 12 June 2010, two days before the publication of the Saville Report.

Kay Duddy and her brother Gerry, pictured with the infamous white hankie waved by Bishop Daly as he and others carried Jackie's lifeless body out of the Bogside on Bloody Sunday.

An emotional reunion at the Bloody Sunday Memorial, as survivor Joe Mahon meets Liam Wray, brother of Jim Wray, on the morning of 15 June 2010. As a terrified sixteen-year-old, Joe had feigned death after witnessing the murder of Liam's brother Jim, just a few feet from where he himself lay in Glenfada Park.

Relatives of the dead and wounded, accompanied by Derry's Mayor, make their way towards the Guildhall for the pre-read of the long-awaited Saville Report on 15 June 2010.

Thousands throng into the Guidhall Square on 15 June 2010 to await Saville's verdict.

Relatives and campaigners symbolically tear through a paper copy of the Widgery Report as they march towards the Guildhall Square on the afternoon of 15 June 2010.

Thousands congregate outside the Guildhall in anticipation of the findings of the Saville Report into Bloody Sunday on Tuesday 15 June 2010.

The vindicated families of Bloody Sunday address a jubilant crowd in Guildhall Square after Lord Saville exonerates all those killed and injured on 30 January 1972.

A delegation of relatives and campaigners travelled to Dublin the day after their vindication, where they personally delivered a copy of Lord Saville's report to Taoiseach Brian Cowen. From left: Linda Roddy, Conal McFeely, Kate Nash, Robin Percival, Taoiseach Brian Cowen, Kay Duddy, Mickey McKinney, Leo Young, Gerry Duddy.

Bloody Sunday families, survivors and campaigners are invited to meet Irish President Mary McAleese and her husband, Dr Martin McAleese, at Áras an Uachtaráin in September 2010.

says, 'we asked them to draw up a compendium of all the new evidence, including Don's book, Professor Walsh's report and the other new documents that had emerged. We met with the men appointed to draw up the assessment a few times and we were, basically, on the same side. They agreed they were going to submit the end result to the British government and were keen to get that done.'

Eamonn McKee and Gerry Cribbin, of the Irish Department of Foreign Affairs, were the civil servants who set about compiling the report.

'Given the renewed questions about Bloody Sunday prompted by *Eyewitness Bloody Sunday*, the Irish government decided that this new material should be assessed,' Eamonn McKee remembers. 'Obviously, the "new" material was, in fact, eyewitness statements taken at the time but it shed a very different light on the account given by Lord Widgery in his report.'

McKee, now Irish Ambassador in Seoul, Korea, alongside Gerry Cribbin, now working for the Department of the Taoiseach, assessed the new material against the evidence presented to the 1972 Widgery Tribunal.

He says that, at that point, Widgery's report was still 'a key document as far as the British government was concerned because it was the official account of the atrocity. 'As long as it stood, there could be no second official narrative, no new inquiry. For all the nationalist scorn about the Widgery Tribunal, its conclusions were based on a public inquiry which had the full authority of British law, conducted under the chairmanship of the chief law officer in the land. Clearly, it would not be possible to assess the new material through any evidentiary process *per se*. The challenge facing the Government was how then to give the new material weight and authority.'

McKee and Cribbin decided to go back to the primary source of the contending narratives and go through the entire Widgery Report. 'It was an illuminating exercise,' McKee remembers.

'Rather than find a crude whitewash, it was, in fact, a richly detailed account and, to the uninitiated, an apparently exhaustive and compelling one. However, the critical details that sought to apportion blame on the victims and exculpate the perpetrators lacked credibility when closely read and reread against the account in the eyewitness statements. These fractures necessarily ran through the whole narrative, but this was disguised by the careful selection of evidence.'

They surmised that Widgery had created 'a complete and polished alternative narrative parallel to but divorced from what had actually happened in the name of exonerating the security forces.'

The pair's most critical insights arose from taking the Widgery Report itself as the framework for assessing the new material. They studied each of Widgery's paragraphs, re-evaluating them with insights and perspectives drawn from the new material.

'Cumulatively, this overwhelmed Widgery's official narrative and, ultimately, his conclusions,' McKee says. 'In so doing, one also created in effect an alternative narrative that would be weighed in the scales of history should the British government reject the new assessment and let Widgery stand.'

Don Mullan speaks of Eamonn McKee with great admiration: 'To know you have someone of his calibre gives you confidence. He and Gerry Cribben did a wonderful job.'

At the beginning of March 1997, a former paratrooper who had served on Bloody Sunday admitted to BBC Radio Ulster's *Talkback* programme that he had seen nothing to justify his colleagues opening fire on marchers. Referring to himself as 'John', the ex-para said he spoke out of a 'sense of remorse' and described Bloody Sunday as 'very regrettable'. He said he couldn't condone what had happened, and urged an official apology to the families of the dead.

'I can't speak for other individuals, I can merely report what I saw myself, and I certainly did not think that there was justification. Even if there had been the odd weapon or the odd round fired at the soldiers, it still didn't justify the response,' he said.

'John's story would not be the only account from a soldier to emerge admitting army wrongdoing over the deaths and injuries on Bloody Sunday. Only weeks later, an explosive newspaper report by journalist Tom McGurk would cause huge controversy, and bolster the families' campaign yet further.

Meanwhile, Don Mullan and a delegation of relatives and supporters prepared for a week-long lobbying trip to the US. While hopeful of an audience with US president Bill Clinton, any exposure, they realised, would be welcome.

'When Don suggested some of us go to New York for the St Patrick's Day parade, I thought it was a great idea,' Mickey McKinney says. 'It was important that people in America knew what was going on. We really needed them on board. We secured funding from various sources and the AOH helped us with flight tickets. We were there for a week, but for some of us, our feet never touched the ground.'

Says John Kelly: 'We flew into New York, and the wife and I stayed in a penthouse owned by a friend of Don Mullan's. One of the things we were hoping for was to get on the New York St Paddy's Day parade, which we did, and then we went to Boston and got on the parade there too. In both cities, the point was to insert the Bloody Sunday issue into Irish-American politics.'

In New York on 12 March, the group attended the US launch of the 'Breglio Report'. They also attended a dinner hosted by the Irish-American Top 100, a prestigious occasion in the US, where several references were made to Bloody Sunday. Families were also introduced to Senator Edward Kennedy, who assured them of his concern and support, and his sister, the Ambassador to Ireland, Jean Kennedy Smith. Edward Kennedy would later visit the families in Derry and lay a wreath in memory of the dead.

Next stop was Boston, where the families and Don Mullan took part in the city's St Patrick's Day parade and held a press conference attended by three US televisions stations and reporters from the main Boston newspapers, the *Globe* and the *Herald*. They then returned to New York for a reception hosted by long-time supporters, the Ancient Order of Hibernians (AOH).

On St Patrick's Day itself, the relatives had a prominent position in St Patrick's Cathedral for Mass. Afterwards, they were greeted by Derry *Eurovision* winner Dana and former Taoiseach Albert Reynolds. They also met the Mayor of New York, Rudy Giuliani, and presented him with a copy of *Eyewitness Bloody Sunday*.

'We spoke to the chief marshal of the parade, who allowed us to go on the march there and then,' John remembers. 'That turned out to be something of a coup in itself – the fact that we were just off the boat and were slotted in and welcomed. It meant we had been given recognition.'

While some family members were marching in New York, others flew off to Washington. Don Mullan had arranged through a friend, a Washington lobbyist, that he and John Kelly would have access to the White House. They found themselves at a reception alongside Irish luminaries such as Derry composer Phil Coulter and Belfast flautist James Galway. President Clinton was upstairs resting a broken leg: Al Gore played host instead.

Before the event, they met Senator Edward Kennedy and his niece Kerry Kennedy Cuomo, who, as a former director of the Robert F. Kennedy Memorial Centre, accepted an offer to become a patron of the Bloody Sunday Trust.

John Kelly recalls the scene. 'I remember walking down the front of the White House and I saw John Hume standing there with Teddy Kennedy and he recognised us straight away. He said 'What are youse doing here?' I said we're over for the St Paddy's Day parade and me and Don's going in to a reception. Hume said, "If only I had known, I would've got you all in!"

'That was the only time we were in the White House. But, then, not many people can say they were in the White House at all. It was a major step forward.'

Later, they met with Congressional leaders who vowed to write a letter in support of a new inquiry. The letter was eventually signed by seventy-two Congressmen.

Kay Duddy addressed the gathering. 'The reaction from the senators was overwhelming, I cried my way through talking and some of them were crying along with me. You could tell they were genuinely affected.'

'Speaking at Capitol Hill was incredible,' John Kelly reflects. 'To actually be in the heart of the American government and get to speak to senators, it was wonderful.'

Having conquered America, the families flew home content. As they did, news broke of another development.

The *Sunday Business Post* in Dublin splashed in their 16 March edition with the story of a former para admitting that unarmed civilians had been deliberately killed on Bloody Sunday. Reporter Tom McGurk identified the soldier only as 'Para AA'. Documents in the reporter's possession confirmed his real name and the cipher given to him during the Widgery Tribunal – Soldier 027.

The soldier alleged that Support Company of the First Paras, of which he was a member, had been told by their Lieutenant the evening before Bloody Sunday to 'get some kills'. He also alleged that some of his colleagues had been in possession of their own additional ammunition, including lethal dum-dum bullets. He further claimed that many soldiers' accounts, including his own, had been doctored by lawyers to tally with the version of events favoured by the army at the 1972 Widgery Tribunal. He claimed that his original statement had been torn up during the Widgery Tribunal hearings and a revised statement provided to him by Counsel for the Tribunal. Both these documents had been among those recently discovered by Patricia Coyle.

Two days later, the story took another turn. Channel 4 News broadcast an interview with an anonymous paratrooper who revealed an uncannily similar account to that of Soldier 027. Disguised in silhouette, the paratrooper admitted that 'shameful and disgraceful acts' had been committed in Derry. He described the situation that had unfolded in the Bogside as 'something of a shambles in every respect' and, more importantly, revealed that 'there was certainly no order to fire.'

Regarding the original Widgery Tribunal, he told Channel 4 News: 'My experience of it was that you said what favoured the line they wished to take or you tended to be ignored. The officers present looked through my statement, removed it from the room and returned some time later with a second statement, which had various changes made to it. It wasn't exactly what I had previously said. In the event, I wasn't called forward to give evidence anyway.'

The striking similarities between the accounts in the *Sunday Business Post* and on Channel 4 led naturally to speculation that McGurk's Para AA and Widgery's Soldier 027 were one and the same.

Describing the paratrooper's claims as 'very serious', Taoiseach John Bruton said that this latest account would be included in the Irish government's assessment being prepared for presentation to the British government: 'The evidence is very strong and very specific as to what happened and when,' Bruton declared.

Around this time, too, another eighteen-strong group of US Congressmen wrote to Prime Minister John Major, urging a new investigation, citing the fact that 'recent evidence raised serious questions as to whether British soldiers fired on demonstrators from the vicinity of Derry's walls. This information alone should be more than enough to warrant a reopening of the investigation.'

Meanwhile, the Bloody Sunday Trust was concentrating on putting support systems for the families in place. Funding from the Peace 1 Programme of the European Union made it possible to employ John Kelly and Mickey McKinney as the first family liaison workers.

In Derry, a major petition was launched through both BSJC and the Bloody Sunday Trust as a mechanism for pulling together the increasing support for a new inquiry. The petition was based on the now-standard demands for repudiation of Widgery, a new investigation and for the perpetrators to be made accountable. The point was not just to gather signatures but to engage in large-scale, face-to-face campaigning.

'It was before everyone had computers so we went door to door,' Kay Duddy remembers. 'We must have talked and explained where the campaign had reached to thousands of people. I'm still using one of the clipboards as my bingo board!'

Eamonn McCann credits the family members themselves as being the campaign's primary source of strength. 'There were others around, but if there hadn't been that group of relatives at the centre of everything, the rest of us wouldn't have been grounded. We wouldn't have been authentically rooted, as it were. People like Mickey McKinney were holding the show together. Mickey is not a flamboyant character by any means, but he was always one of the most determined campaigners, always focused, always with his eyes on achieving the campaign's objectives and clearing his brother's name. Even now, he is more determined than any of the others to have charges brought against those responsible.

'Going out with a petition sheet, you needed to be able to say to people on the doorsteps that you were here about the case of Mickey McKinney's brother and other relatives and nobody else.'

In spite of this, there was still a degree of edginess in the public's response. Liam Wray recalls: 'I remember me, Banty Nash and my wife Doreen and others were allocated Carnhill and Shantallow and we went around two people to a door, knocking and asking for signatures. Even in your own area, you got abuse and were chased. But you carried on regardless.'

'Even our own people were still telling us it was a lost cause,' Geraldine Doherty adds. 'It was annoying at times, but you battled on, hail, rain and snow. I do remember one door I went to, they shouted stuff about "you murdering b**** you killed my son" and so on. I walked away shocked.'

'Whatever spare time you had, you were out getting signatures,' Gerry Duddy remembers. 'I had doors slammed in my face in the Bogside and Creggan and everywhere. People told you "get away from my door. I don't want anything to do with you." That was our own people. Even when we were doing flag days to raise money, people would walk past and refuse you. They were blatant about it too. But you get both sides of the coin, some people are nice to you and others are just ignorant. We persevered, but some people can tell you that it more or less took up our whole lives.'

Older sister Kay reports a more positive reception: 'I'm sure there were people out there who thought, "For Christ's sake, give it a rest." But I have to say I had very little abuse. I found that people wanted to tell you their own story, where they were on Bloody Sunday and what they were doing when it started to happen. I think the whole of Derry was in shock after Bloody Sunday and people often didn't realise. There must be scores of people who have suffered from post-traumatic stress and have never been diagnosed. I know people who couldn't cope with it all and became alcoholics.'

Says Eamonn McCann: 'I think there were some people who thought that the relatives were Provos or were being manipulated by the Provos. But, probably, a bigger number just wanted to push the Troubles away from their doors, which was a perfectly reasonable attitude to take. If you don't think the campaign had a chance of succeeding, despite whatever support it was getting from abroad or whatever, then you wouldn't see the point of involving yourself with it. It wasn't hostility in the vast majority of cases, more a feeling of futility.'

As well as walking door to door, campaigners maintained a city centre presence. 'On Saturdays, me, my mother and Kay sat, sometimes under umbrellas, at a pasting table in Waterloo Place with sheets of petitions and black ribbons to sell,' Geraldine Doherty recalls. 'People would question what we were doing and most people wanted to sign it. I think people seemed less likely to refuse you in town than they would at the door, as though you were intruding on their privacy on the door to door.'

South of the border, the mainstream media were beginning to move into alignment with the campaign's perspective. A *Sunday Tribune* editorial on 25 March 1997 branded British troops on Bloody Sunday as 'a gang of murdering thugs'.

In May, Labour leader Tony Blair succeeded John Major as British prime minister. Almost immediately, pressure was put on him to begin to resolve the Bloody Sunday issue. At the time, there was a noticeable thaw in British-Irish relations. A meaningful peace process loomed. In the following months, Sinn Féin would be brought into all-party talks at Stormont. The Good Friday Agreement would be signed a year later.

Embroiled in the peace negotiations, Martin McGuinness – later to become Northern Ireland's deputy first minister – frequently travelled to see Blair at Chequers. He reveals that Bloody Sunday often slipped into the conversation.

'Bloody Sunday came up in quite a number of conversations,' McGuinness says. 'Gerry Adams and I would travel over to London without the media knowing and then on down to Chequers and meet Tony Blair there. We had many soul-searching conversations about the conflict in Northern Ireland and spoke openly of Bloody Sunday.'

Days after Blair was appointed prime minister, Derry MP John Hume tabled a second Early Day Motion in the Commons urging the new prime minister to 'recognise that, having a full examination of all the relevant evidence, including the army's radio traffic, the fresh medical evidence and unexamined written statements of witnesses, is the best way to exorcise the bitter memories of twenty-five years'.

'The aim', he explained at the time, is to get this Government to take the step towards truth which its predecessor resisted. I believe the truth matters to Tony Blair. I also know that without the truth there can be no honest reconciliation or meaningful healing.'

Back in Derry, the campaign demanded that the Labour government's approach to the issue had to be 'radically different' from the previous Tory administration's.

Throughout this period, the families were kept abreast of progress by Hume and McGuinness: 'The British were already floating the possibility of a formal apology,' Tony Doherty remembers. 'But by then we were getting regular access to the airwaves and we made it clear on numerous occasions through radio, TV and newspapers that an apology would not be acceptable and would make matters worse. An apology would be appropriate only after we got the truth.'

'What we were talking about was having to undo an aspect of history which was morally, politically and judicially wrong and had caused great hurt to Irish people over decades. It was an aspect of history that remained an obstacle in terms of the peace process and everyone knew the positive effect that a successful resolution of Bloody Sunday would have on that process.'

As the summer of 1997 drew nearer, Eamonn McKee and Gerry Cribbin finalised the Irish government's assessment of the new evidence. Don Mullan was given the opportunity to preview it before completion.

'I was invited to the Department of Foreign Affairs to read through the penultimate draft of the document,' Don recalls. 'I was given an office over two days to read through it. Any comments I had were incorporated into the final draft which was to be handed over to the British government. It was a very comprehensive report, and the Irish government included relevant documents from their own archives, too.'

'Eamonn McKee described the assessment to me as "the anatomy of a whitewash",' Jane Winter remembers. 'We worked very closely with him.'

The Irish government eventually presented its assessment to Tony Blair's government in June 1997. It's widely believed that the Irish government had to threaten to publish the assessment in order to persuade the British government to make decisions. It was now a question of politics.

Taoiseach John Bruton noted the 'double injustice' suffered by the victims and families of 30 January 1972. In a covering letter accompanying the document, Bruton made it clear that the Irish government shared the national and international concerns about the 1972 tribunal. 'I believe that your approach to this issue can help to remove a source of profound distress not only to the relatives but to the nationalist community generally' he told Tony Blair. 'There is now an opportunity to lay to rest this most troubling and disturbing episode of the terrible history of the past twenty-seven years.'

Bruton described those killed and wounded on Bloody Sunday as a 'unique group in that the injustice of their fate at the hands of those whose duty it was to respect as well as uphold the rule of law, was compounded by a second injustice arising directly from the Widgery Report.'

Don Mullan says: 'John Bruton would never have been seen as a friend of Northern nationalists. But when we went to Dublin and made a presentation, he took on the Bloody Sunday issue whole-heartedly. It was his initiative to have the assessment done.'

Bertie Ahern succeeded John Bruton as Taoiseach on 26 June 1997. The new administration was equally supportive of the campaign. 'Bruton was determined that the assessment be handed over to Tony Blair before he left office,' Don Mullan says. 'Bertie Ahern took over as Taoiseach shortly thereafter and, so, unfortunately, he gets all the credit when, in fact, it was entirely down to John Bruton.'

As Taoiseach, Ahern was to prove a valuable asset in the campaign because of his particularly strong views on Bloody Sunday. Jane Winter reveals: 'The Department of Foreign Affairs told me that Bertie Ahern had phoned Tony Blair and said something along the lines of "never talk to me again in my political life unless you do something about Bloody Sunday". At that point, I knew we had reached critical mass. Bloody Sunday was right at the top of the political agenda. That's really how we got the inquiry.'

Just days after taking office, Bertie Ahern presented the McKee/Cribbin critique to Blair's government. 'You could tell that we were close to something,' Tony Doherty reflects.

Although this increased pressure on the British government bolstered hopes of a new inquiry, the BSJC also endured disappointment when the United Nations rejected the BIRW application that Jane Winter had earlier made. It was a blow to the families, but the campaign decided to present the BIRW report submitted to the UN to the Prime Minister anyway.

Families became adept at withstanding knock-backs and rejection. Gerry Duddy acknowledges the constant highs and lows that shaped so much of the campaign. 'As soon as we thought we were getting somewhere, it would get wiped from under our feet. But we kept at it. We had to.'

In late summer 1997, leading global human rights groups threw their weight behind the campaign. In an open letter to NI Secretary of State Mo Mowlam, Amnesty International, Human Rights Watch and the Lawyers Committee for Human Rights urged a British response and called for an independent, impartial public inquiry.

The families had already travelled to London to meet with Mo Mowlam while she was Opposition spokesperson on the North. John Kelly speaks fondly of her: 'Mo Mowlam, initially, was difficult. A batch of us travelled to London to meet her in Mill House after the election. We talked to her and she became enlightened to what we were trying to achieve. It was a very positive meeting.'

Jane Winter also speaks of the important role Mo Mowlam played. 'She became spokesperson in Northern Ireland for the Labour Party and, when it became clear that Labour was going to win that election, she asked for a seminar to brief her and her team on human rights issues in relation to Northern Ireland – which shows that she was interested in human rights.

'I was asked to chair that seminar in the House of Commons, and I said to her afterwards "When you're secretary of state, there are two things that are going to land on your desk immediately; one is Bloody Sunday and the other is Patrick Finucane. You have to do something". I think she heard what I said and she did do something about Bloody Sunday. It was her who persuaded Blair and the rest of the Cabinet to listen about the issue of Bloody Sunday. #In my view, she was the best secretary of state this place ever had. She also tried on Patrick Finucane, but she didn't succeed. It is a great shame that she is no longer with us.

'There were so many people involved in this campaign – we were just a cog in the wheel,' Jane adds. 'But I do think that we made a difference, because our efforts helped uncover the evidence and it shows that using the law and using human rights mechanisms is a good way of getting to the truth. We have done this with many other families since. It's never easy, but we know it works in the end. It did work in the end.'

[chapter nine]

'A thorn in their side'

It was becoming increasingly clear that those campaigning about Bloody Sunday would not give up. Despite the occasional differences and disagreements, the families maintained their collective strength. Every week brought new revelations, more influential supporters and a slow but steady surge in numbers. In Derry, the families continued their postal onslaught.

In July, human rights watchdog Amnesty International called on the British government to repudiate the Widgery findings. In its report, 'United Kingdom: An Agenda for Human Rights Protection', it said that the 1972 report should be 'quashed' and an immediate and full inquiry established so 'that the full circumstances of the killings be known.'

Growing speculation about Irish/British peace talks and the possibility of an acceptable settlement played its part in propelling the issue forward. 'The campaign and the peace process worked hand in hand,' Gerry Duddy says. 'Martin McGuinness and Sinn Féin and Mark Durkan and the SDLP, they really pushed the case every chance they got.'

The nationwide petition gathered pace throughout the summer of 1997, with relatives travelling to Belfast, Dublin and many other cities. The number of signatories grew to tens of thousands. The number had topped 40,000 by July 1997 when the families travelled to London to present it to Downing Street.

The hand-over outside 10 Downing Street drew considerable media attention. 'That felt amazing,' Kay Duddy remembers. 'Standing there together outside Number 10, with Hume and other MPs backing us up, I felt proud.'

While in London, relatives also held 'positive and constructive' talks at Westminster with Mo Mowlam. They left London full of hope and confidence. The same week, relatives met with Taoiseach Bertie Ahern in Dublin. He, too, assured them that the new Irish government would pursue the case 'with vigour and determination'.

In London, tentative peace negotiations rumbled on behind closed doors. The leaders of Northern Ireland's political parties regularly met with Tony Blair and government ministers. While Bloody Sunday was not officially on the agenda, local politicians ensured the issue crept into discussions. From the outset, Tony Blair seemed malleable and willing to consider the case.

'Ultimately, I don't think a Conservative government would have ever contemplated an international inquiry,' Martin McGuinness says. 'It was only when Blair was elected in the summer of 1997 that we had some sense that there might be a government that would genuinely put its shoulders to the wheel to develop a meaningful peace process.' McGuinness credits Blair for the 'great contribution' he made towards the resolution of the Northern conflict.

'I had a good understanding that we were dealing with someone who wanted to make a real contribution,' McGuinness reveals. 'Blair recognised that the British government bore huge responsibility for partition, for the creation of a state in which Catholics, nationalists and republicans were discriminated against.'

Martin McGuinness discussed the families' demands with Blair many times. 'Eventually he accepted that this would form a very important part of furthering the peace process. He took a brave step and it took a long time.'

At a meeting of the Anglo-Irish Inter Governmental Conference in Belfast in November 1997, Irish Foreign Affairs Minister David Andrews expressed concern about the time it was taking the British government to respond to their dossier on Bloody Sunday. Mo Mowlam, in reply, conceded that Bloody Sunday was a 'difficult, complicated issue' that the British government was devoting a lot of time to. 'We will reach a conclusion, I hope, sooner rather than later,' she said.

Towards the end of November, John Hume travelled to Westminster with a number of relatives and Derry city councillors to lobby for a new inquiry. More than sixty MPs had by now signed Hume's Early Day Motion demanding the truth into the 1972 killings. And Hume raised the issue yet again during Prime Minister's questions in the Commons.

'Would you tell us what steps you are prepared to take to establish the truth?' Hume asked. Blair replied that the government 'recognises the pain and distress of the events of 30 January 1972, and recognises, what's more, that they're still there after twenty-five years or more.'

The Prime Minister told the Commons that the new material before his government was 'extensive and detailed' and promised that his administration would 'consider it fully'. 'No options have been ruled out, but all the material must be fully examined first,' he added. 'When it has been examined and conclusions reached, we will announce them.'

In a statement the following day, the campaign described Blair's remarks as 'important', and added, 'The British prime minister cannot acknowledge pain and suffering without taking action.'

December was fraught with challenge and counter-challenge. Spokesperson Tony Doherty pressed Tony Blair to 'lead by example' and take risks for 'peace and justice,' and accused the Blair administration, despite its assurances, of continuing to fail to act. However, he also spoke of the families' hopes that truth was now within their grasp.

'Bloody Sunday is no longer a relatives group scoring an achievement here and there, mostly at local level. We have come a long way, but there is some distance to go yet.'

December also brought news that, having waited for a response, the Irish Government intended to publish their report on Bloody Sunday in the New Year. Taoiseach Ahern told the Dáil: 'It would be my intention to publish the assessment of the new material relating to the events of Bloody Sunday in the early months of 1998 . . . I believe it's important the truth is told about those events, and I believe the best way to achieve this is through an independent inquiry.' The pressure on Blair's government to act was continuing to build.

The Taoiseach said he was expecting a clear reply to the Irish government's report. 'They [the British government] know that we believe the Widgery report is fundamentally flawed and that the correct decision is to have a new inquiry. It is a matter of whether they will answer in the positive or the negative.'

In response, Mo Mowlam said that the British government was planning to respond to the families' call 'very soon'.

The following week, a Day of Action took place across Britain in support of the Bloody Sunday Justice Campaign and backing the demands for action. Protests were held in several major cities, including Birmingham and London, organised by the Troops Out Movement.

John Johnston, fifty-nine, was the oldest victim of Bloody Sunday. He is widely regarded as the fourteenth victim, having died from his injuries some five months after the shootings. John had no children and his wife had died. But his heartbroken in-laws fought to clear his name. Brother-in-law John Duddy became heavily involved in the Bloody Sunday Justice Campaign. His tireless crusade was to see no end, however: John passed away in May 2010, a month before publication of the Saville Report. Jimmy Duddy had accompanied his father to campaign meetings for many years and now stepped into his role.

'Johnny was such a jolly man,' Jimmy remembers. 'Because he had no children, we were like a family to him and his wife, Margaret. He was much more than an uncle. I remember him always singing to our aunt, songs like "You Are My Sunshine" . . . Johnny believed in equal rights, and supported the civil rights movement, although he never spoke about it much.

'He was always a big healthy man but he went downhill rapidly after being shot. Even when he seemed to be on the mend, he just wasn't the same. If Bloody Sunday had never happened, who knows how long he would have lived?'

Jimmy says his father had become involved in the campaign from the moment he heard about it. 'Bloody Sunday wasn't just about the families, everybody was affected by it. The whole town felt it badly and it rippled outwards and affected people far beyond Derry. My father strongly believed in justice and was very passionate about the campaign. He thought that, without justice, we were back where we began – as second-class citizens. He would come home from meetings and tell me everything that happened.

'As my father's health deteriorated in the last few years, I took over and got involved when I could. I went to London a few times when the Saville hearings moved there. When I wasn't able to go, I followed the hearings with transcripts of the evidence.'

The substantial progress the campaign had made created a new set of problems. 'The numbers involved were increasing to a degree that it was nearly causing problems,' Kay Duddy reveals. 'Not in a bad way, but with a bigger group there were different opinions and there was a lot of clashing of personalities, which I suppose is par for the course. I remember once saying that, for the next meeting, people should bring a punch bag and a pair of boxing gloves! I think frustration started to set in because no-one was sure what we were doing at times.

'Sometimes, you would have to stand up and say, "Hold on, let's not lose sight of what we are fighting for here!" To begin with, we were almost too afraid to take on any political support because we needed to be non-political. That was difficult to maintain because we needed balanced support on all sides while maintaining independence.'

Olive Bonner (née Gilmour) wasn't put off by the arguments. 'There was always the odd raised voice or difference of opinion and breakaways. That didn't bother me. We were essentially united, and wherever we went we put on a good show for the sake of the cause. There might have been arguments going on in the background, but we never let anyone see that side of things.'

Olive pays tribute to the core campaigners. 'The main families behind the campaign did their very best. They had a lot on their plate at times – then they organised the meetings and contacted everyone – all the rest of us had to do was turn up. They had all the hard work done, organising things, writing letters and coming up with new ideas. They did a brilliant job, didn't they?

'We suffered rejection from time to time, of course, but I believe that, basically, Derry stood behind the families since the beginning. Even a few years down the line, people would still stop you in the street and ask how the campaign was going. People remembered and cared.'

Some family members remained critical of the process that was unfolding. One dissenting voice was Liam Wray. 'Somewhere along the line there seemed to be this notion that we had campaigned for an inquiry. We did *not* campaign for a new inquiry, it was not one of the campaign's three aims – that still annoys me to this day. My view was that a new inquiry would be conducted under the same 1921 Act that had failed us so spectacularly with Widgery.'

Liam believes that the new inquiry was a 'politically orchestrated deal' done beyond the families' remit. 'I was very unhappy with it, but I stayed in solidarity with the other families. After all those years, I understood how important it was to them and how it could lead, in a sense, to the three aims.'

The period leading up to the inquiry had seen a dramatic increase in archive material with a huge volume of documents and evidence unearthed from various sources. It became necessary to develop a structured system of gathering and storing this vast archive. The Bloody Sunday Trust's vision of a central archive suddenly became a priority.

Tasked with collating the archive was local man Colm Barton. In 1997, he became the first Bloody Sunday Trust employee. Having been a member of the group since its inception a year earlier, he gave up Trust membership to take on the role of Project Coordinator: 'The role was essentially a historical one, gathering material and looking after the archive, with a potential for a history centre,' Colm explains. 'There was so much information coming to light, it all needed properly collated and organised, so that was my job.'

It was not long after Colm took up his post that the prospect of a new inquiry began to come into sharper focus. When the demand for an inquiry was finally met, his job widened in scope, being now directed towards the needs of the inquiry.

'I ended up based in Belfast for a couple of months with Madden and Finucane. They had employed a professional archivist from Dublin, so we were literally up in the attic of Madden and Finucane surrounded by box-loads of material which had been gathered over the decades, putting it all together for the inquiry,' Colm remembers.

Years of planning and development would eventually lead to the creation of the Museum of Free Derry in Glenfada Park – housed in what once were homes scheduled for demolition: the museum is located on the ground where some of those it commemorates were gunned down. All the material which had been gathered was subsequently submitted to the inquiry. Ultimately, it would end up back where its journey began, as part of the repository of the Museum of Free Derry.

Colm now reflects on his involvement. 'I held the role in a paid capacity for a few years and then felt the time was right to step back. When I did resign, I was delighted to be invited back on board as a member of the Bloody Sunday Trust and I am proud of my long involvement with them.

'I'm also proud every time I walk down Rossville Street and see the Museum of Free Derry, which now stands as a testament to the people of Derry and tells their story through their own voices.'

The campaign continued to take its message far and wide. Family members who had once been reluctant to speak publicly became surprisingly adept at addressing the public. As well as speaking at rallies, one-to-one interviews, TV news programmes and talk shows were all utilised. For many of the main campaigners, courting the media became a necessity and a way of life.

John Kelly admits that campaigners were wholly unprepared for the spotlight thrust upon them. The unfamiliar media industry daunted them at first. 'We had to learn to do the interviews as best we could,' says John. 'We're only ordinary people. Mickey McKinney is a butcher, Gerry's a plasterer, Kay's a housewife. Geraldine was a shop assistant, Mary was a housewife, I'm an engineer, Tony Doherty's a joiner. As campaigners, we never had any experience – we were all doing it completely raw.

'It was always the same core people that did the interviews. As to techniques and so on, we had no idea! My fear was always the worry of saying the wrong thing. I don't think I ever did, but you need to be very careful.'

Building a rapport with the public was just as important. Gerry Duddy vividly recalls one occasion when he was due to speak in Birmingham. Just as he was about to begin, dozens of police came charging into a room. 'I was there to give a talk and suddenly these cops burst in. There was a bomb scare and they evacuated us all. The organiser, Mary Pearson, started to apologise to me and I said, "Don't worry about it". I asked her to go grab me two crates. I went into the car park, put the crates on top of each other, threw my arm around a lamp-post and went on with my meeting!'

'It worked,' he adds, with a smile. 'I was literally hanging around up a lamp-post, and to start the meeting, I said sorry if we seemed nervous because we weren't used to things like bomb scares back home – that broke the ice nicely.'

Gerry was continually harassed and searched. 'I would always get stopped when they sent me to England, but that was more publicity. Usually it would make the papers. From the very start, I was getting pulled in at the airport. I was a Bloody Sunday relative simply going over to talk about Bloody Sunday and I was still getting hassled. Even when I travelled over with junior football teams, nothing to do with Bloody Sunday, I was still pulled aside and harassed.'

The far-right National Front made trouble at many Bloody Sunday commemorations in England. 'At one stage it got quite scary in Glasgow and London,' Gerry recalls. 'The police treated us terribly. They would have side streets cordoned off but, then, every so often they would move the barriers and the National Front would attack the marchers and, then, if the marchers retaliated, the police would appear again and arrest the marchers. It happened quite a few times because the National Front was always out.

'One of the scariest places I've been was Glasgow. Once, on a march of about five or six thousand we were faced with 1,500 National Front. There was about two thousand police there, but it's still scary when there are women and children with you, to imagine – if that crowd got loose . . . They had me leading the march and I'm thinking, "What am I doing here!"'

The National Front also threatened Gerry personally. 'They made death threats to me when I was in Birmingham; they also got hold of Mary Pearson's number and were phoning her every hour on the hour. Once, when I was on a radio show for a two-hour question and answer session, they kept phoning up and saying, "we're going to get you Duddy, you bastard."'

The campaigners' fearlessness and passion earned them admiration. They were held in increasingly high esteem wherever they went. 'It was clear to me that the families were always the powerful voices in terms of articulating what had happened that day,' Martin McGuinness says. 'Our role was simply to support their demands – they had to retain the dominant position. All credit to them, they got the support of everybody everywhere who came to believe that what happened was a blatant act of murder by state forces on a particular community.'

Another dedicated member of the Bloody Sunday Justice Campaign was Damian 'Bubbles' Donaghy. A cousin of fellow victim Gerald Donaghey, Damian was the first person shot on Bloody Sunday and today, almost forty years later, the physical and psychological effects continue to plague him.

'I was only fifteen at the time and I remember how happy and positive everyone seemed as we set off from the Creggan Shops,' he recalls. As the march neared William Street, Damian remembers seeing British soldiers hiding in a derelict building. 'People were throwing stones at them, which was pretty normal in those days. Then a few rubber bullets were fired, one bounced off the wall and I dived to get it as a souvenir. The next thing I knew, a shot rang out and I was on my back. I saw the blood and knew I was hit. People came over to lift me, one of whom was John Johnston, and they shot him, too.'

Damian underwent emergency surgery before joining the other wounded men on a ward. Only then did he learn the full magnitude and scale of the shootings. 'I was in total shock – I thought it was maybe just us who were shot. I remember there were a couple of British soldiers at the far end of the ward laughing about what had happened. They weren't paratroopers but they still gave us abuse – so I grabbed the crutch and went for one of them.'

Damian spent seven months in hospital. However, the leg injury has never healed properly and, only recently, doctors suggested reconstructive surgery on his knee.

'At times, the pain is still terrible,' he says. 'The bullet had fractured my right femur and, even to this day, I can only bend my leg 30 percent. I have a seven-inch scar up the side of my leg and I had one of those big bolts put in to strengthen it, and then a calliper. I was only a teenager when it happened, but it has never really healed.

'We campaigned to get everybody cleared but we didn't really think we would get it, to tell you the truth. Well, I didn't think we would anyway.

'I didn't talk about Bloody Sunday much, I resented the fact that we were named in the wrong and, for years afterwards as you know, people still saw us as terrorists. Many in the Protestant population thought we were all nail-bombers and gunmen. The army seemed to know who you were, and they stopped you steadily when you went out. During Operation Motorman in August 1972, when the barricades around Free Derry came down, I was still on crutches and they would have singled me out because of who I was.'

Damian is now married with four children, but he still finds it difficult to talk about his experience: 'To be truthful, I never really talk about Bloody Sunday unless it's coming up to an anniversary or something. Although I suppose it is different for me than for the people lying up there in the cemetery – at least I can talk about it.'

[chapter ten]

'Into the unknown'

As the twenty-sixth anniversary loomed, relatives and campaigners were more hopeful than ever of news from the British government. By now, support for the campaign had reached unprecedented levels. Bloody Sunday was being reported and debated all over the world.

The prospect of a new inquiry had regularly featured in the talks which were to lead to the Good Friday Agreement. It was evident, particularly to the nationalist population, that action on Bloody Sunday was necessary to facilitate a successful and lasting peace process.

The Irish government's commitment to the campaign made headline news on 23 January when Taoiseach Bertie Ahern visited Derry and laid a wreath at the Bloody Sunday Memorial on Rossville Street. The following day, London supporters took to the streets for their own Bloody Sunday march. Momentum was gathering pace. Campaigners, families, friends and citizens across Ireland felt that an announcement was imminent.

Tony Doherty recalls: 'By then, there was practically no doubt that there would be a second inquiry; the marches had been getting bigger and bigger. There were very high expectations.'

Peter Cassells, General Secretary of the Irish Congress of Trade Unions, wrote to John Kelly on 16 January to let the campaign know that the ICTU had pursued the families' demands with both the British prime minister and the Irish government. They had received a reply through Secretary of State, Mo Mowlam. In the reply, dated 24 November 1997, Mowlam assured him that the government was examining a range of new material and that, if there was indeed new evidence to warrant an inquiry, appropriate action would be taken.

'I fully understand that the events of 30 January 1972 known as Bloody Sunday still arouse great pain and sorrow; I met the relatives of some of those killed in my office in July and saw just how much pain remains after the passage of so much time,' Mo Mowlam wrote to the ICTU.

Towards the end of January 1998, the families received dramatic news.

'We found out a few days beforehand that the British government was planning some kind of announcement,' Tony Doherty reveals. 'There was a fair idea it was going to be significant, and it turned out to be a new inquiry. Nothing like this had ever happened before, so no-one was really sure until we got the phone call.

'Mo Mowlam rang me at home and, as I remember, it was quite a short conversation and she wasn't giving much away, but she said Tony Blair's announcement was going to be a new inquiry.'

Mickey McKinney takes up the story: 'Mo had said we wouldn't get what we wanted – an international independent inquiry – but probably something close, with a British judge and two Commonwealth judges. It was suddenly very real.'

On a cold but sunny Thursday morning on 29 January 1998, the families, survivors and campaigners huddled around televisions in their usual meeting place at Ráth Mór to await the announcement. The following day would be twenty-six years since Bloody Sunday and almost six years after that first campaign meeting in the spring of 1992.

'We were all to meet at 10.30 AM that Thursday morning,' Tony Doherty remembers. 'We didn't do any media interviews on the morning of the announcement, and it seemed as though we were basically locked away up in the Ráth Mór, waiting. Some media knew we were there, but we had already organised a press conference at the Guildhall for later that day.'

Solicitors Patricia Coyle and Peter Madden joined the families and survivors for the announcement, alongside representatives of the Irish government and Bloody Sunday Trust members. They awaited a speech that was soon to make British legal history.

In a 'Breaking News' bulletin, Tony Blair announced the establishment of a fresh public inquiry into the events of Bloody Sunday. He told the House of Commons that, because 'much new material has come to light', there were 'indeed grounds for such a further inquiry.'

'We believe that the weight of material now available is such that these events require re-examination. We believe that the only course which will lead to there being public confidence in the results of any further investigation is for a full-scale judicial inquiry into Bloody Sunday to be set up. We have therefore decided to set up an inquiry under the Tribunal of Inquiry (Evidence) Act 1921. The inquiry will have the power to call witnesses and obtain production of papers.'

As required by the Act, a resolution was passed in the following terms: 'That it is expedient that a Tribunal be established for inquiring into a definite matter of urgent public importance, namely the events on Sunday, 30 January 1972 which led to loss of life in connection with the procession in Londonderry on that day, taking account of any new information relevant to events on that day.'

The prime minister also acknowledged the long campaign for truth and paid tribute to the Derry families and campaigners: 'I have heard some of their remarks over recent years, and have been struck by their dignity,' Blair said. 'Most do not want recrimination. They do not want revenge. But they do want the truth. I believe that it is in the interests of everyone that the truth is established, and told. It is also the way forward to the necessary reconciliation, which will be such an important part of building a secure future for the people of Northern Ireland. I ask all sides of the House to support our proposal for this inquiry.'

In Derry, relatives were both buoyant and nervous. 'I remember thinking, thank God this is it – everybody will know now,' Olive Bonner says. 'We were really relieved there was finally an end in sight, that we might actually be told the truth at last.'

Kay and Gerry Duddy were cautiously hopeful. 'We weren't sure at that early stage what to think about the inquiry news, but we hoped it was a means of achieving our aims,' Kay said. 'It was like a sigh of relief.'

'I couldn't really believe it,' Jean Hegarty adds. 'I was really quite amazed. I suppose I was quite sceptical that the British government would give us a second inquiry at all.'

Feeling an unfamiliar mixture of pride and apprehension, Tony Doherty remembers: 'Our family was quite excited about it all. We knew that, even though we had many people working and campaigning on our behalf, that we, the families, were at the forefront and core of this. That was a great feeling.

'If we hadn't been active within the campaign, we wouldn't have been where we ended up in 1998. It took six years of very, very hard work. Seemed a longer time, but it was six years almost to the day from the twentieth anniversary to that announcement at the House of Commons. It was a great time, I have to say . . . There was a real sense of achievement and breakthrough and possibility – and there's nothing better than feeling the sense of possibility about you.'

Patricia Coyle, who was with the families when the news broke, remembers: 'It was a real moment in time and an unprecedented moment in legal history. One inquiry was overturned and another was announced. My sense that day was that the families were delighted – and also nervous. Not just because of the announcement, but also because of the job that would follow. The announcement of the new inquiry was not the end but the beginning of another, much more difficult phase.'

The Inquiry was to be chaired by the Right Honourable Lord Mark Saville of Newdigate – a respected British Law Lord. The other tribunal members would be the Honourable William L. Hoyt, former Chief Justice of New Brunswick, Canada, and the Right Honourable Sir Edward Somers, from New Zealand.

Tony Doherty was content with the idea of the three judges. 'The campaign had been pushing for an international inquiry and not a single British judge and that's what we got, two judges from Commonwealth countries, which were independent so that was okay.

'I think any doubts people had at that time were largely dispelled by the government agreeing to make it international.'

Geraldine Doherty was elated. She knew how important it was to her mother to have Gerald's name cleared. 'Some thought we'd get nowhere with the government but we proved it, we kept on. We took the knockbacks, and we got there! When the new inquiry was announced, more of the families who had preferred to be discreet and private started coming on board.'

Once the families and wounded had digested the news, they prepared to address the media. Because Blair's announcement had broken with all precedent and constitutional tradition, it was an international news story. The Guildhall was packed with the press.

Tony Doherty remembers the event. 'We knew nothing of Saville or any details at the time, and we hadn't much to say for ourselves apart from recognising it as a major breakthrough. It was an honourable thing that Tony Blair did. He may have gone on to do a lot of terrible things in the world, but, from our point of view, it was the right thing to do and a very brave thing to do, and we gave him genuine credit for that on the day.'

To mark the announcement, the BBC repeated its controversial 1992 documentary 'Remember Bloody Sunday' in which Lieutenant Colonel. Derek Wilford, Commander of the 1st Battalion Parachute Regiment, insisted, 'I don't believe my soldiers were wrong'.

On Sunday 1 February, more than 30,000 people wrapped up warm and came together at the Creggan Shops to commemorate the twenty-sixth anniversary. As always, the march traced the original 1972 route. A jubilant mood prevailed, the crisp winter air electric with possibility.

The nature of campaign meetings changed after Blair's announcement. Having achieved so much, many campaigners were, to some extent, at a loss. Leo Young says it was the announcement that made the difference to him personally. 'After Bloody Sunday, I never would have dreamt of a campaign. I suppose the first time I did consider it was when the Saville Inquiry was announced. It was only then I started thinking we might get somewhere. My sister Maura would have been more involved in the campaign before that. Naturally, human nature and different opinions means there were arguments and disagreements over the years. Still, they stayed with it until the end.'

Leo praises the campaigners who had led the way. 'They persevered when everybody else was taking a step back, they were moving forward all the time. They were very positive thinkers, and they spun even the smallest negative reaction into positives for the campaign. And it was worth it.'

Leo would become a regular fixture in the Guildhall throughout the Saville hearings.

Survivor Mickey Bridge was less than confident that a new inquiry would uncover the truth and maintained a lack of trust in the British establishment as a whole. 'We were granted a second inquiry for one simple reason. The Public Records Office was being thrown open after thirty years and there were papers there that British Irish Rights Watch and Patricia Coyle were made aware of. The British government knew we were going to find something and this forced their hand. They couldn't get rid of it – so they addressed it by taking control and establishing an inquiry, just like they did in 1972.'

Mickey Bridge had rarely dwelled upon his injuries or the massacre that had unfolded around him. 'Bloody Sunday was different. Nobody could ever have seen it coming – we had no concept of something like that ever happening on our own streets. My family never even knew I was shot, it was a teacher who told my daughter at school. I didn't talk about it and wouldn't have talked about it if it hadn't been for the inquiry. I had tried to keep my family distant from it all.'

Mickey was aged twenty-five in 1972 and was one of many stewards on duty during the march. Having successfully shepherded marchers along the route and towards William Street, the Bogside quickly descended into pandemonium. Marchers fled advancing troops and ran for shelter towards the Rossville Flats and the rally point at Free Derry Corner. Mickey was among those who ran. He was targeted as he confronted soldiers in the courtyard of the Rossville

Flats – indignant at seeing the shooting of teenager Jackie Duddy, someone he had known through boxing circles.

'When I saw young Duddy fall, I went back towards the soldiers, probably shouting obscenities at them, and they shot me, quite deliberately.' He remembers hearing bullets whizzing past. The bullet hit Mickey just below the hip. 'It split my leg in two halves,' he says. He spent two weeks recovering in Altnagelvin Hospital. 'In the beginning in the hospital the wounded had no idea how many people had been shot. We didn't know the full extent of what had happened until the next day. It was only when I saw the newspapers that the reality began to hit me.

'Me, Joe Friel, Mr Nash and Patsy O'Donnell were on a ward together. We were still in hospital for the funerals. The nurse actually stole the TV off the soldiers on the ward and brought it up to us so we could follow the funerals on TV.'

Mickey recalls his fury after Widgery cleared the soldiers and British authorities of any blame. 'I was angry about Widgery, everyone was, but we couldn't do anything about it. They avoided the wounded like the plague. They ignored witnesses and important evidence. They were aware of police reports and did nothing and they got rid of the survivors as quickly as possible. The RUC investigating officer at the time said that the shooting of Jackie Duddy was murder. He also said that I was innocent – facts which were never brought to the Widgery Inquiry.'

'Overnight, Bloody Sunday changed everything. They branded us. They labelled us terrorists just to justify the killings. Even to this present day, that bothers me. Because of the environment we were living in – if I strayed into a staunch Protestant area and they found out who I was – I was often targeted for being Catholic. It restricted where you could work. That was a reality then.'

This distrust persists today, as Mickey reveals. 'Once you were identified, the army took it upon themselves to stop you every time they saw you. Once I was stopped seven times in one week! I was a name they recognised; they checked my ID and they thought, "There's that nail-bomber from Bloody Sunday".

They held me in security for hours every time I went to England. We had to live with that for years. It affected your personal life, everything. It never leaves you.' Mickey was to relive his experiences when he gave evidence to the Saville Inquiry.

It was in preparation for the inquiry that the Bloody Sunday Trust appointed Mickey McKinney and John Kelly as family support workers.

'Jane Winter and British Irish Rights Watch secured money for family liaisons, and it ended up that John and I got the posts,' Mickey recalls. 'We liaised with all the families, something which we had done in a way from the beginning of the campaign, but it was much more important to the group now while the inquiry was on.'

Mickey would again take up the liaison role in the months before the inquiry reported in 2010.

Legal teams also began preparing for the inquiry. As solicitors, Derry brothers Ciarán and Fearghál Shiels, were to play integral roles, collectively representing ten of the families and deceased.

Ciarán Shiels recalls how he became involved in March 1998, shortly after Tony Blair announced the inquiry. A last minute interview with Madden & Finucane Solicitors proved life-changing for the young solicitor. Today he is a partner with the same firm. 'I travelled to Belfast and was interviewed by Peter [Madden] one Saturday afternoon for about an hour or so and was offered the job to start that Monday at 9 AM,' Ciarán says. 'It all started quite quickly.'

The responsibility of representing the families was evident to Ciarán and his brother. They had attended the annual march as children and maintained interest in the case as they grew up. 'Obviously the case was hugely important to me and I was honoured to be involved in it,' Ciarán reflects. 'I was from the Creggan estate as were my parents and both sets of grandparents. My father and grandfather were significant witnesses who were interviewed by the *Sunday Times* Insight team in 1972. My mother's family all grew up beside the Duddy family in Creggan and were very good friends with them. So you can imagine how pleased, and nervous, I was to be helping out and offering what contribution I could.'

Ciarán says the Saville Inquiry featured a 'cast of thousands'. 'What we were dealing with was mass murder perpetrated before the world's media. It took place over a period of about ten to twelve minutes, within a geographical area not much bigger that two football pitches, with the British army's Commander of Land Forces and an Assistant Chief Constable of the RUC in close attendance.

'Initially, the Madden & Finucane team immersed themselves in the detail of the case starting with the Widgery Report, which, by dint of the Saville Inquiry being set up, was effectively already consigned to the dustbin. But it was a good place to start as far as official British documentation was concerned.' Ciarán was already familiar with the Walsh Report, the Irish government's report and the witness statements collated by NICRA.

Those first months saw the energies of the legal team devoted to summarising Widgery's evidence and identifying issues for counsel. 'In those early days there was a very small team working on the case,' Ciarán Shiels continues. 'There was Peter and Patricia who were combining the work along with their other case loads, myself working full-time and an archivist from Dublin called Lawrence Doyle who M&F engaged to start properly collating all of the material that we had gathered into a proper archive in the office in Belfast. The only counsel in those early days was Seamus Treacy who was then a junior counsel who had assisted and prepared the families' application to Strasbourg the year before the inquiry was announced.'

Campaigners continued to meet regularly, but relationships were gradually becoming more strained. 'You spoke your mind and moved on,' Geraldine Doherty remembers. 'If there was a problem, you tried to talk it through. Everyone was so highly strung at times, but people said what they had to say.'

Gerry Duddy doesn't regret the sacrifices he made for the campaign, but admits that Bloody Sunday dominated much of his life.

'When I first got involved, I vowed to do everything in my power to see it through and I stuck to that commitment. Any of the core members of the campaign will tell you the same – it consumed us . . . Our spouses and partners always gave their full support. Throughout the campaign, they became one-parent families because, at the drop of a hat, we could have been anywhere. If we didn't have their backing, we couldn't have done it.'

Despite a new inquiry being announced, Gerry and the other core campaigners continued their work behind the scenes, taking their message as far and as wide as they could. 'It didn't just stop because we had a new inquiry, you know. There was still work going on behind the scenes. All the time, we still had to get our message out there.'

Elsewhere, behind the scenes, Jane Winter recalls how the unexpected help of a former British army captain produced hours of transcripts of army radio messages.

'The Porter tapes were hours of British soldiers talking in code and using ciphers but nobody had ever transcribed them. It took months, and I thought we would never get there until one day a former army captain from Derry, who wasn't here on Bloody Sunday but had served in the army for many years, phoned me in tears. He said his mother had just died and on her deathbed she had passed him a copy of *Eyewitness Bloody Sunday* and asked him to read it and he had just finished doing so. He was devastated and wanted to do something to help, so I said, as it happens, we're trying to decipher these military tapes and, so, he came to help.

'He understood all the military jargon, and spent hours recording it all. Not only that, but, because he was ex-army, this man went to the regimental headquarters of all the regiments present on Bloody Sunday and asked to look in their libraries, providing us with loads of information. That was brilliant and unexpected and we should be grateful to him.'

An open appeal for eyewitnesses was also underway in Derry. 'We had to encourage people to attend the inquiry,' Kay Duddy remembers. 'We put out an appeal in the paper for witnesses to come forward and give evidence. Then we sat at tables in the Guildhall foyer encouraging people to take part and we took their names and addresses.

'It seemed to me that Derry people very much wanted the opportunity to tell their experience of the day. It appeared to be really important that people get it off their chest. Although it was really emotional at times, it was probably a release for them, as they had never had the chance to tell their story.'

Campaigners collected well over a thousand names of potential eyewitnesses. Now those who had come forward, who had witnessed the horror first-hand, would have to give an official statement to Eversheds, the legal firm tasked to take the thousands of witness statements for the inquiry.

Initially, lawyers from Eversheds' team expected the process to last two months. But the mammoth task of collating was to span seven years. By the end, the fifty-strong team had taken statements from over 2,200 witnesses, including civilians, military, police, politicians and a former British prime minister.

Two months after being set up, the Bloody Sunday Inquiry prepared to open proceedings in the Guildhall. Brutal deaths would be discussed in the basest of terms, lives publicly dissected and desperate last moments revealed. For many, it would reopen deep wounds. 'We really were going into the unknown,' Kay Duddy says. 'We literally had no idea what was ahead of us.'

On Friday 3 April 1998, dozens of nervous relatives, survivors and supporters gathered at McCool's Shop on William Street, the location of the British army's barricade fourteen on 30 January 1972. Theirs was to be a symbolic procession to the Guildhall for the first day of the new Bloody Sunday Inquiry – finishing the march they had begun in 1972. Uneasiness pervaded the silence as they approached Guildhall Square under a grey sky and surrounded by photographers and well wishers. It was a moment of mixed emotion after two decades of disappointment. Many dared to hope, while others were naturally wary of Lord Saville and the British judicial system that he represented.

Formally opening the inquiry, Lord Saville addressed the Guildhall's opulent main hall by means of a simple introduction. 'My name is Mark Saville. I am an English Law Lord.'

Saville's dedication to the job was evident from the start – to many, he seemed to grasp immediately the significance of the inquiry and the crimes of which the British army stood accused. Although seemingly kind and personable, Saville did not satiate anyone – it would only be after a thorough investigation and the truth declared that the families would be able to rest.

'Our task is to try to find out what took place in this city that Sunday afternoon,' Lord Saville told the hall. 'It would be foolish for us to ignore the fact that there are allegations that some of those concerned in the events of Bloody Sunday were guilty of very serious offences, including murder. Whether there is any substance in those allegations remains, of course, to be seen.'

Although now opened, the inquiry would not begin its oral hearings for another two years. In the interim, legal teams and researchers would spend thousands of hours collating evidence and gathering testimony. Few in Derry imagined the scale of the operation ahead and the families felt wholly unprepared for an operation of this magnitude.

'We were dealing with something completely different here,' Kay Duddy admits. 'Especially when you consider that the entire Widgery "farce", as we can call it now, actually lasted a shorter time than the opening address of the Saville Inquiry!'

Speaking prior to the opening of the public hearings, Linda Roddy (née Nash) told a reporter: 'My father didn't want to live after Bloody Sunday.' Linda's father, Alexander coped not only with his own wounds, but with the murder of his son, William, on Bloody Sunday.

'How can the truth be divisive?' she asked. 'My brother was never interested in the IRA. We were actually a military family because two more brothers were soldiers in the British army. William was murdered when he was totally innocent of any crime and I want that recorded once and for all.'

Reflecting on the responsibility of the new tribunal, Linda's brother John Nash told press: 'In my opinion, the Widgery Tribunal was a complete and utter travesty. This was compounded by the abuse and harassment my family received from the security forces after Bloody Sunday for many years and forced me to move with my family to England for eight years. I expect this new tribunal to properly investigate my brother's death and my father's wounding.'

Just six days after the Bloody Sunday Inquiry opened, a historic break-through in Anglo-Irish relations took place with the signing of the Good Friday Agreement on 10 April 1998. Optimism was a rarity for Northern Ireland and, although the peace process was still in its infancy, the region was already beginning to transform and claw back its own identity.

[chapter eleven]

'Lie still – pretend you're dead'

The thought of reliving the long-suppressed horrors of Bloody Sunday proved difficult for many as the inquiry got underway. Joe Mahon had been among a group running from the chaos in the Bogside when the gunfire began. 'They just started firing at us – the only para I saw in action was holding the gun at his hip and just firing into the crowd.'

As Joe lay shot in Glenfada Park, he heard a voice just behind him. He later found out it was William McKinney. 'He just said to me "I'm hit, son, I'm hit!" I could see another pair of feet nearby too.' This was Jim Wray. 'Then I heard a woman's voice saying, "Lie still – pretend you're dead." That woman saved my life. Just as the paratrooper approached me – God rest Jim Wray – he moved and the paratrooper stopped, and fired twice more, right into his back. I saw his coat rising twice. Then he moved on.'

Had he not feigned death himself, Joe has no doubt the paratroopers would have finished him off too. Joe's internal organs were seriously damaged. In Altnagelvin hospital, the shock hit him badly. 'The bullet went through my hip, through the stomach and lodged in the other hipbone. In casualty, people say I never spoke or moved, but I can remember being half-aware of what was going on. Apparently, they thought I was dead until they found a pulse in my neck.'

Joe never spoke of his experiences, even to his own children, until the new inquiry began and their mother thought they ought to know.

Now in his fifties, Joe faced his demons when interviewed by Eversheds for the new inquiry. 'The experience of recounting it took me right back to the day and I broke down. It was the first time I had ever cried about it and that has been in the front of my mind since. I was seeing a psychologist after it, that's how bad it was. My whole personality changed, I became more withdrawn. I still find it difficult to speak out and to this day, I avoid confrontations. It all stems from Bloody Sunday.'

As the new inquiry became reality, campaign meetings saw a surge in numbers. Other relatives as well as disenchanted survivors like Joe Mahon began to trickle into meetings at the Ráth Mór centre. Solicitors Madden & Finucane were representing all of the victims at the time. Some relatives and wounded would eventually decide to seek their own legal representation.

The M&F legal team met regularly with their clients in a crowded room at the Ráth Mór centre. It soon became clear that the firm needed a full-time presence in Derry. They eventually opened an office in the new Bloody Sunday Centre in Shipquay Street.

Ciarán Shiels explains: 'The offices became a focal point for the families and the wounded. Over the years of the process, I became very good friends with all of them, in particular with Gerry Duddy, Bubbles Donaghy, Joe Friel, Mickey McKinney and others. We had many an afternoon going through material that had just come to hand or discussing issues which had just arisen. And occasionally we had a good night in a bar in Derry or later in London. At times it was exhausting. But it was all extremely rewarding. The families were never slow in giving their views, or telling us that we were missing something or that we could emphasise a point in another way.'

'Ciarán and Fearghál Shiels were great fellas,' Damian Donaghy says. 'They knew more about Bloody Sunday than all the other solicitors put together.' Similarly, Mickey McKinney acknowledges that despite an initial unease with solicitors and barristers, the families learned to relax in the company of the legal teams, 'I think there were friendships struck up. It just took time for them to realise we were no threat.'

Mary Doherty attended the inquiry as much as she could, despite fighting cancer. 'She was going through chemotherapy at the time,' her daughter Geraldine remembers. 'We would have gone for the first chemo appointment early on a Wednesday morning so we could make it back to the Guildhall for hearings. Even through all that, she wouldn't have missed the inquiry.'

'The campaign was always subject to people's jobs, babysitters and the amount of spare time people had to devote to it,' says Mickey McKinney. 'The inquiry itself was just the same.'

Leo Young was impressed by Lord Saville's tenacity and attention to detail. 'I had great faith in him once I saw him in action – he knew everything and missed nothing. I saw him on his own one morning in the Bogside walking around Glenfada Park – that's how thorough he was – exploring the Bog on his own.'

The inquiry courted controversy from the outset. Lord Saville had insisted that soldiers called to the inquiry should testify at the Guildhall. However, the soldiers appealed Saville's ruling. The issue would continue to divide opinions for years to come.

Having witnessed the bloodshed from her home in the Rossville Flats, Olive Gilmour was one of over five hundred eyewitnesses to testify in the Guildhall. She had already given evidence to the Widgery Tribunal. 'Before I gave evidence to Saville, they gave me the statement I did for Widgery, but I didn't even look at it. I just went in there and told the same story. I wasn't afraid of giving evidence, even though this was so much bigger than the Widgery Tribunal, and you knew the whole world was watching. Not one minute did I ever flinch. I saw how they were with some people, but I didn't let them worry me.'

Several survivors who had previously preferred to stay out of the spotlight also came forward to testify before the tribunal. Michael Quinn, now living in Dublin, was seventeen and still at school when shot on Bloody Sunday. He was fleeing Glenfada Park when gunned down. The bullet hit his shoulder and exited through his face.

Joseph Friel, twenty-six, was also running across Glenfada Park towards his home in the Rossville Flats when he was shot in the chest. Apprehended on the way to hospital, the army accused Joseph Friel of being a gunman.

Patsy McDaid, twenty-five, had just helped carry the injured Peggy Deery to safety when he was hit in the back as he sought refuge from the incoming fire. He was crouching down when the projectile cut across him, exposing the bone on his spine. 'Every time I pass the Bloody Sunday monument, I think to myself "your name could have been on there", because it so nearly was. It wasn't difficult to give evidence. I have nothing to hide, I could only tell the story of what happened to me'.

Madden & Finucane had worked with the majority of the families until this point, but now some families questioned the logistics of one firm representing twenty-eight families. Tony Doherty remembers: 'At the beginning, everyone was with Madden & Finucane but then some people wanted to do their own thing – and that was fine.'

The Wray family were the first to break away. 'Our family withdrew after a short period of time,' Liam says. 'We sent a letter to Saville on 15 September 1998 saying, "I, Liam Wray, on behalf of the Wray family, whose brother Jim was murdered by British paratroopers on Sunday 30 January 1972, since known as Bloody Sunday, and whose reputation was tarnished by Lord Widgery in 1972, would like to inform you that we have no confidence in the inquiry that you presently chair.'

The Wrays spent six months outside the tribunal. Then, Liam recalls, 'One of the solicitors at the inquiry started to discuss Jim's case. We got very annoyed at that, because we were not participating in the inquiry.' He took advice from another solicitor. 'We wanted to make it clear to Saville that we didn't want Jim mentioned again by anyone – they had no right to do so. The solicitor told us that we had no control over this. The inquiry was entitled to investigate the death of all involved, and that was the end of it.'

The solicitor, Greg McCartney, indicated that he would gladly represent the Wray family if they were allowed to return to the inquiry with separate representation.

For lawyers, the inquiry was the hottest ticket in town – 'the FA Cup Final for solicitors', as Liam put it.

After much negotiation, Lord Saville agreed and the Wray family returned to the inquiry with their new legal team. Liam is aware of the tension the dispute created at the time. 'Most of the families were nonplussed but I'm sure there were a few who thought: "Who do you think you are?" Then other families followed suit to find their own representation- the McGuigans, the Dohertys, the Nashs, Mickey Bridge and Mickey Bradley. I thought that was the healthiest thing in the world.'

Liam attended almost every day of the Saville Inquiry. 'I was working at the time and had to plan my work around the hearings. It was tiring at times and hard to concentrate and keep focus. Then other times it could be quite exciting and you'd think you were getting somewhere. Then of course, it could be quite painful. Someone would say something you thought you had dealt with decades ago, but it cut you deeply.'

As media interest grew, so did the need for a co-ordinated press operation. Eamonn McCann gladly took up the challenge and secured office space in Guildhall Street, mere feet from proceedings.

'Once the inquiry was up and running, it was necessary to have some system of getting news out and making sure the families point of view was heard,' he says. 'If the media centre hadn't been specifically organised, that wouldn't have happened. And it wasn't all that organised, as I recall! There was no designated boss. I advised people on what to do, and sometimes it worked and sometimes it didn't.

'One of the important jobs was trying to get other journalists interested – phoning them up, saying, "you really should look into this". We needed as much interest and coverage as we could muster and eventually a number of journalists, particularly British journalists, became very interested and very positive.

'It's interesting that, as in the case of the Guildford Four and the Birmingham Six, in the end it was British journalists, not Irish journalists, who kept at it. That says something. Until the subject became mainstream, I don't think there was a single programme devoted to Bloody Sunday made by an Irish television station.'

Things were changing for the campaigners. As the inquiry progressed and the press operation was formalised and developed, it also became apparent that the family group had become too large to be accommodated in West End Park. In late September 1998, they ended their tenure there.

The establishment of the new inquiry did not engender harmony among the families. In the months following Blair's announcement, meetings were often argumentative and tiring. Mickey McKinney, chair of the campaign during this period, recalls: 'There were personality differences, and things could get a bit heated at meetings. You have to remember we began all this essentially as strangers. We had a common goal, but we'd never been together in any organised way.'

'We didn't know where we stood now as a group.' recalls Tony Doherty. 'The campaign of old had actually outlived its usefulness. Some of the meetings after that were difficult, argumentative and rancorous at times. We decided after a particularly bad meeting in one of the city centre hotels that enough was enough, that we were advising that the campaign go into cold storage until after the inquiry, and that's effectively what happened.'

On 27 November 1998, the tribunal announced that the soldiers would be offered immunity if they testified – not a guarantee of no prosecutions but an assurance that nothing which they said in evidence would be used as a basis for prosecution. Meanwhile, debate rumbled on over anonymity for soldiers giving evidence. The tribunal asked the various legal teams to make submissions on the issue.

Before the tribunal had come to a decision on soldier anonymity, and five days before the anniversary of the day of the massacre, another of the Bloody Sunday parents passed. Alexander Nash died on 25 January 1999. He hadn't lived to hear his injuries explained or his son's name exonerated.

In his statement to the inquiry, dated 15 June 1999, John Nash recounted the events surrounding his father's wounding and his brother's murder. Their mother was in Altnagelvin hospital with a heart condition when it happened. John had got married just the day before. William had been his best man.

'I didn't see and I don't know of anything which would have justified Willie being shot at the barricade,' John said is his statement to Eversheds. He recalled his slain brother: 'Willie was only once in trouble with the police. He was politically naive and not interested in that sort of thing. He was hard working and always worked at least five days a week, usually six. He was into boxing and could have been a good boxer. It was just sport and work and Saturday, or Sunday night dancing. He went out that day dressed in his brown suit, which he had worn to the wedding. This was his Sunday best. He was carrying nothing with him but a can of Budweiser.'

On 5 May 1999, the tribunal rejected requests for automatic anonymity for all soldiers giving evidence, but confirmed that individual soldiers could apply for anonymity based on individual circumstances. Seventeen of the soldiers who had fired live rounds on Bloody Sunday immediately sought a judicial review of the ruling.

Two months later, the Court of Appeal reversed Saville's ruling and decided that military witnesses would be entitled to withhold their identities. Families in Derry were furious.

More tragedy befell the family of Gerard McKinney that summer. Gerard, a man with a passion for roller skating and football, had been thirty-five on Bloody Sunday. He died with his hands in the air as he moved to help the mortally wounded Gerald Donaghey, leaving his heavily pregnant wife Ita and seven young children behind. In August 1999, Gerard's youngest son Gerry, born just eight days after his murder, was killed in a car accident on the Glenshane Pass between Derry and Belfast. In an unsettling parallel, Gerry's wife was pregnant with their first child when he died.

Young Gerry never had the chance to meet his father, but he had become involved in the campaign and had followed the inquiry closely. After his death, older sister Regina McLaughlin cautiously stepped forward to represent the family.

'We were all kids when Daddy was killed,' Regina reflects. 'I suppose I only got involved after Gerry died. I stepped up because I had the most time of the family members to commit to it. We were always behind the campaign as a family and stood as one. But some people are better doing the legwork and talking to people, whereas our family were very reserved and shy so we stayed very much in the background. We didn't need anybody to tell us what happened, we already knew. The only thing we wanted was for our Daddy to be declared innocent before the world – and eventually we got that.'

Tragically, Regina would also become a widow at an early age while heavily pregnant. 'It's strange that there are three of us in one family, but again you learn from things. I've learned to appreciate life since I was a young child because you don't know what it'll throw at you. I understand how my mother felt to be suddenly widowed and pregnant. You cannot comprehend the grief that you feel, bearing a child with your husband not there to share it. I can see now how hard things were for my mammy. I can say it is heartbreaking.'

Regina McLaughlin forgives those responsible for the death of her father. 'I wouldn't wish what we went through on my worst enemy. We all forgive. It doesn't mean we like or accept what they did. You can forgive and still have justice.'

It was clear as the tribunal hearings approached that the families and wounded would need strong support around them. Core to this would be a city centre base. 'We negotiated with Garvan O'Doherty of [property company] the Garvan O'Doherty group, and asked him to help us find a building,' Conal McFeely, vice-chair of the Bloody Sunday Trust remembers. 'He gave us his 39 Shipquay Street – we paid a penny a year for the duration! That was his personal contribution and it was an enormous gesture.'

The building on Shipquay Street was a grand, if somewhat dilapidated Georgian structure in the heart of the city, just metres from the Guildhall. Colm Barton is certain that the city centre presence heightened the public's awareness of the campaign and increased local support for the inquiry. 'Its prominence in many ways reflected the increasing respectability of the Bloody Sunday issue. It was a great resource to have at the time. My brother Sean was a supervisor with Enterprise Ulster at the time and painted the building from top to bottom for us too.'

Mickey McKinney remains appreciative of scores of other local business people, too, for their generosity. 'We owe them a huge debt. Conal McFeely was brilliant at organising important things and he was a fantastic help to us over the years.'

Jean Hegarty shares Mickey's appreciation for McFeely. 'Some people were central to the campaign and Conal McFeely is one of those core people who kept everything going, alongside Kay, John, Tony and the others. If these people hadn't done their bit, where would we be?

'There are tonnes of individuals who lent support over the years, too, and deserve much credit – people like Pat Friel, who volunteered for years in the Shipquay Street centre and then in temporary premises in Foyle Street. Pat was always dependable, never let us down. It was a great help to have someone like that.'

In February 2000, shortly before oral hearings began, an admission came from the British Ministry of Defence (MoD) that of the twenty-nine rifles fired on Bloody Sunday, ten had been sold and a further fourteen destroyed. Now the MoD admitted that somehow they had destroyed two of the five remaining rifles kept at an army storage facility.

The loss of these items sparked severe criticism on all sides. Saville had given explicit instructions that the rifles were to be preserved as evidence. John Kelly claimed the destruction of the rifles was part of a MoD conspiracy to cover up evidence. 'They were told to do a job — to hide or destroy the evidence — and they did it.'

The inquiry began its public hearings on 27 March 2000 in the Guildhall. The opening speech by Inquiry Counsel Christopher Clarke QC lasted forty-two days and remains the longest in British legal history.

The night before the public hearings began, thousands gathered for a candle-lit vigil in the Bogside and then walked to the Guildhall. They held a short rally in the square, speakers making final pleas for truth and transparency. Conor Duddy, nephew of Jackie Duddy, asked the people 'who have stood by the Bloody Sunday families and sustained the struggle for the truth for twenty-eight years' to attend the tribunal whenever possible. 'We have come this far. We have some distance still to go. The Bloody Sunday families ask you to maintain the pressure. Be vigilant. Demand the truth. Justice demands it.'

In August 2000, one of the three judges, Sir Edward Somers, stepped down and was replaced by Honourable John L. Toohey, former Justice of the High

Court of Australia. In the same month, the inquiry ordered that paratroopers who had opened fire must return to Derry to testify. The soldiers swiftly appealed the ruling, citing fears of reprisals from dissident republicans – an appeal they later won.

The first civilian witness was heard on 28 November 2000. In total, the inquiry interviewed and received statements from around 2,500 people, 922 of whom were called to the witness stand.

The tribunal would hear from 505 civilian witnesses; 9 experts and forensic scientists; 35 IRA activists or former IRA activists; 49 reporters and photographers; 245 military witnesses; 33 members of the Royal Ulster Constabulary (RUC); 39 politicians, civil servants and intelligence officers and 7 priests.

Liam Wray remains critical of the way civilian witnesses were treated when testifying: 'All the other parties had legal representation, but civilian witnesses had nobody backing them up. Anthony Gifford was the only QC who stood up for them. Saville, of course, went through him like a ton of bricks and he sat down a bit flustered. I walked down from the family area, through the double doors and onto the floor of the inquiry where I walked right up to him in front of everyone and shook his hand.'

Few appreciated the personal trauma experienced by eyewitnesses, who were often berated and ridiculed by lawyers trying to undermine their accounts. At times, Derry's collective wounds felt as raw as ever.

Other interesting issues emerged during the first years of the inquiry. The tribunal was shown two minutes of black and white aerial footage shot by the army of the advance into the Bogside. It ended somewhat conveniently as shooting began and the crowd scattered.

Mickey Bridge is still angry at the 'blatant deceit' of the helicopter film footage. 'That army camera goes continuously when they're monitoring a march. Yet at the tribunal, they only produced a couple of minutes and that was the end of it. I still find it unbelievable that Saville accepted that. The deceit was blatant.'

Photographs would prove elusive too. Despite ten army photographers and a camera crew deployed in the Bogside, the Ministry of Defence claimed none of the photos survived. Only forty-eight arrest photos of soldiers with their detainees and ten low-quality photocopies were produced to the tribunal.

Mickey McKinney lived and breathed the tribunal. Every day for five years, he got up, dressed, ate breakfast and headed for the hearings. If not in the Guildhall itself, Mickey followed proceedings on a special screen in the family room of the Bloody Sunday centre across the square. The centre hosted a permanent exhibition about Bloody Sunday and a thick, heavy curtain cut the room in half, concealing the families' screening area from public view.

Most evenings, mentally fatigued by the day's evidence, Mickey would go out to work, driving his taxi. Driving allowed him to mull over the day's events and the progress or problems within the case. 'The inquiry definitely took over my life,' he remembers. 'It was pretty lonely at times but I had made my choice and committed myself to it. I didn't realise it at the time, but for five years there was no getting away from it. I wasn't consciously thinking about it, but it was there all day every day.'

The lives of many family members fell into the same pattern.

Damian 'Bubbles' Donaghy was the first of the wounded to give evidence. He was just fifteen when, reaching to retrieve a discarded rubber bullet as a souvenir, he was shot in the leg. The first casualty of Bloody Sunday, Damian is still in pain today. 'I don't think my evidence lasted longer than half an hour. Right at the start of the hearing, the lawyers for the soldiers said they knew I hadn't done anything wrong on Bloody Sunday, so that might be why my testimony was so short.'

After his evidence and unexpected exoneration, Damian left the Guildhall on a high and told reporters: 'After twenty-nine years this burden has been lifted from me. I'm on top of the world.'

On 6 February, retired Bishop Edward Daly took the stand. He told the tribunal how he had helped carry the dying Jackie Duddy through the streets to escape the gunfire. He said he was 'absolutely certain' that the boy had nothing in his hands. He also spoke of the shooting of Mickey Bridge, of crowds fleeing the scene and of no-one posing any threat to soldiers.

At the time of Bloody Sunday, Dr. Daly was a curate in his late thirties at St Eugene's Cathedral in the Bogside. By chance, he was caught up in the commotion as marchers fled the troops. He administered last rites to many of the dying. Speaking of Jackie Duddy – he still has a framed photograph of the boy in his study – Bishop Daly told the *Catholic Herald* in summer of 2010: 'I didn't know him at the time, but I spent the last three minutes of his life with him. I feel I've come to know him very closely over the last forty years.'

Alana Burke also gave evidence, but it wasn't the catharsis she had hoped for. 'I never got the feeling of relief that I had always expected. When they got up to cross-examine me, I almost felt like saying, "how dare you question me? If you knew the half of what we saw that day!" I was so angry. But they kept pressing me and pressing me under cross-examination and, eventually, I just fell apart. They just didn't get it.'

Mickey Bridge testified in March 2001. 'I was disappointed in myself after giving evidence as there was much more I wanted to say. But it's difficult. They were very clever people and they sidetracked witnesses.' Mickey missed very few sessions at the Guildhall. 'We often sat downstairs in the family room. We needed to be there – there were things that they got wrong, including basic inaccuracies like the exact location of old buildings. I remember Joe Friel corrected them when they showed a photograph of a fella with a gun in the high flats – Joe could tell straight off that this photo wasn't even Derry – it was of the Divis high flats in Belfast. We let the lawyer know and they corrected it. That's an example of why it was important that we were there.'

Another survivor, Daniel Gillespie, never attended the inquiry and dreaded testifying. The horrors of Bloody Sunday were not a memory he wanted to revisit. 'Danny had to re-live it all,' his widow, Frances, recalls. She told him just to tell the truth, that he saw no weapons, nor nail-bombs, but did see the lifeless body of Michael Kelly being carried out on the street.

While much gut-wrenching eyewitness testimony was widely ignored by the press, Martin McGuinness's first appearance in November 2003 caused a media storm. At the time, McGuinness was both Sinn Féin deputy leader and NI education minister. Testifying had risky implications for both his party and the peace process.

Ahead of his appearance, McGuinness admitted at a press conference that he had been the second-in-command of the IRA's Derry unit at the time of Bloody Sunday. The revelation caused a furore. However, he reiterated that the IRA had obeyed orders to stay away from the march.

Having won a ruling to remain anonymous, in summer 2001 soldiers challenged the inquiry's decision that they should testify in Derry. By Christmas that year, the Court of Appeal had overruled Saville: the soldiers were to be allowed to give their evidence in London

Two films were made about Bloody Sunday in the period between 2000 and 2002. Both were screened in Derry before being shown on television in January 2002.

Sunday was from the team behind *Hillsborough*, writer Jimmy McGovern and director Charles McDougall. They spent three years researching and interviewing relatives, survivors, priests, politicians, paramedics, journalists, eyewitnesses and British soldiers. The film was shot in Derry. Poignantly, many relatives had prominent roles. Paul Campbell played his uncle Jackie Duddy, Niall Kelly played his uncle Michael and James Wray played his uncle Jim Wray.

Bloody Sunday, written and directed by Paul Greengrass, featured Northern Irish actor James Nesbitt as well as Bloody Sunday relatives, including Declan Duddy in the role of Gerald Donaghey. The film was inspired by *Eyewitness Bloody Sunday*. Don Mullan himself co-produced the film.

Throughout February 2002, a photographic exhibition, 'Hidden Truths', in which Bloody Sunday featured prominently, ran at the International Centre of Photography in New York, curated by Tricia Ziff. The exhibition was praised by critics for its artistic achievement but for the families, the main point was to keep the message out there

Meanwhile in Derry, the inquiry was delving into the case of Gerald

Donaghey. Widgery's report had labelled Gerald a nail-bomber, the official record insisting that he had had nail-bombs in the pockets of his tight denim jeans. The tribunal explored the case in detail, revealing significant evidence that the bombs had been planted. Leo Young, who had run to young Donaghey's aid, insisted: 'He had nothing in his pockets. I know because I searched his pockets looking for ID when we brought him into a house.'

One of those who attended the hearings daily at great personal cost was Mickey Bradley. Mickey had been one of the survivors, but the trauma and injustice was to preoccupy him for decades to come. All those years, his family life suffered and determined to see the inquiry through, Mickey immersed himself in the minute detail. Unable to work because of his injury, he was often found deep in papers and research, analysing the evidence word by word. 'Mickey lived through every single day of the inquiry. He held on to that lifeline believing that maybe, just maybe, this time they would be proven innocent,' his step-daughter Jackie Bradley says.

'Sometimes I wished Bloody Sunday would just go away. It caused a lot of arguments. Our house was a nightmare. We had doctors here at times because Mickey really relived every minute of it. He had anxiety attacks and would wake up in the night screaming. As the tribunal went on, his depression and mood swings got worse instead of better. It was terrible.'

Another of the wounded, Daniel McGowan, was too apprehensive to go to the inquiry. 'Danny would ask about it when I got home, wondering what happened that day,' his widow Teresa remembers. 'He was interested but just too fearful to go himself. It's a pity that most of the wounded have died before they ever heard the truth. You never imagined that the inquiry would go on so long.'

Teresa pays credit to the families whose voices were often the loudest. 'I don't think we would have got anywhere without them. I was so proud of the way that John [Kelly] and Kay [Duddy] and the others could speak, I always wondered if they had elocution lessons! I always felt better being at the Guildhall with them.'

By March 2002, Lord Saville, after tense negotiations with legal teams, the Ministry of Defence and the British government, announced that the inquiry would transfer to London to hear evidence from soldiers and senior British officials. No paratrooper would ever set foot in Derry to give evidence of why he'd gunned down Derry people in 1972. Relatives felt crushed by the news. Some refused to attend London hearings. Others planned reluctantly for a weekly commute to Methodist Central Hall in Westminster.

The Derry families were about to walk in some notable footsteps. Central Hall was the venue where the Suffragettes had congregated, Mahatma Gandhi gave his first speech in England and the newly formed United Nations held its first General Assembly in 1946.

[chapter twelve]

'The black, black days'

After two years of mostly civilian evidence heard in Derry, the Inquiry relocated to London at the end of 2002 to hear from around three hundred military witnesses.

'It was hard enough hearing all the evidence in your own town, but in London we felt like strangers, isolated and out in the cold,' Geraldine Doherty remembers. For thirteen months, normal family life would cease for many as daily routines were shattered. Geraldine and her mother Mary were just two of those who would commute to England every week. The disruption would be unprecedented, but necessary. Mary's brother Gerald had been one of seven teenagers murdered on the day.

The great majority of the soldiers who gave evidence were known only by cipher. 'We really thought we would get a chance to look them in the eye,' Kay Duddy says. 'But most felt the need both to hide their identity behind numbers and talk behind screens. Bloody Sunday happened in Derry and the soldiers should have been brought back to testify. We tried everything to make that happen, but it just didn't work. Instead, we went to London for over a year.

'I never envisaged living in a hotel for the best part of a week, unless I was on holidays. But for all that time we had to commute there and back every week. London took its toll on everybody.'

Despite misgivings, the relatives' fears of hostility in England were to prove, for the most part, unfounded. Kay recalls just one negative encounter during their time in the British capital, on the first day of the hearings. 'A big lorry drove past and circled twice, and the driver shouted out "up the paras" while we were laying a wreath at Westminster Abbey for all the victims of the Troubles. But incidents like that were few and far between. We tried not to let them bother us.'

The inquiry facilitated the presence of two relatives per family at all times, paying travel costs and accommodation. The proceedings were also relayed back to the Guildhall in Derry, and to the family room in the Bloody Sunday Centre, where many relatives also watched.

The London hearings opened on 24 September 2002. Retired General Sir Frank Kitson was the first military witness. Later that month, Brigadier Maurice Tugwell apologised for telling the BBC on the evening of Bloody Sunday that four of the men shot dead were on a wanted list. He told the tribunal it had been a 'mistake'.

Mickey McKinney was one of those who became a long distance commuter. He rarely missed a hearing. 'It could be a very isolating experience. Some people went to dinner and had a drink after hearings, but others, myself included, preferred to stay in most of the time digesting the day's events.'

Mickey says that Cúnamh, a Derry-based group which counselled and supported families throughout the inquiry, were of great help. 'Cúnamh were a listening ear for anybody there who needed someone to talk to. They had at least a couple of counsellors in the Guildhall with us every day, and they travelled to London with us too. Of course, there were times you did get emotional, but I didn't let the hearings get me down completely. The worst had already happened in 1972, so it couldn't get any worse.'

London could be an unforgiving city. Often the reluctant commuters would rotate the weekly visits, sharing the burden out among as wide a group as possible. Some attended every week, while others saved up their annual leave to attend hearings when they could. 'I was in London as often as possible,' Kay Duddy says. 'It was important we had a presence at all times.'

Jackie Bradley travelled to London as often as she could alongside her stepfather Mickey Bradley, but she thought the move unfair. 'I thought it was scandalous that they took the inquiry to England. My mother went a few times but it was too hard on her. She had lived through the effects of Bloody Sunday with Mickey and saw everything that he suffered, but then when she was really needed beside him she couldn't be there.'

Joe Mahon was also angry about the inquiry's relocation and refused to take part. 'I didn't agree with the changes that were happening,' he says. 'I never went to England once. It happened here and they should have investigated it here.'

In October 2002, 'Soldier 027' testified. He was the soldier whose interviews with Tom McGurk and Channel 4 News had proven significant. He told the inquiry that some of his colleagues had opened fire on civilians 'without justification', that at no time had he seen any gunmen or bombers. 'I looked through my sights, scanning across the crowd. I was as keen to find a target as anyone, but I just could not identify a target that appeared to justify engaging. I did not see anyone with a weapon or see or hear an explosive device.'

Soldier 027 also described the shooting in Glenfada Park, where four people were killed, and revealed details of a briefing the night before, where colleagues remarked on how they could be 'getting kills' in the Bogside.

'Unspeakable acts took place on Bloody Sunday. There was no justification for a single shot I saw fired.' He said he had been living under a witness protection scheme for two years because he was worried about possible reprisals from former colleagues.

Jane Winter confirms that Soldier 027 was 'traumatised' by the time he came to give evidence, having lived under constant threat. 'He had to keep moving every time they found his address and once his landlord was beaten up and hospitalised in mistake for him. A few other paras were truthful in the end, but he was the first soldier who really told it as it was. It was very brave of him and it ruined his life.'

Olive Bonner never missed hearings at the Guildhall and often commuted to London with her brother Bernard and sister-in-law Kathleen. 'My wains are grown up, and I was retired, and so my children and husband were quite happy for me going to London from Monday to Thursday every week,' says Olive.

'It wasn't all doom and gloom, you know. We did have laughs. As for a tour guide, you couldn't ask for anybody better than Gerry Duddy. He knew every street in London and insisted on showing everybody the sights. He waited for me every morning too, calling "c'mon, ma!" and we walked to the tribunal together and walked back again. We made the best of it.'

Olive particularly missed her brother Floyd, who had campaigned tirelessly but died before the inquiry could conclude. 'I was doing it as much for Floyd as for anybody. He started it and I wanted to make sure somebody kept it going. My brother Bernard and his wife Kathleen did a brave lot too. Poor Kathleen, she didn't see the end of it either.'

Caroline O'Donnell, daughter of Patsy O'Donnell, one of the wounded, attended the London hearings when she could, pooling her annual leave at work to be in London for any evidence relating to Glenfada Park, where her father was shot.

The families made many friends in England. John Kelly remembers: 'We were very well looked after in London. Jim Redmond of the Connolly Association, Charlie Cunningham of the Wolfe Tone Society, and others like Danny Burke made our time there much easier. Sometimes they held events to make life in London more bearable.'

The families also came up with novel ideas when attempting to organise everyone. 'London is a big place, and although Gerry was the real tour guide, I remember he gave Mickey and me two table tennis bats to wave and help keep everyone together – one of them said Dumb and the other, Dumber! We still have them to this day,' laughs John.

When a date was set for the evidence of General Robert Ford, relatives flocked en mass to be there. Ford had written a memo shortly before Bloody Sunday saying that some Derry rioters might have to be shot to restore law and order.

However, he told the inquiry that this was just an initial idea and one that would have needed government clearance to be carried out. As Commander of Land Forces, General Ford was responsible for the day-to-day conduct of army operations throughout Northern Ireland.

He told the inquiry that he had been in Derry on Bloody Sunday merely as an observer, and insisted that he did not put pressure on the local brigadier to send the paras into the Bogside. He said that he had been mistaken when he told a journalist in 1984 that he'd sent a message to Brigadier Pat McLellan suggesting he 'get a move on' and use the paratroops that he, Ford, had deployed to the city.

In evidence in November, Brigadier MacLellan said while he gave the order for the Parachute Regiment to move into the Bogside, the tactics on the day were left to their commander, Colonel Derek Wilford. He added that it appeared the Parachute Regiment disobeyed his orders, and agreed with Saville that it appeared that the paratroops had gone deeper into the Bogside than he had ordered.

Former prime minister Sir Edward Heath gave evidence in January 2003. He denied pressuring Lord Widgery into exonerating the soldiers who fired the fatal shots. He rejected a suggestion that the conversation documented in the memo unearthed by Jane Winter – urging Widgery to remember that there was a propaganda war as well as a military war to be fought in Northern Ireland – was a signal that 'England expects every man to do his duty'.

'The people who were involved in the appointment wanted it to be absolutely plain that there was no pressure on whoever did it to reach a particular conclusion. They all knew that was the last thing that I would tolerate . . . To suggest that Lord Widgery, of all men, would be browbeaten into finding conclusions which he did not think were genuine is malicious and it is completely unjustified.'

Asked by a barrister whether innocent people were murdered on Bloody Sunday, he said that he had not made a statement at the time and would not do so now. He went on to refuse to apologise to the families of those killed on the grounds that he had already expressed regret at the time.

Kay Duddy recalls her frustration: 'Ted Heath's disdain when giving evidence was infuriating. This arrogant "how dare you speak to me like this" attitude he had the whole time – he just didn't want to be there. His reactions could be hard to take.'

Families were continually frustrated by the lack of media interest in the inquiry. 'I would have thought that press would have been swarming around Westminster when the soldiers were giving their evidence, but it got very little coverage,' Mickey McKinney recalls. 'The English press didn't want to know,' Kay Duddy adds. 'It was always the same.'

In March of that year the soldier in charge of the Parachute Regiment on Bloody Sunday gave evidence. Colonel Derek Wilford insisted that his men had acted in a professional manner; his troops had been shot at and had returned fire within the rules of engagement. Wilford said he saw or heard nothing which led him to believe that paratroopers were out of control at any stage. 'Nor did I see any shameful and disgraceful acts.'

Lord Gifford put it to Colonel Wilford that the paratroops had fired first, aggressively and at anybody who moved. Wilford responded that this was entirely untrue. He rejected another suggestion that the paratroops had been sent into the Bogside to kill people.

In April 2003, Britain's top soldier, General Sir Mike Jackson, chief of the general staff, told the inquiry that there had been no plan to tempt the IRA into a gun battle on Bloody Sunday. General Jackson had taken time off from supervising the war in Iraq to give evidence. He had been a captain and second in command of the First Battalion of the Parachute Regiment in January 1972, prior to his ascent to the pinnacle of the military hierarchy.

Kevin McDaid had attended the inquiry every week when it was in the Guildhall, but refused to travel to London. 'None of my family went to England – we didn't think it was right. London cost them big time, even though it was the cost that they cried about for years, money this and money that. I could see no justice in moving it there for any reason.'

John Campbell, son of Bloody Sunday survivor Patrick Campbell, also refused to attend hearings in London. 'They were big enough to murder people, they should be big enough to come back here and answer for it, not hide behind screens and claim amnesia. It's like Michael Mansfield said – how come the people of Derry can't forget and the paras can't remember?'

Mickey Bridge recalls seeing Soldier N and others give evidence in April. 'The whole stance was that they didn't remember much. Instead of saying they shot a person, they shot a target – a nail-bomber or a gunman. Even at the hearings in Westminster, Lieutenant N refused to acknowledge that I was the person he shot. I was the only person there – he shot me – that is a fact.'

Lance Corporal V claimed during evidence in May that he shot a petrol-bomber near the Rossville Flats and then saw a group of people, including a priest, going to the body. The boy was Jackie Duddy. Believing Jackie's killer to be one of two soldiers, Soldier V or Private R, most of the Duddy family travelled to London to attend the hearings of both. 'It felt like we were getting somewhere when we actually got to see them,' Gerry Duddy recalls. 'You always have this impression that the paras are going to be huge, broad-shouldered men, but on the stand they're just wee skinny men. Their gun made them ten feet tall.'

Gerry admits it was difficult to contain emotions at times. 'Naturally, there was anger. We'd have loved to have shouted at them at times. But if we had let our anger get the better of us we would have ruined it for the rest of the families. They would have put us all out of the hall and that would have defeated the whole purpose of being there,' he adds.

In June, a former Parachute Regiment commander rejected suggestions that he had not been in control of his men on Bloody Sunday. Major Ted Loden was in charge of the company which fired more than one hundred shots on the day. He also refused to apologise to the family of one of the men killed by the shots.

Michael Mansfield QC told Loden that Barney McGuigan had been shot dead at the Rossville Flats as he waved a white handkerchief, and asked if he would like to apologise to the family of the forty-one-year-old father-of-six. Loden said he'd prefer to 'await the outcome of the inquiry'. He rejected a suggestion that the plan on Bloody Sunday had been to teach a lesson to nationalist residents of the Bogside area.

In July, Soldier P, suspected of having killed one or all of John Young, William Nash and Michael McDaid, told the inquiry that he did not remember firing his rifle on Bloody Sunday. He said that he had to rely on evidence he gave to the Widgery Tribunal in 1972 for confirmation that he had shot a nail-bomber and a gunman on Rossville Street before firing a number of shots over the heads of a crowd of rioters. He also said that Bloody Sunday was the only occasion in his army career in which he fired live rounds. 'Are you really saying that, despite this, you remember practically nothing of the day?' Christopher Clarke QC, counsel to the inquiry asked him. Soldier P replied: 'That is correct, yes.'

Lord Saville would later conclude that Soldier P 'shot at least one of these casualties and may have been responsible for all three.'

'I saw Soldier P in the stand with his para tie and badge on him,' Leo Young remembers. 'He looked like an old man, but that's irrelevant, because if you commit a crime then you should be brought to book for it no matter what age you are. They are still chasing people for war crimes fifty or sixty years ago. If he was a soldier who was doing his job in a war situation, it might have been acceptable, but this was no war. To shoot someone who poses no threat is murder, pure and simple. These people were sent here to protect us and they killed our own people.'

Regina McLaughlin was frequently in London and forewarned her family back when the evidence concerning the death of her father, Gerard McKinney, began. Most of the family flew to London to hear the evidence and, although Private G was dead by then, the experience proved harrowing. Regina remembers: 'It was quite hard, especially watching mammy – that was awful. She was just heartbroken all over again.'

Despite being robbed of a father at such an early age, Regina feels no anger. When speaking of the man who killed her father, compassion shines through. 'To forgive him doesn't mean it's right, but it means I'm not going to hate him the rest of my life either, because in a way they've won if they have ruined my life. The soldier that killed daddy is dead and already before God and there's no higher justice than God. But it was heartbreaking to sit and watch the other families. Having soldiers come in and be disrespectful, insulting, or with selective hearing, it was hard to take, the way they looked at you – like you were scum. This was their opportunity to put it right. But to hide it a second time publicly, to me that's a greater sin and a greater insult than the first time.'

For forty years, Bridie McGuigan never spoke publicly about her husband Barney's death. After publication of the report in summer 2010, she finally broke her silence in an interview for the *Derry Journal*. Her words dominated the front page. She remembered how Barney had 'a smile that could light up a room . . . My heart broke that day and it has never healed. We were madly in love. We got married in 1953. He was such a handsome man, a great dancer and he was everyone's friend.'

On Bloody Sunday, Barney McGuigan had been among a group of marchers huddled around a telephone box behind the high flats, sheltering from the gunfire. The body of teenager Hugh Gilmour was lying nearby. The group watched in terror as several men in the distance crawled to safety, almost flat on their stomachs, Paddy Doherty among them. He was shot in the buttock, the bullet travelling up through his body and exiting his chest. He was bleeding to death. Barney could hear Paddy calling out repeatedly, 'somebody help me, please – I don't want to die on my own.'

Barney could take no more. He reassured those holding him back that he would be safe to venture into open ground. He would wave a white hankie. The army would know he was going to help someone. With the hankie held high, Barney took a few steps forward. He was shot in the head. He died instantly, blood seeping over the pavement in a crimson halo where his head lay. All around, people screamed.

After Barney's death, Mrs McGuigan relied on family and friends to see her through what she called 'the black, black days.' 'I insisted on telling my children myself. We had three boys and three girls – the oldest was sixteen and the youngest was just six. I brought them into a room and told them their father was dead.'

In October, the man responsible for Barney's death and many others testified in London. He was told he faced allegations of murdering four people on Bloody Sunday, and possibly more. Soldier F agreed that he killed four people, but insisted he did not murder them – he fired only at two nail-bombers and a man carrying a pistol. He admitted killing Michael Kelly, Barney McGuigan and Paddy Doherty and an unidentified man in Glenfada Park. It was suggested to him that the unidentified man may have been William McKinney.

Earlier that day, he had agreed – under a barrage of questioning from Michael Mansfield QC – that he killed Barney McGuigan at the Rossville Flats. The inquiry stopped for a few moments as Bridie McGuigan was taken from the chamber in tears.

Speaking outside, Barney's son, Charlie, said: 'We have been fighting this case for almost thirty-two years, which is a lifetime for some people. I feel happy that we've got to this stage, and I'll feel happier when we see the final report, where we may have the justice that we require.'

Bridie McGuigan reflected on her emotions at that time in her later newspaper interview. 'I just wanted to be there when this man was giving evidence. But sitting there listening to him speaking with no remorse was just awful. I was thinking to myself: that man put a bullet through Barney's head – and it was just too much.

'I don't want prosecutions. What is the point in prosecutions? What would be the point in him going to jail? Would it take away my pain? No, it wouldn't. We, as a family, do not want Soldier F's family to go through what we went through.'

John Kelly recalls the day Soldier F first took to the witness stand. 'I think there were as many as 130 family members in London to hear Soldier F testify. The family seating area was packed and so I ended up in the public gallery with a few others.' Just as John settled into his seat, he was summoned outside to assist with a security problem. As family liaison, it was his job to help.

'I had waited for thirty years to see Soldier F and then, just at the last minute, I had to leave. I couldn't believe it. I remember Gerry Duddy coming out to me telling me to get back into the hall – he would take over. "This is your day," he said, which I always remembered. It just shows the level of support that we gave each other. He wouldn't hear of me missing Soldier F taking to the stand, for any reason.'

Gleann Doherty was in London to face his father's killer – also Soldier F. He was just an infant when Paddy was killed as he crawled away from the gunfire. A series of telling photographs show the father of six crawling along the ground to safety just before being shot.

'When Soldier F as much as admitted to killing my da and I was sitting there with the McGuigan family, everything hit me like a ton of bricks,' Gleann remembers. 'I was happy, if you can say that word, that he admitted to shooting people, but I just sat there stunned. Even afterwards in the hotel when everyone seemed pleased with a good day at the inquiry, I wasn't pleased. It wasn't great, someone telling you that your father was dead.'

Mickey McKinney and his family had always believed Soldier F was the man responsible for Willie's murder, and was glad to finally see him take the stand. 'I went to every day of the inquiry and I saw them all. For Soldier F's testimony, I sat in the public gallery because there was no room in the family area. He was very broad, stout with a broad back, but when he opened his mouth to speak, I remember he had a high, feminine voice. It wasn't what I was expecting. He was solid throughout. They all were – none of them flinched or showed an ounce of emotion. That was so frustrating – the fact that they didn't show a flicker of regret or remorse.'

Reflecting on his personal London experiences in a 2010 piece in the *Guardian*, Paddy Nash said: 'In London for the soldiers, you didn't know where to put your rage. You would go home or back to the hotel and you wouldn't feel too well. You felt you had no redress. Maybe as young men they didn't think, but at middle age you imagine they're going to feel some sorrow. But we saw what I would call genuine sorrow, maybe once or twice.

'I don't think the inquiry was for us at all. It wasn't for Derry people, it wasn't for Ireland. I think it was done for Britain's world standing. It's a whole lot of people playing little games in offices and getting paid for it.'

Tony Deery was six when his mother Peggy was maimed for life on Bloody Sunday. He never missed a day of the Saville Inquiry. Peggy Deery was the only woman shot on the day. She died in 1988 having never known of an inquiry. 'She always talked about the boy who shot her. She always said she knew his face and that he had reddish hair. The soldier I saw testify in the stand had sandy reddish hair too, so she was probably right all along.'

On October 9, the inquiry heard from a former soldier who had driven the body of Gerald Donaghey to an army post at Craigavon Bridge. Soldier 150 from the Royal Anglicans told the tribunal that he didn't see any nail-bombs on the dead boy's person and that if he had seen nail-bombs he wouldn't have driven the car.

As hearings in London wound down, plans to create a central archive in Derry continued. Adrian Kerr began work as researcher for the Bloody Sunday Trust in September 2003. He was eventually to become manager of the Museum of Free Derry.

On 15 October 2003, Lord Saville recalled General Sir Michael Jackson, Britain's most senior soldier, to the tribunal. The Chief of General Staff was summoned a second time after revelations that he was in fact the author of several key documents drafted by the army in the hours after Bloody Sunday. The most notable document in his handwriting was a 'shot list', purporting to specify where each shooter had been standing when he fired and the location of his target. Each target was identified as either a gun-man or a bomber. Every detail on the list had been shown in the interim to be wrong.

Jackson insisted that he had simply noted down what his senior soldiers had told him and explained the inaccuracies by reference to the fact that the document had been written in the early hours when he had been rather tired.

The hearings concluded in London on 21 October 2003, beginning again in Derry on 29 October to hear the remaining oral evidence. For the families, it signalled the end of a long year. They had put lives on hold, cancelled family events and missed family birthdays to follow the case. Now, finally, they could bid farewell to London.

[chapter thirteen]

'Lord Saville – set the truth free!'

The inquiry returned to Derry's Guildhall from 29 October 2003 for the final phase of evidence.

Much of the remaining testimony concerned the role of the IRA on Bloody Sunday. In November 2003, Martin McGuinness told the tribunal that within two weeks of the massacre, he was leading the IRA in Derry. Speaking of the Bloody Sunday victims, he said: 'These people were heroes because they were prepared to march on the streets to defend the rights of their fellow citizens. For that they were murdered and massacred.'

As the New Year began, two Channel 4 News journalists feared prosecution after refusing to hand over the names of confidential sources to the inquiry. Lena Ferguson and Alex Thompson insisted that they would rather go to prison than break the journalistic code of ethics and name sources. Lord Saville later announced there would be no prosecution.

Campaigners remain appreciative of all those who gave statements or braved the witness box. 'The people of Derry were absolutely brilliant coming forward to give evidence,' says Geraldine Doherty. 'They put themselves through so much for us. The legal teams tried to confuse people and sometimes made them out to be liars – you got the feeling that some eyewitnesses left the Guildhall feeling as though they had let us down. Of course, they hadn't – it was a big enough step for people to go in there and withstand all the harsh questions. They wanted the truth as much as we did.'

Alana Burke is equally appreciative: 'Bloody Sunday is something that has affected the whole city. Everyone had such traumatic stories to tell at the inquiry. I'm so proud of Derry people coming to help us in any way they could by giving evidence in the Guildhall.'

On 13 February 2004, the tribunal heard its final witnesses. There was then a lull of several months before the inquiry resumed in November for closing speeches. On 22 November, five years after Lord Saville had opened proceedings, counsel to the inquiry concluded the hearings with a two-day summation. Then began the wait for answers. It was to prove long and torturous.

Liam Wray found adjusting difficult. 'When it all stopped in 2004, your life in a sense became very empty. All of a sudden, all that energy, work, investigation and communication was gone and I didn't expect that. It had become nearly addictive, then just ended. I'd say for about three or four months after the inquiry ended I was totally agitated. I didn't realise what it was at first, but suddenly my whole routine had changed and I had to adjust to that.'

Liam reflects: 'It was a long six years, full of frustration. You wouldn't believe the amount of hours, from 1998 right up to 2004, that my wife Doreen and I spent researching and sifting through documents every week, every night, hours and hours at a time. God bless her, what a stalwart!

'Sometimes we came in from work and spent eight hours sifting, particularly in the early stages, looking through documents we had never seen before. My wife was fantastic. We examined all the old videos and paused them painstakingly. It was Doreen who found the footage that shows Alex Nash waving his hand from behind the barricade before he was shot. We had watched that video about thirty times before and then she suddenly picked it out in the corner of Glenfada Park. No-one had noticed it before, and it was later used as evidence in the inquiry.'

By now a reluctant expert on the subject of Bloody Sunday, Liam never truly believed the tribunal would deliver on the families' expectations. 'All the way through the inquiry, I made it quite clear that I did not trust Saville. I wanted to see if he had the ability as a British judge to be fair and impartial and to come to the right decision, which I think he failed on, to be quite honest.'

Elsewhere in Derry, work continued on the Bloody Sunday Trust's museum. The Trust had its sights set on a disused housing block in Glenfada Park, over-looking the spot where Soldier F had fired repeatedly on an unarmed crowd

Adrian Kerr explains how the Trust came to buy the property: 'The Glenfada building was totally derelict and was being used as a drinking den – it was a real pit of a building. We approached the Housing Executive, whose only intention was to demolish it, and bought it off them at a much-subsidised rate because of what we were going to use it for. The surrounding area had undergone a radical transformation since 1972. The only reason the building had survived was that Saville had placed a preservation order on it – not for any historical value but to preserve the physical geography of the area for the inquiry.'

With initial funding from Derry City Council and the Department of Foreign Affairs, the Trust began a process, which hopefully would culminate in a £1.5 million museum.

'I suggested that we should develop the project in stages and do what we could immediately', says Adrian. 'The Trust agreed straight away and we started planning. We costed the building, and how much money would be left over. Then we sat down with an architect, and worked out a design based on what we could achieve now with the money we had. It made sense, instead of hanging around for years, waiting for money that may never come.'

The building was gutted and its internal walls removed to leave a basic shell. The Bloody Sunday Trust opened it with a temporary exhibition in January 2006. 'It still had bare walls, no paint and concrete floors but it was something to work with, and it showed other people that we were capable and serious about doing this,' Adrian says.

Funders and authorities were impressed and additional funding soon be-came available, with the Northern Ireland Tourist Board and the Department of Social Development contributing. The premises closed at the end of 2006 for major work, including proper flooring and the first set of glass display cases for exhibits. 'Everything came together in stages, if and when the money came in,' says Adrian. 'But at least we had proved we knew what we were doing and were doing it properly. We reopened in January 2007 as the Museum of Free Derry.'

Preparations for Phase Two are continuing. In the meantime, the modest museum, its poignant artefacts and rich Bloody Sunday archive has earned international recognition. It is not something separate from the campaign, says Eamonn McCann: 'In a sense, we want the museum to house the truth which so many have fought for so long to wrench from the authorities. The Museum of Free Derry will be a living thing, both a symbol and the substance of a struggle.'

Bloody Sunday was never far from the headlines, with frequent, and often negative, press reports lambasting Saville and his team and questioning the inquiry's cost and necessity. The inquiry process itself became the subject of a play in April 2005 when Richard Norton-Taylor's *Bloody Sunday, Scenes from the Saville Inquiry* opened at the Tricycle Theatre in London. The production later travelled to Derry and played to widespread acclaim.

Months became years and, in the end, the wait for Saville's report proved too long for some. Willie McKinney's mother, Anne, died in July 2005 having never had the truth about her son's death acknowledged.

The same week saw the demise of Edward Heath, British prime minister at the time of Bloody Sunday. His death filled newspaper columns, but there were many in Derry who did not mourn his passing.

Later that year Eamonn McCann's *The Bloody Sunday Inquiry: The Families Speak Out* was launched, which delved into the complexities of the inquiry process, its legal teams and its repercussions from the perspective of the relatives. Whispers of a completion date came and went. By now, the families were well used to delays and disappointments.

Patsy O'Donnell, one of the wounded, died on 1 May 2006, on his wife's birthday. He was seventy-four years old and hadn't heard himself declared 'innocent'. Caroline O'Donnell says Patsy was never the same after Bloody Sunday. He was forty-one when shot in Glenfada Park, the bullet piercing his shoulder.

'Realising he had been shot, the paras came after my father and used the butt of their rifles to batter his head in,' Caroline recalls. 'They kicked him with steel toecaps and ran away, leaving him for dead. The head injuries alone could have killed him, but some taxi men came out and dragged him in off the street, and got him help.

'He came back a different person. Before that, he was very outgoing and loved going out, bringing his friends back. We always looked forward to Saturday nights, everyone sitting around chatting while my mum made a big pot of homemade soup. All that stopped after Bloody Sunday. My father became afraid of crowds, and we always had to plan family functions at one of our houses.'

Caroline recalls how she became involved with the other families. 'I took over from my daddy, because I had an active interest. He would phone to tell me there were meetings on, and I would go along. Caroline feels blessed in her good fortune. 'I feel for those who were robbed of a daddy – I can't imagine that. It was totally different for us, because we still had our father. We went on to have a great life. We were so lucky really. When the inquiry started, my daddy thought Saville had a lot of integrity, but he feared the British establishment would do anything to cover up the truth.'

A television documentary about the Bloody Sunday Inquiry was broadcast on the Irish network, RTÉ 1, on 6 February 2007. It helped keep the subject in the headlines and to the forefront of people's minds. *Bloody Sunday: A Derry Diary*, produced by Derry film-maker Margo Harkin and her production company, Besom Productions, followed the lives and experiences of several relatives and campaigners as they attended hearings in both Derry and London.

Another of those wounded on Bloody Sunday, Daniel Gillespie, died in August 2008, without hearing a declaration of his innocence. Daniel Gillespie had been a milkman. As a young man, he took work in England so he and his fiancée Frances could afford to be married. They would have celebrated their ruby wedding anniversary in 2010.

Frances Gillespie becomes emotional remembering how Bloody Sunday affected her husband. 'Had he lived, Danny would be seventy-four today. I still put out his cup of tea every morning. He always said he'd be dead and buried before they'd get justice. It's a fight with the British government – they'll admit nothing even when they're wrong.

'His own daughter was twenty-eight before she discovered Danny was injured on Bloody Sunday. He never talked to them about it – I suppose he didn't want them to grow up bitter.'

Danny was wounded in Glenfada Park and lay unconscious for the duration of the shootings. 'He had head injuries and some men carried him home,' Frances remembers. 'I saw them coming towards the house and I didn't even recognise him – his face was covered in blood and looked all battered. He cried and cried saying they'd killed "weans . . . bits of weans"'.

Having heard that his own brother had been shot, Danny went to the morgue at Altnagelvin Hospital. The room was filled with bodies, on stretchers and laid out on the floor. His brother was not among them. 'I always remember Danny telling me that he saw policemen standing in the doorway of the morgue afterwards, singing "I'd Like to Teach the World to Sing". He never forgot that.'

Danny took to the stand to testify to the murder of his fellow civil rights marchers and the maiming of himself. He, too, would die without hearing the truth.

Kay Duddy remembers how difficult the intervening years were. 'We were very frustrated because that void was there again, and it was just more waiting, waiting. Sometimes, it seemed like it would never end. We had to keep highlighting it, in the meantime, to try and keep the subject in the public eye.'

On 6 November 2008, Lord Saville broke the news that his report wouldn't be ready for at least another year. 'We have always found it difficult, given the scale and complexity of the material with which we are dealing, to predict accurately how long it will take us to complete our task,' Saville wrote to the families.

The families had little choice but to keep waiting, and worrying. 'It was delay after delay, and we were tired, but we just hoped it would be worth the wait,' Mickey McKinney said.

Eamonn McCann said the families were losing confidence in the inquiry. 'This is an enormous task and it's understandable it should take some time, but this amount of time? The publication date has been pushed back repeatedly, and I think that some people are beginning to ask themselves, what's going on?'

Autumn 2009 brought with it yet more dismay. On 23 September, Lord Saville said he was 'extremely disappointed' but the Bloody Sunday report would not be ready and delivered to the British government until March 2010. Saville claimed that the delay was due to unforeseen difficulties involved in the intricacies of printing a report running to several thousand pages. Parliament was to go into the Easter recess on 22 March and there was a distinct possibility of an election being called without it ever reconvening. That possibility, said Tony Doherty, was of 'grave concern' to families.

Mark Durkan warned that, 'This will have severe implications and could create many complications.' Himself a Derryman, SDLP Leader Mark Durkan had supported the families throughout the inquiry and the long wait thereafter. 'Derry is a small place and, working in John Hume's office from 1984 onwards, I would have got to know many of the family members individually. I became increasingly conscious of not just the family but the personal dimensions of Bloody Sunday and the report. I don't think any person of my generation could grow up in Derry and not feel it personally.

'I was eleven when Bloody Sunday happened and was out playing football when I heard there was shooting up the town. I remember running home, and seeing people drifting past who had been on the march. I remember one man in particular, who just called, "It was a massacre, a massacre". Between the radio and scraps of TV news, the death toll mounted and it was a sense of numbing shock, but also a pounding anger that I felt, and I knew everybody else felt that as well.'

As an MP, Durkan was regularly involved with the families and wounded. 'I was in the background if they needed me, and often spoke with them. They would share some of their feelings on particular evidence they had heard that week and you saw how much it affected them all individually. I learned a lot about them. Absolutely, I admired them – and I feared them! They were absolutely straight up. Setting out as they did, then progressing to getting an inquiry, then the twists and the lies of the inquiry, they have stayed strong throughout.'

Mickey Bradley died on 2 May 2009 at his home in Osborne Street. He had been left permanently disabled by Bloody Sunday and a compulsion to uncover the truth had dominated his life since 1972. 'Mickey had been almost obsessed by Bloody Sunday,' Jackie Bradley remembers. 'And although that calmed down when the inquiry ended, he then threw himself into researching every word that was spoken during the inquiry, analysing who said this and that – he never took a break from it.'

When Mickey died, Northern Ireland's deputy first minister led the tributes in praising his unwavering dedication. 'Although carrying the physical symptoms of that attack ever since, Mickey never ceased in his efforts to fight for the full truth of what happened to be revealed.'

Five years had passed since Saville had retired to compile his report and still no completion date was in sight. Frustrations grew. Mickey Bridge described the constant delays as 'nonsense'. 'A five-year wait for the report? That is just utter nonsense. The evidence was clear – six months would have done it.'

Addressing the 2010 rally, relatives urged Lord Saville to publish his report without delay.

In February 2010, the families and Bloody Sunday Trust decided to draw upon the strength of the original campaign and establish a movement to 'Set the Truth Free'. This initiative had one aim – that the families should see the entire Saville report without redactions.

Families and legal representatives were concerned at news that the British government intended to hold the report for at least two weeks after receiving it from Saville to proof it for any potential breaches of 'Article 2' of the Human Rights Act (the right to life). Many were incredulous. The proofing would require 'specialists' who would most probably be staff from the Ministry of Defence or MI5 personnel. 'It was ridiculous,' says Kay Duddy. 'I thought, "Are they out of their mind? Have they lost the plot?" It undermined everything we had fought for.'

Conal McFeely recalls: 'The "Set the Truth Free" campaign had a very simple message which worked because it captured the human side of what we were fighting for – the truth. We used very simple imagery – for example, a close-up representation of Gerry Donaghey's eyes coming out from a huge poster.

'We were also aware that 2010 would be a very traumatic year for the families and we needed to put their needs first. We thought it was time to try to re-establish a family support programme. We engaged Julieann Campbell as a press officer because we felt that we needed her to bring a freshness to the campaign. Instead of focusing on the negativity and old photographs, to show the victims and the families in a very different light – as ordinary folk gunned to death or injured on their own streets and entitled as of right to the full truth about themselves.'

The families and wounded released a statement on 23 February, entitled 'Lord Saville – Set the Truth Free!' Noting that it was now more than twelve years since Tony Blair had announced the inquiry, they insisted that 'time and timing are now very much of the essence.'

Campaigners voiced concerns that a general election could delay the report by months. 'The report will be in the hands of officials within the NIO for a period of several months without any political control from above. This is a frightening prospect for the families, as we believe that the report will fall victim to selective leakage and other partisan usage long before the full report sees the light of day . . . In short, the inquiry process, detailed, meticulous and painful as it was, could become a total mess and a travesty in the final few weeks before it becomes public.'

The Pat Finucane Centre remarked that to justify further delay, 'the government is apparently implying that Saville and his team are not competent to Article 2 proof the report.'

On 4 March, the families met with Secretary of State Sean Woodward at a city centre hotel, accompanied by Martin McGuinness and Mark Durkan. Top of the agenda was the need for relatives to receive Saville's report at the same time as the government. Woodward explained to families that, due to legal constraints, this would not be possible.

'I will get the report to the families and the other parties as soon as possible so there will be no time for leaks or spin, but for security and legal reasons, I, and my team of solicitors must see it first.' He added that, 'I respect the families enormously. They have been through a hell of a lot over the years.'

Woodward was challenged in the hotel foyer when leaving by more relatives, among them Linda Roddy and her sister Kate Nash, all wearing 'Set the Truth Free' campaign T-shirts.

With the families becoming increasingly tense and anxious, the Bloody Sunday Trust received funding from the Irish Department of Foreign Affairs to establish the Bloody Sunday Family Advice Centre in Ráth Mór Centre, Creggan. With Mickey McKinney resuming his role as family liaison officer and Julieann Campbell now in place as press officer, the new space provided a central meeting point for all the relatives and wounded as publication date loomed.

The centre was officially opened on 11 March 2010. Saville's report was now tantalisingly close. But age and illness continued to claim the lives of some of those still fighting for vindication. By now, half of all the Bloody Sunday wounded were dead. Only one bereaved parent survived – Lawrence McElhinney – Kevin's father.

chapter fourteen

'Reclaim the history of Bloody Sunday'

Caroline O'Donnell was just thirteen when her father, Patsy was wounded on Bloody Sunday. Now a mother and grandmother, Caroline was very happy to be included among a small group of relatives plotting an adventure in Westminster on St Patrick's Day 2010.

Saville's report was in sight, but government protocol and endless red tape delayed publication yet further. The families had resurrected the justice campaign for one final push. Their 'Set the Truth Free' campaign would put pressure on the government to publish the report in full, with no redactions. Campaigners announced their intention to visit London to 'reclaim the history of Bloody Sunday' and highlight concerns over the delays.

Before 8 AM on St Patrick's Day, 17 March, a dozen campaigners met at City of Derry Airport. It was bitterly cold before the dawn, but an air of mischievousness warmed the bones. The plan was London and back in one day, so the schedule was tight.

At 11 AM, campaigners arrived at 10 Downing Street, where, supported by MPs Mark Durkan and Conor Murphy among others, they were to hand back an original copy of the Widgery Report. Tony Doherty and John McKinney slowly pushed the thin blue report through Downing Street's shiny black railings, into the hands of a waiting security officer.

The group received impromptu invitations to the St Patrick's Day celebrations inside the Houses of Parliament that afternoon. Tony, Gerry, and Caroline were selected to attend. Prime Minister Gordon Brown was to host the event. Tony seized the opportunity to hand-deliver the campaign's letter. Caroline recalls their amusement at attending such a star-studded event. 'There we were, at a party in parliament, and there was a green theme, tricolour cocktails and a free bar! We spoke to loads of people, explaining why we were there.'

Then it was on to Ministry of Defence building on Whitehall. Tony and Caroline made their way up to its huge doors to hand back General Jackson's infamous 'shot list'. The others sprang into action, chalking the outlines of fourteen bodies on the pavement, symbolising the fourteen dead of Bloody Sunday. The group were moved on within minutes, but not before leaving a dozen chalk bodies on the Whitehall pavement.

The next destination was to be Buckingham Palace, but relatives had discovered that Gordon Brown was to drive past the MoD shortly. Unfolding a long banner saying 'Set the Truth Free', the group dominated the roadside as Brown's cavalcade passed. The demonstration had not gone unnoticed. As the group walked through the Mall towards Buckingham Palace, it became apparent that police were tailing them.

'Don't you worry, we're well used to being watched,' joked Gerry Duddy.

Tourists thronged the wide mall around Buckingham Palace, awaiting the changing of the guard. Before the campaigners reached the palace, a noticeable police presence spoke in hushed tones into walkie-talkies.

One half of the group were apprehended before they reached the palace gates, but Tony, Gerry, Stephen Gargan and Paul O'Connor made it across the road, holding their Set the Truth Free banner up at the palace gates for the milling tourists to see. They also delivered to the palace a list of the dead and injured to remind the British Monarch of the real heroes of Bloody Sunday, – not Para commander Lieutenant Colonel Derek Wilford, on whom she had bestowed an OBE after the massacre.

Tony Doherty said: 'Wilford was no hero – the dead and the injured were the real heroes who went out that day to demand civil rights and ended up as targets for the paras. Wilford should be stripped of his honour.'

A heavy police presence soon escorted the campaigners away: 'When they were moving us on, I remember one policeman said he supported us and wished us all the best of luck for the cause,' says Caroline. 'That was nice.'

After lunch in the Methodist Hall in Westminster, where they had spent so many hours at the hearings, the delegation walked across the square to the Houses of Parliament where Mark Durkan had organised an audience with MPs. Tony conveyed the case clearly and with emotion. One MP in particular, former Ulster Unionist MP Sylvia Hermon, showed genuine interest and stayed behind afterwards to talk further.

After the discussion, Durkan organised for the families to be allowed into the members' bar. Caroline recalls: 'Most of us stayed outside because the smoking area was the balcony of parliament that you always see on TV – overlooking the whole of the Thames. I remember Gerry saying to me, "Will you pinch me?" and me replying, "Will you kick me?" It really was a brilliant day's craic.'

The families were warned more than once by the Metropolitan Police that their actions were in breach of new legislation banning any demonstration within one kilometre of parliament. It would take more than that to scare the well-seasoned campaigners: 'Highlighting Bloody Sunday at Buckingham Palace, the Ministry of Defence and Downing Street was more important on this occasion than any alleged technical breach of this new law. We will demonstrate where and when we want and that's what we did.'

Meanwhile, John Kelly and Jean Hegarty had flown to Washington. At the White House, they met with senior US politicians to voice their concerns about the imminent report.

In a campaign statement released on the eve of their trip, John said: 'We feel that it is very important to take our just demands of truth and justice at this time to both Britain and the US. Just hours after our loved ones were mown down on the streets of Derry by the Parachute Regiment, the British Embassy in Washington were able to describe and condemn the dead as gunmen and bombers. We cannot allow an open field for the British government to stage and manipulate the release of the report for their own ends. The next few weeks will be crucial in seeing the hated Widgery Report entirely repudiated.'

In Washington, the campaigners also met congressmen in Capitol Hill and attended functions at the American Ireland Fund, at which Hillary Clinton was honoured at a Northern Ireland Bureau Breakfast and where both Martin McGuinness and First Minister Peter Robinson spoke. They also attended the unveiling of a portrait of Pat Finucane.

In support of the families, both the *Derry Journal* and *Derry News* began carrying the campaign's new 'Set the Truth Free' banner on the front page of every edition and would continue to do so until Saville delivered. Thousands of campaign leaflets were also distributed throughout the north-west and, on Saturday 20 March, a rally was held in the Guildhall Square to highlight the issues over the report's publication and the need for parity with the British government. Speakers included Eamonn McCann, now chair of the Trust, relative Tony Doherty and several local politicians.

The annual Bloody Sunday lecture was given on 20 March at the Guildhall by renowned civil rights lawyer, Gareth Peirce, who had been crucial in both the Guildford Four and Birmingham Six cases. More recently, she had represented former Guantanamo Bay internee Moazzam Begg and the family of Jean Charles de Menezes, the young Brazilian man shot dead by police officers in the London underground after they wrongly identified him as a suicide bomber.

'I have a great admiration for Gareth Peirce. *The Name of the Father* is one of my favourite films,' Kay Duddy says. 'Her lecture was wonderful and afterwards I said to her "I wish we had you on board during the campaign" and she said, "You didn't need me – you did it all by yourselves." Wow, I thought that was fantastic.'

On 22 March, the tribunal released a statement confirming it had given final approval to the proofs of its report. Its publication was now the responsibility of the Secretary of State. Two days later, and despite the months of protestations from relatives and campaigners, the entire report was handed over to British government lawyers for checks on national security. Families felt powerless to intervene. If the checks took too long, families knew there was a very real possibility that the report would be shelved until after the general election – which was still months away. All they could do, as ever, was wait.

In the months preceding the report, parliament had decreed that only one member of each affected family would be allowed to see it before publication. An ongoing battle was waged over the issue with families engaged in negotiations with the Northern Ireland Office. They felt outraged that the authorities could expect them to face such an arduous task alone and demanded that the numbers allowed to preview the report be increased. Under pressure, on 1 April, Shaun Woodward confirmed that the Speaker of Parliament had agreed to allow two people per family a preview of the findings.

Gerry Duddy said the news, while far from ideal, would 'certainly ease the burden' of examining the final report. 'How they expected one person to absorb the findings is beyond us, especially considering that it is taking up to two weeks for legal experts to scrutinise these same documents. Our families, the wounded and the wider population of Derry have waited over thirty-eight years for the findings of this inquiry.'

After the intense period of campaigning, Secretary of State Woodward also informed the families on 8 April 2010 that no redactions were made to the report: 'I can confirm that this checking process has now been completed and I have received advice from the checking team which confirms that there is nothing in the report which, if published, could breach article 2 of the European Convention on Human Rights by putting the lives or safety of individuals at risk, or put national security at risk. I am therefore satisfied that the report can be published in full and I have advised Lord Saville of this.'

However, there was a sting in the tail. Woodward revealed that, given the time needed to print the report, 'it will not be practically possible to publish the report to Parliament before this Parliament is dissolved for the general election.'

'We were so close, almost at the finishing line, and now we will be made to wait even longer,' John Kelly said.

The families insisted the report stay in the possession of Saville until its publication to safeguard against potential leaks. They also insisted that any new government should honour the agreements reached with the current Secretary of State, Woodward.

A few days later, on 13 April, Bloody Sunday Trust member and MLA, Raymond McCartney, highlighted the families' concerns during a debate at Stormont. There, the subject proved as contentious as ever.

Just weeks before Saville delivered his verdict, John Duddy died. John had given years to the campaign, desperate to remove the stain upon his brother-in-law, John Johnston's, name. 'My daddy died on 3 May 2010, six weeks before Saville,' Jimmy Duddy reveals. 'It was very hard for me, after all those years discussing the campaign together and him phoning me to fill me in on meetings. Suddenly he wasn't there anymore, and I had to take his place.'

With Conal McFeely taking the lead in the practicalities and logistics of publication, there followed further months of tough negotiations. 'Preparations for the report involved negotiating with several bodies at once – Derry City Council, Police Service of Northern Ireland (PSNI), Northern Ireland Office (NIO), Department of Social Development, as well as the international media. Our focus throughout was to do all this from the families perspective. They kept talking about their needs, and we had the confidence to say "No – it's not about the BBC or UTV, it's about the families," remembers Conal. In discussions with the families, it was agreed that Mark Durkan would make himself available in Westminster for the publication.

'There was a lot of suspicion around the report, and how it was going to be handled and the plans for its publication,' he recalls. 'When we discussed what should happen on the day of publication, it was clear that I should be in Westminster. A big part of me would have preferred to be in Derry, but the families were clear that my station that day, as their MP, was to be in the Commons. Of course, when we agreed that, we had no idea what Saville would find, how David

Cameron would address it, or how the House of Commons would receive it.'

Durkan reveals that the original plan was that the secretary of state would address the Commons, not the prime minister. 'Under Labour, it was going to be Shaun Woodward who addressed the Commons and published the report, but when the Conservative government came in, the prime minister decided to do it himself.

'A foreign office minister had asked me earlier who should make the statement, and I said I thought the prime minister should. He replied, "That's what he's wondering..." Everybody knows who David Cameron is, unlike the secretary of state, and so when he decided to do it himself, it gave the statement much more credibility. In fairness, Cameron got the measure of it.'

Looking back, Olive Bonner believes the issue of money is irrelevant. No costs could equal the murder of her little brother, Hugh. 'People like Ian Paisley and Gregory Campbell, they were talking about money constantly, they weren't concerned about what the army did, just about how much this all cost. The truth costs nothing. If they had told the truth in 1972, none of this would have been necessary. I couldn't care how many millions it cost – these were human lives they took, married men with families and babies, gunned down in their own streets.'

As final preparations got underway, Derry found itself in a flurry of excitement and trepidation. The families and injured were being sought for press interviews and comment around the clock.

'It was the longest week of my life waiting for it,' Kay Duddy recalls. Kevin McDaid says he had trouble sleeping and lost his appetite. 'My nerves were wrecked.' Jackie Bradley felt terrified and asked her son, Pio, to attend the report's pre-read with her. 'I didn't sleep a wink the night before. I sat up and cried and cried – crying for Mickey because he wasn't there for it, and wondering if I would be able to do it for him. The thought of the walk over to the Guildhall the next morning terrified me, I was too nervous and thought my legs would never take me. I just asked Mickey for the strength to get there, and to see him proven innocent.'

Meanwhile Mark Durkan prepared to travel to London. In Westminster, he would attend a controlled reading of the report and later speak in parliament. He had also been granted the only phone call into the Guildhall that day – through a secure line – to gauge families' reactions there before addressing the Commons.

Durkan says: 'It was terrible leaving Derry the day before the report. You felt this sense of trepidation, you hoped for a good report, but had all those natural suspicions and doubts.'

Alana Burke's son Gareth, a solicitor, was supposed to go into the pre-read with Alana but a serious accident had left him fighting for his life. At the last minute, Alana asked her brother to accompany her to the preview.

'It was all tinged with sadness for me, because of what was going on with Gareth at the time. I remember John Kelly phoning me to the intensive care unit the night before telling me they needed me at the Guildhall. I said "The British army or every army in the world wouldn't stop me from being there tomorrow, John."'

'I remember telling Gareth when he was unconscious, "I won't be here tomorrow, I've got a very important day." It made me feel better telling him all about it; I wonder if he could hear me.'

As publication day finally arrived, Kay Duddy woke too early. Despite being deeply anxious about the hours ahead, she had agreed to allow an ITV camera crew to shadow her for the day. They hoped to capture the personal anguish behind the colossal inquiry. Kay showed them the true face of Bloody Sunday, the genuine apprehension and fear of herself, Gerry and their twelve brothers and sisters.

Although not in the least bit hungry, Kay struggled over a small breakfast, trying desperately to ignore the television crew fussing around her. A camera was the least of her worries this morning – all she could think about was getting through today. All she could see was Jackie's face, smiling.

The ITV news crew finished temporarily, Kay readied herself, hugged her sister Susie next door, and set off towards the city centre to meet Gerry at the memorial. Susie and all the other Duddy brothers and sisters would join them later. Throughout, Kay carried an old white handkerchief marked 'Fr Daly' in her pocket. It was the hankie used by the young priest to stem the blood flowing from Jackie, the one waved frantically at soldiers. A simple square of cotton that somehow made her feel close to Jackie. She needed its strength today.

'All that morning I had butterflies' Kay says. 'I was nervous but I was quietly confident because I had this belief in Saville. Throughout the whole inquiry, as much as we were watching him, I knew he was watching us. I was confident that Saville had done what he set out to do.'

Across the city, Gerry Duddy left home early and visited Jackie's grave in the cemetery before walking downhill towards the Bogside. 'I walked to town because I wanted to keep my head clear. I had a lot of thinking to do. It made it harder for me and Kay to go into the pre-read, with all the others from our family left outside. I thought that was terrible, I thought everyone should have been allowed in, but the best thing we could get was two people, which put a lot of pressure on me and Kay.'

Kevin McDaid was distracted on the morning of the report. 'I got up really early, before 7 AM, and I wondered did we need milk? We didn't need milk, but I went out looking for it anyway. I didn't come back for an hour, but I couldn't tell you where I went. The wife said people were phoning looking for me, but I took my time getting ready and polished my shoes and sorted myself out. You didn't know what to expect and you wanted to look half decent.'

Nerves had woken Alana Burke too. 'I got up at 4.30 AM as I couldn't sleep and I was really scared.' Before Bloody Sunday, Alana was a vibrant young girl. The injuries she suffered from the Saracen persist, still causing daily anguish. 'That whole morning was surreal and full of trepidation. I know that I wasn't shot on Bloody Sunday, but the impact of the day will stay with me for the rest of my life, it really will.'

Jean Hegarty had responded to one of the many press requests for early morning interviews and spoke with BBC crews high on the Derry Walls, the sun rising over the Bogside.

Jean was shocked to see the massive media operation unfolding in the city centre. 'I was really very surprised how important the occasion seemed to everybody else. I'm not sure what I expected, but when I did an interview on the walls, you could see the preparations underway all around us, and all the TV stands lined up along the walls – that's when I realised the enormity of it all. I kept thinking – what if Saville doesn't deliver?'

Relatives granted advance sight of Saville's report met at the Bloody Sunday monument in Rossville Street around 10 AM. The Bogside swarmed with press from all over the world.

Tensions were fraught and tears flowed freely. John McKinney remembers: 'Looking at photos of us that morning, you can really see the pressure we were under. This was it. While we were waiting around, I looked to see Joe Mahon with Liam Wray. Joe Mahon was lying beside our Willie in Glenfada Park when he was killed and I saw Joe breaking down and I deliberately stayed away from him because I knew I couldn't handle coming face to face with him. It was hard enough that morning without seeing him so upset.'

The planned silent walk to the Guildhall was permeated by camera clicks and sporadic applause from well-wishers. John McKinney recalls that the decision to walk down the middle of the road was purely impulsive. 'I remember having a conversation with the stewards who were helping organise the occasion, about whether we were going to walk on the footpath and I said, "We're walking down no path – we're walking out on the road!" The traffic stopped for us. The media were everywhere too, so it was good for publicity but pretty nerve-wracking all the same.'

Kevin McDaid remembers feeling amazed that a group of ordinary families had come so far, and regrets not getting involved in the campaign sooner. He met his brother John and sister Bridie at the monument. 'Never in a million years did I think we could ever have done that,' Kevin says. 'Even days before the report came out, we weren't sleeping, just a bag of nerves. When we were walking towards the Guildhall, with everyone watching and cameras everywhere, I was wondering "what would Mickey think?" . . . He would have been amazed.'

Gerard McKinney's daughter, Regina, felt her father's presence throughout. 'I felt him as soon as I got to the point that the march stopped. To finish what he started was the greatest honour for me. We were finishing the steps he took. I felt Daddy there.'

[chapter fifteen]

'The relief of Derry'

'I was shaking. My heart was thumping. I don't even remember going up the stairs, you know. But all of a sudden I was in that big room, with tables everywhere and lawyers all standing around, looking at us . . .'

Olive Bonner held tightly to her brother Bernard as they walked towards their allocated table in the main hall of the Guildhall to find out whether the truth had been told about their brother's murder. 'As soon as we got the report, we just went straight to Hugh's section. I'm sure every family did exactly the same . . . Then I said to Bernard, "Thank God", and we both started crying . . . I looked around and almost everybody around us was crying too. If only my mother and father had lived to see this day. If only our Floyd had lived to see it. . . .'

Mickey McKinney remembers that he felt like a giant as he and younger brother John walked towards the huge neo-gothic door of the Guildhall minutes before, urged on by well wishers. 'The whole campaign was worth it in that one moment of walking through those doors. This was what it had all been about.'

John McKinney felt overwhelming urgency to get inside, 'Everyone was taking their time but I needed to get in, I needed to know and get it all over with,' he remembers. 'The security was fierce and we were searched and put through an electronic scanner and made to hand our phones in.'

Kevin McDaid and his brother, John, were inside. 'Everything seemed un-real, and I kept wondering what Michael would think of all this fuss. I had been off the cigarettes for a year, but I lost count of how many I smoked that day.'

'I was nervous but hopeful,' Gerry Duddy recalls. 'But I still had that nig-gling feeling that they might still wipe it from under us. When we went in, Barry McDonald of our legal team asked us to sit down, I said "I'm not sitting down, tell me straight, is it good or is it bad?" He said it was good, so then we did sit down and he explained everything in more detail.'

Rather than trawl through ten volumes of report, Saville had condensed his findings into one fifty-eight-page summary, the *Principal Conclusions and Over-all Assessment of the Bloody Sunday Inquiry*. The final paragraph in the summary said it all . . .

'The firing by soldiers of 1 PARA on Bloody Sunday caused the deaths of thirteen people and injury to a similar number, none of whom was posing a threat of causing death or serious injury. What happened on Bloody Sunday strengthened the Provisional IRA, increased nationalist resentment and hostil-ity towards the army and exacerbated the violent conflict of the years that fol-lowed. Bloody Sunday was a tragedy for the bereaved and the wounded, and a catastrophe for the people of Northern Ireland.'

'Within about ten minutes it was all over – we got what we wanted, maybe more,' Kevin McDaid says. 'I just read over Michael's wee bit of the report, self-ishly, over and over again.'

'It was an unbelievable feeling,' Damian Donaghey adds 'All of a sudden, everyone was cleared, and we had to sit around like nervous wrecks in that big hall for hours waiting, drinking tea and smoking like trains.'

An overwhelmed Kay Duddy found the enforced separation within the Guildhall hard to handle. 'It was fantastic to be told that Jackie was innocent and that he died unarmed and running away, but all I wanted to do was run downstairs and tell my brothers and sisters. But we weren't allowed near them.'

Alana Burke tried to absorb the gist of the report, but emotions got the bet-ter of her. 'I couldn't see through the tears. 'Then I heard whooping from the back of the hall, and suddenly I realised "everything's going to be ok". I get shivers remembering the feeling that gave me. It was just fantastic, worth every minute, every march, every campaign, every tear.'

'I just burst out crying,' Jackie Bradley says. 'I just kept wishing Mickey was there, he fought so long and hard for this. It was his day but he wasn't here for it. I was so gutted for Mary Doherty and Geraldine Donaghey too.'

Mary Doherty, sister of Gerald Donaghey, was seriously ill and too weak to attend the pre-read. Responsibility now fell to Geraldine, and Gerald's best friend, Donnacha McFeely. Their worst fears were confirmed within minutes of entering the Guildhall – Saville had ruled that Gerald had, 'in all probability' had nail-bombs on his person but had posed no threat at the time of his death. His family were stunned.

'We were the only family disappointed on June 15, says Geraldine. 'Just the week before we had been told that our mother's chemo didn't work and they weren't going to give her any more treatment. She'd put on a brave face, but she was really scared. I saw Patricia Coyle coming towards me and I knew by the look on her face that it was going to be bad news. I asked "What about the nail-bombs" and she shook her head "No, Geraldine". I just broke down, knowing this was my mother's worst fear. "How am I going to tell my mammy this?" I thought. People tried to make us feel better, pointing out that at least Gerald was declared innocent, but that wasn't the point. On paper, his name was still ruined.'

Saville's key findings were that the fourteen Derry civilians died as a result of 'unjustifiable firing' by British soldiers and that none of the casualties were armed or posed any threat. Many pages of the report documented the fact that unarmed victims were shot dead as they tried to crawl away to safety or going to the assistance of others who were dying. The report also found that the British army fired the first shots and did so without warning. It said there had been a 'serious and widespread loss of fire discipline'.

However, the upper echelons of the British establishment and its military emerged unscathed. Key figures like General Ford, Edward Heath and Sir General Mike Jackson were largely cleared of any blame. The only officer singled out for criticism was Lieutenant Colonel Derek Wilford: the inquiry found that the soldiers entered the Bogside 'as a result of an order which should not have been given' by their commander. Saville also found that after the bloodshed, many of the soldiers 'knowingly put forward false accounts in order to seek to justify their firing.'

Martin McGuinness and Sinn Féin MP Conor Murphy were in a lockdown at the nearby City Hotel where later, the media would also be permitted to see Saville's conclusions ahead of publication. All were bound by secrecy until 3.30 PM.

Besides the ruling on Gerald Donaghey, the report was well received. 'We were delighted with it before we had even seen the families' reactions,' Martin McGuinness remembers. 'We knew they would be pleased.'

In Westminster, Mark Durkan had also relinquished his mobile phone and freedom for a few hours. He would address the Commons that afternoon on behalf of the families.

'I phoned home before going into the Cabinet Office and handing over my phone. Even over the phone, you could already sense how the mood was growing in Derry,' says the MP. 'I knew I needed to be in London, but I really wished I was at home.'

A big screen inside the Guildhall broadcast Sky News in anticipation of Cameron's speech. 'The big screen really made it for me,' says Damian Donaghy. 'We could all see was going on outside and watched the big march taking off from William Street and coming through the town and we couldn't wait to get out there.'

Frances Gillespie had a knot in her stomach all day, despite the atmosphere and happiness at the Guildhall. She didn't go for the pre-read – she couldn't. Her son did and burst into tears. She preferred to await the results inside the Guildhall in the mayor's parlour.

The emotion proved too much for Leo Young. 'The doctor on standby in the Guildhall wanted to put me in hospital because my nerves were wrecked,' he remembers. 'My blood pressure soared. I was in a bad way. I thought my heart was going to bust out of my chest.'

Conal McFeely felt mostly relief. He had been instrumental in organising the day and had arrived at the Guildhall at daybreak, around 5.30 AM, to make sure everything was going to plan. 'Truth be told, I was always very anxious,' he reveals. 'The worst case scenario for me was that all the other families would be exonerated and that the Donaghey family would be left on their own, which is sadly what happened.'

A number of Bloody Sunday Trust members were also inside the Guildhall, each with a specific task. Conal, Eamonn McCann, Raymond McCartney and Robin Percival were the main support team for the families, while Maoliosa Boyle was present to oversee the use of the big screen outside, which flashed intermittently with the faces of the boys and men killed on Bloody Sunday.

Inside, the strict security caused some problems. 'We negotiated with Mary Madden, the key player with the NIO, to allow the other families upstairs early as tensions downstairs were escalating,' recalls Conal. She argued that there was protocol to follow, but eventually she relented. I told her "The families are in control of the situation now."

'It was an incredibly emotional day for everyone involved. Every single person in the room was affected – even the hardened campaigners like Eamonn McCann were quite overcome!'

Eamonn recalls he felt a great personal joy. 'I was literally jumping with excitement, I couldn't contain myself and was afraid I was going to make a fool of myself. I felt a great sense of vindication and joy and of relief that it was over. There was also a feeling of gratitude towards the families that they had been so generous in allowing people in. To be allowed into their campaign as deeply as I was allowed in was a great privilege. I was treated as a member of the families and I am deeply, deeply appreciative of that.'

Family members waiting patiently downstairs were on edge and imagining the worst. Around lunchtime, an hour before the formal announcement, families upstairs managed to sneak word out. Huddled in a cordoned-off smoking area off a side door, Gerry Duddy and Kevin McDaid heard voices nearby. Gerry says, 'I knew it was Conal and Raymond, and I think I said something like "alright mucker, everything's great. . . . ."'

'We hoped that if the families knew it was a good report, everyone could relax,' Kevin adds.

Mark Durkan, permitted the only phone call of the day to the Guildhall, nervously rang the relatives. 'Mickey McKinney answered the phone. He asked me what I thought, but I wanted to know his reaction first. "Well, we think it's kinda good," Mickey said. And I said, "Well, I think it's very good," and we started talking from there. It was very emotional. I spoke to John Kelly and Mickey Bridge. John wanted it put to Cameron in the Commons that Widgery was definitely binned, Mickey Bridge reminded me to read the names of the fourteen men out, if Cameron didn't. That was important, so people didn't forget who this was all about.

'I couldn't speak after the phone call, in the full flood of emotion. I didn't know what to expect in the chamber.'

After 2 PM, the remaining family members were allowed upstairs. With them were Bishop Daly, Robert Jackson from the Department of Foreign Affairs and several of his colleagues. A doctor was also on hand, just in case.

Gerry Duddy remembers the relief. 'It was great when the rest of the family came upstairs. Kay was the emotional one with the tears and all – I tried to play it cool as usual!'

While the others swarmed up the Guildhall's opulent staircase, Mary Doherty, too weak for the stairs, took the lift to the second floor. 'In the background I could hear the squeals of others as they heard their good news. Then I saw my mother and she knew by looking at me it wasn't good. "What about the nail-bombs?", and I told her no, they didn't clear him of that – but he still had his innocence declared. She just broke down. While all the families were in the main hall, celebrating, we were given a side room. Arthur Harvey QC came in to explain, almost in tears, and my mother said to him "Just get to the point."'

Mary wanted to go home immediately. But Geraldine was needed on the platform outside. 'We decided not to mention the nail-bombs in the speech as it would put a dampener on the occasion for everyone else. We didn't want to spoil their happiness. My mother was heartbroken. Why declare him innocent but leave the stain of those nail-bombs? It just doesn't make sense, especially when Gerald was shot through the same pocket that they claim held nail-bombs. My mother always said that the British military would never hold their hands up and admit to planting bombs. She always feared they would use Gerald as a scapegoat – and they did.'

Derry writer and dramatist Dave Duggan was there with practical advice and reassurance for the relatives due to speak. Conal recalls the scene: 'In the midst of all this emotion, Dave had the foresight to calm family members, telling them not to be afraid of expressing things in their own words and to relax. The hall was a pressure chamber, and here was Dave and Maoliosa sitting in a corner talking quietly and reassuring everyone.'

With the report embargoed until after the prime minister's speech at 3.30 PM, the NIO tried to maintain total isolation. Jubilant relatives, however, saw little point in adhering to parliamentary law.

With a few minutes to go, the thousands outside the Guildhall erupted into cheers as hands emerged from beneath iron window grills to give the thumbs up to the crowd. One by one, the hands appeared, some holding copies of Saville's summary against the windows, waving them excitedly. Cameras spun around to capture the moment.

'The people who stole the show were those who put their thumbs out the window,' Conal McFeely marvels. 'That to me was the story of the day.'

Moments later, a hush descended as David Cameron appeared on the screen in the Square. The prime minister told MPs and millions around the globe watching the live coverage: 'What happened on Bloody Sunday was both unjustified and unjustifiable. It was wrong . . . what happened should never have happened.' Cheers filled the air.

Cameron acknowledged that the government was ultimately responsible for the conduct of its armed forces, 'And for that, on behalf of the government, indeed on behalf of our country, I am deeply sorry.'

Mickey McKinney relives his joy and relief at hearing a British prime minister finally admit responsibility for Bloody Sunday. 'When Cameron apologised on behalf of the government, that was fantastic; but when he apologised on behalf of the country, I thought Jesus, he's really doing it. From inside, you could hear the cheers from the square, it was brilliant.'

'My jaw dropped when I heard Cameron's speech,' Kay Duddy recalls. 'I couldn't believe that someone had the guts to stand up and say what really happened – and in the House of Commons of all places – it was incredible.'

Gerry adds: 'I never thought I would enjoy one word from the English dictionary so much as "innocent" . . . It made all the hard work worthwhile.'

Adds Tony Deery, son of Peggy Deery: 'She would have been over the moon about it.'

'I couldn't stop crying,' admits Alana Burke. 'I was dumbfounded. I just couldn't wait to get out to the daylight, to get air.'

Joe Mahon says that Cameron's apology meant little to him personally. 'They could have said sorry at Widgery but instead they put the families through so much over the years. And what about Gerald Donaghey? They got their pound of flesh.'

Liam Wray describes Cameron's speech as 'a great moment of satisfaction. My great joy was watching a British Conservative prime minister having to get up in the mother of all parliaments and saying the shooting was unjustified and unjustifiable and wrong. It was a hollow apology but it's an apology that went out worldwide. It vindicated the victims, the families, the Derry people who for thirty-nine years were right behind us and were called liars. It vindicated all those people internationally who supported us.'

For Kay Duddy, the entire day was 'tinged with sadness' but adrenaline kept her going. 'There was such a calm in the air, a strange elation that you couldn't put into words. I lost Gerry on the way out of the Guildhall, and that really annoyed me because I wanted to walk out hand in hand with him like at the end of *In the Name of the Father*, "I'm going out the front door with Gerry!" He had worked so hard, and I wanted to walk out that door with him.'

With almost 150 people making their way tentatively out of the Guildhall to face an expectant, electric crowd, the critical moment had arrived – sharing the news with Derry and the world.

Damian Donaghy remembers how nervous they were. 'I said to Alana Burke on the way out "If the Birmingham Six can do it, we can do it!"'

Mickey McKinney was to be the first to address the square. 'I remember very vividly that Mickey was actually shaking from head to foot,' Conal McFeely says. 'Maoliosa Boyle had to grab his hand and lead him to the podium.'

'I couldn't believe it when I saw how many people were waiting,' Mickey McKinney adds. 'They all seemed so close and I remember thinking "Jesus, look at the emotion on their faces." I realised at that moment how much this all meant to them too.'

Olive and Bernard Gilmour held their heads high and fought off nerves. Olive offered up the moment to her family. 'When I walked outside my first thoughts were of them and of Hugh and I said to Hugh "I hope you're happy now." I was oblivious to the crowd, I just saw my mother and father and Floyd and Hugh.'

Jean Hegarty could scarcely believe the support. 'I'm not sure there are words to describe how it felt – it was mind-blowing.'

Leo Young, who had needed medical assistance inside, was likewise in awe: 'It was a fabulous day – a day of days. It was history.'

After Mickey opened proceedings, Tony Doherty addressed the thousands. 'Unjustified and unjustifiable. Those are the words we've been waiting to hear since 30 January 1972. The victims of Bloody Sunday have been vindicated, and the soldiers of the Parachute Regiment have been disgraced. Their medals of honour have to be removed.'

Emotions spilled over as each chosen family member declared their loved one 'Innocent' to the world. Gerry spoke for the Duddys, Bernard for the Gilmours, Kathleen Cooley for the Kellys, John McDaid for the McDaid family, Kate Lyons for the Nash family, then Leo Young, Jean Hegarty, Joe McKinney, Liam Wray, Geraldine Doherty, Regina McLaughlin, Gleann Doherty, Charlie McGuigan and Jimmy Duddy.

Jimmy Duddy recalls: 'I was in tears . . . I couldn't get over the fact my father wasn't there to see it . . . just six weeks. If the report had come out in March, like it was supposed to, he would have been alive to see it.'

Caroline O'Donnell then took to the podium and slowly read out the names of the wounded who did not live to see this day. 'Michael Bradley – innocent; Patrick Campbell – innocent; Peggy Deery – innocent; Daniel Gillespie – innocent; Daniel McGowan – innocent; Alex Nash – innocent, and Patsy O'Donnell – innocent.' Then Alana Burke named her fellow wounded survivors: 'Michael Bridge – innocent; Damian Donaghy – innocent; Joe Friel – innocent; Joe Mahon – innocent; Michael Quinn – innocent, and Patsy McDaid – innocent.'

John Kelly thanked the people of Derry, Ireland and the world for their support. 'We would never have made it without you.'

Kay Duddy gets tearful remembering: 'When I saw the sea of faces and the sun shining down, I got shivers down my spine. You could almost see the big black cloud lifting from over the people of Derry. I was thinking "thank you so much". This was so, so important.'

Regina McLaughlin was oblivious to the thousands. 'I saw nothing but the images of my family watching the news wherever they were. I spoke to each of them individually and I was so aware of mammy and the fact that she was going to hear me say that Daddy was 'deliberately targeted'. That's the words I used, they are the words that struck me and that broke my heart. It needed to be said. We never knew daddy had been deliberately targeted. . . .'

Liam Wray, while dissatisfied with many key aspects of Saville's conclusions, knew he had to bide his time. Now was not the time for anger. Instead, he revelled in the euphoric wave sweeping the city. 'I came out onto the Guildhall Square and just thought, "My God, I am not raining on this parade." And so instead I said, "Thank you, Derry people, for what you did . . ." I will deal with any negativity thoughts in my own time in years to come.'

'It's the feeling I remember, not the scenes as such,' Eamonn McCann remembers. 'These were emotions I had never felt before. A buzz spread across the families and the crowd and enveloped everybody. My thought in the Guildhall was just "Jesus, we've done it!" It had taken so long, but to finally be there and see the families so deliriously happy was tremendous, just tremendous.'

Devastated at the ruling on her uncle Gerald and worrying about her mother, Geraldine Doherty still braved the public and stood alongside the other families. 'When they opened the gates of the Guildhall, my stomach was jumping. I was nearly in tears and froze so they pushed me out and I saw everyone clapping.'

Mary Doherty sat despondent inside the Guildhall, waiting for her daughter to fulfil her obligation on the podium and take her home. Theirs was to be no celebration. 'Most people didn't know about the findings on Gerald until they saw the papers the next day,' remembers Geraldine. 'My mother hid her feelings but inside she would have been hurting a lot.'

The sole surviving parent of Bloody Sunday, Lawrence McElhinney, had suffered a heart attack and had been in hospital for a number of weeks. While his children emerged from the Guildhall to a crowd of thousands, he would learn of his son's innocence from a hospital bed.

Martin McGuinness had charged over to Guildhall Square to catch the families coming out. 'It was just an incredible day. Seeing the square thronged with citizens showed how much all of this meant to the people of Derry and all people over Ireland.'

Across the water, Mark Durkan addressed the House of Commons as MPs still reeled from the candour of Cameron's speech. Fulfilling his oath to the families, Durkan spoke with eloquence and great emotion, becoming visibly moved when reading out the names of those who had lost their lives on Bloody Sunday. 'The people of my city did not just live through Bloody Sunday; they have lived with it since.'

After his address, Durkan made his way out of the chamber to meet supporters and friends who were in the Gallery, along with the Irish Ambassador. 'There was a lot of acknowledgement from other MPs,' Durkan said later. 'Thumbs up, hugs, tears, arms gripped, hands shaken and sincere emotion voiced. John Kelly's son, Niall, said the hairs had stood on the back of his neck as he sat in the Gallery. I said to Niall that he must really miss not being in Derry because I did.'

For Solicitor Ciarán Shiels, the only disappointment was the finding on Gerry Donaghey. 'We established beyond doubt that Gerry was shot without any justification by Soldier G. But there remained that stain on his character. There is no Court of Appeal and there will be no rehearing of this issue. I think that we have come as close as we ever will.'

'I think 15 June 2010 will remain with me for the rest of my days, as it will with most people there,' Ciarán added. 'There hasn't been another case like it. Ever. It was an epic,' he says. 'I don't think we will ever see the likes of it again.'

Bishop Daly was also present for the publication. In his subsequent piece for the *Derry Journal*, he recalled: 'It was theatrical, spellbinding and hugely powerful. There was no triumphalism, no gloating – just sheer unadulterated joy and delight . . . I am filled with joy that the families and the injured have been so utterly vindicated. Their Trojan efforts in pursuance of justice and truth over so many years deserved such a result. They deserve the gratitude and admiration and respect of all of us. Widgery and his disgraceful findings, which caused so much hurt, have at last been consigned to the dustbin where they belong. It is a wonderful blessing to live to see this day.'

Jean Hegarty says: 'It's hard to know what Kevin would make of all this. He was only seventeen when he died, but I think he would be proud of us and proud that we fought on and on. There were times I doubted we would achieve it, but people like John Kelly never doubted it for one minute.'

NIO official Nadine Brown was also caught up in the emotion of the day. 'The most powerful moment for me was witnessing the families' reactions to David Cameron's statement in the Guildhall. When we heard the words "unjustified and unjustifiable", the tension lifted and the sense of relief was plain to see. The day left a lasting mark on everyone, and I hope the experience brings comfort to the families.'

Likewise, solicitor Patricia Coyle revelled in the families' vindication 'For me personally, the publication of the Saville Report in Derry was a very emotional day and marked the end of something very close to my heart. It was fantastic to see the families and wounded so happy and so relieved. They were phenomenal – they persevered with what must have felt like a great responsibility, not just to themselves but all involved. That must give great satisfaction to them now.'

Leo Young says: 'Cameron had no choice but to say what he did – it was so damning a report that the government had to accept it and admit to it. It's sad that there will never be another tribunal like the Bloody Sunday Inquiry, nobody else will ever reach those heights. This was unique in our lifetime.'

The McDaid family preferred to escape the cameras and crowds. 'That night I just sat with my wife talking about it all, was it real or was it not real?' Kevin says. 'We sat around, trying to let it sink in. The feeling of relief was brilliant.'

After the furore, Kay Duddy went straight to her twin sister, Bernie's house for a drink. 'When we were watching it on the news, the enormity of it all finally began to hit me. Kevin and I went to the Collon Bar for the quiz later that night for a bit of normality, and, when we walked in, we got a standing ovation. I cried!'

'The whole day was unbelievable,' says John McKinney. 'I think Derry has never seen a day like it since Dana came home from winning the Eurovision! But seriously, there was a fantastic feeling in the air, everyone was smiling and crying. The whole world was watching, and it was all worth it.'

'Thankfully, we were able to do everything our way,' Conal McFeely says. 'Many dedicated volunteers on the day deserve great credit: Colm Barton, Adrian Kerr, Dave Duggan, Eimear O'Callaghan, Paul McFadden, Raymond McCartney, Robin Percival, Maoliosa Boyle, everyone from the Pat Finucane Centre, Paul, Maggie and Geraldine and workers from E&I Engineering. There was so much going on, but everyone pulled together and it worked.'

Professor Dermot Walsh, who wrote the influential 1997 report, says that he feels 'profoundly humbled and privileged' to have been involved in the campaign. 'Looking to the future, I believe one of the most important and lasting legacies of Bloody Sunday will prove to be the example set by the victims' families. The dignity, determination and sheer humanity with which they pursued justice in the face of the most powerful and intimidating opposition will always shine like a beacon of hope and encouragement for oppressed individuals and communities throughout the world.'

While overjoyed at victims' exoneration, many family members still hope for full justice. 'We still have another step to take,' says Gerry Duddy – of soldiers being prosecuted 'We started this campaign with a set target and we're not at our target yet. We have one last aim to achieve. If we can even prosecute one soldier for Bloody Sunday, I'd be happy.'

Kevin McDaid shares Gerry's hopes, but doubts any soldier will ever serve time for Bloody Sunday. 'Not one soldier has done one second of time for killing my brother or the other thirteen people. We need the equality anyone else would get from the law.'

With emotions running high in Derry, few had time to consider the military pre-read in London or how soldiers may have reacted to the report's findings. Mark Durkan says that that not one soldier took up the offer to see Saville's findings in advance. 'As I understand it, only one soldier took their pre-read in the Ministry of Defence, and that was General Mike Jackson.'

Liam Wray recognises Saville's report as an important historical document. 'The great beauty of this inquiry is that this report will last for generations. That material gathered together is vitally important and in a sense, it immortalises the subject of Bloody Sunday and the victims and the truth is self-apparent.'

Teresa McGowan smiles broadly recalling how it felt to hear Daniel exonerated. 'It's sad that Danny wasn't there. It was the most wonderful day. I will never forget it. Now we can live with a lighter feeling.'

As evening descended on Derry, so did a distinct calm. Most of the families had long since left the city centre, but several still milled around, fulfilling an endless list of press and TV requests. It was almost midnight when Tony Doherty conducted the last interview of the day with a BBC reporter on a bastion of the city walls overlooking the Bogside. He believed the report in general to be 'heavy on innocence, light on blame . . . The apology was vital, but I didn't expect Cameron to use the words that he did. There's a palpable sense that we have experienced humanity at its worst and today, we have seen humanity at its best.'

'An Enduring Legacy'

'The heavens wept the day Barney was buried, and the sun shone the day he was cleared,' said Bridie McGuigan.

The dust had barely settled on Guildhall Square when a small group of families met the following morning to travel to Dublin to hand-deliver a copy of the report into Bloody Sunday to Taoiseach Brian Cowen.

In Derry, a second historic event was underway. Three Protestant church leaders, Bishop Ken Good, Church of Ireland Bishop of Derry and Raphoe, Reverend Norman Hamilton, moderator of the Presbyterian Church, and Methodist Church president, Reverend Paul Kingston, visited the Bogside and met with the Bloody Sunday families and wounded at the memorial. The church leaders presented the relatives with a replica of Derry's 'Hands Across the Divide' statue, by local artist Maurice Harron. They expressed their hopes that 'a cloud that has been hanging over this city for almost four decades has begun to lift.'

'We believe that the Saville Report presents a challenge and an opportunity for new and closer relationships within our wider community. Recognising the goodwill and the significant efforts already made by many people from all sides, we dare to believe that this can be a decisive turning point in reaching out to one another.'

Bishop Edward Daly was also in the Bogside the next morning and describes the presence of the other Christian church leaders as 'a sign of great hope for the future.'

The families were still digesting the events of the previous day. Many could still hardly believe what had transpired. Although it had taken years for their campaign to be recognised, Kay Duddy insists that 'it means such a lot that we didn't have to pass this on to another generation. With only one parent of Bloody Sunday left by then, it had already taken too long.'

'My father would have been in disbelief,' Caroline O'Donnell says. 'To walk around and not be seen as an IRA terrorist or a gun-man would have been brilliant. He had to live with that reputation all those years.'

'Was it worth it?' asks Liam Wray. 'Well, there has been no soldier prosecuted as yet, it certainly hasn't affected the career of General Michael Jackson, the architect of the cover-up. Colonel Wilford still has his OBE and his pension, and Soldier F and his cohorts have gone unpunished. Did we get justice from it? No. Will those responsible, in reality, ever be brought to book? I very much doubt it. Does that make me pull my hair out at night? No. The prime minister had to apologise, the Parachute Regiment will always carry that badge of shame. My hope was that the true epitaph of Bloody Sunday would be that our loss would affect these politicians and military people so much that it would never happen again. But judging by the news we see with the British army in places like Iraq and Afghanistan – that's the true sadness – that they haven't learned from any of it.'

'It just shows you what ordinary people can do if left alone with the will-power and the drive to do it,' says Joe Mahon. 'You have to admire them – people talk about the likes of Nelson Mandela and others, but the campaigners in Derry were fantastic. They don't even realise how much they achieved.'

However, while Joe believes the campaign was worthwhile, he recognises that the British army will probably never be punished for their crimes on Bloody Sunday. 'Will the army learn? They will learn, yes, but they'll learn the wrong reasons – they will learn to cover things up better. They'll learn no moral lessons from Bloody Sunday.'

'I already felt peace, but we needed to fix the official record,' says Regina McLaughlin, daughter of Gerard McKinney. 'The history books are claiming that these men were IRA men or terrorists. Now they have to put their records straight, because when we are dead and our children are dead, who would carry on and insist that those men were innocent? The history books needed to be rewritten now.'

John McKinney remembers the elation of fellow Derry people. 'Even the next day, when I was walking through the town with Tony, different people came over to us to shake our hands! It was a great feeling. That lasted for months. It felt as though a weight had been lifted from your chest after years and years. Saville may not have gone far enough, but the whole world now knows the British government were responsible for Bloody Sunday and that's what matters.'

For Geraldine Doherty and her family, the legacy of Bloody Sunday and Saville's report will be very different. Mary, Geraldine's mother, lost her battle with cancer on 3 November 2010, just as MPs began a debate on the Report in the Commons. Mary's passing was announced in the Houses of Parliament.

Geraldine reveals Mary's final wishes. 'A week before my mother died, she said to me "Geraldine, will you fight on?" and I said, "Of course I will." And I will. All I can do is keep highlighting Gerald's name and reminding people about his case. At least we got a declaration of innocence, and I'm just glad my mother was there to see it.'

Fellow campaigners have vowed to support the Donaghey family fully. 'In the campaign we were like Musketeers – all for one and one for all – and so if Geraldine wants to do something about Gerald she will have the backing of the families,' said Kevin McDaid.

'There's something else you have to remember, too,' says Eamonn McCann. 'Not nearly as much would have been achieved without an awful lot of people who are rarely mentioned, the weekend committee, for example. They had been organising the annual march and the various events around it for years, and they naturally came forward to organise, for example, the relatives' march to the Guildhall on the morning of publication and much else. In every campaign, there are always people working tirelessly and with little recognition in the background. The weekend committee came into that category and no account of the campaign is complete without them.'

Some months after the publication of the Saville Report, Bloody Sunday campaigners learned they had won the RTÉ 'People of the Year' Award. Several relatives travelled down to attend the glittering televised ceremony and accept the award. Singer Christy Moore performed a tribute, and film footage detailed the campaign and the emotional scenes in Guildhall Square. After so many years spent struggling for recognition, the families received a standing ovation south of the border.

In September 2010, families were also invited to Áras an Uachtaráin, where President Mary McAleese thanked the families and wounded for 'an absolutely outstanding contribution to the peace process.'

'Your resolve and your dignified determination inspired everybody and it made Ireland very, very proud of each and every one of you,' said the President.

With the Bloody Sunday Justice Campaign essentially at an end, many families have since lent their support to the Ballymurphy families in Belfast, whose lives were shattered by the Parachute Regiment just months before Bloody Sunday. The same group of paras murdered eleven unarmed civilians there in August 1971, the dead including a parish priest and a forty-five-year-old mother of eight. No investigation has ever taken place into the Ballymurphy Massacre. Their families fight on.

In Derry, thousands of relatives, survivors, campaigners and citizens marked a fitting finale to their struggle with a final Bloody Sunday Commemoration March in January 2011. Almost 30,000 took to the streets one last time. Unlike any year since 1972, the huge gathering was cause for shared relief and celebration. Never again need Derry folk congregate in Creggan to walk the long and winding route down Southway and on towards the Bogside.

The permanent legacy of Bloody Sunday, the Museum of Free Derry in Glenfada Park, continues to thrive. Plans to expand the museum are under way. It is now a member of the International Coalition of Sites of Conscience.

'We have attracted around 80,000 visitors since opening and the number's going up every year. We're very proud of it,' says Adrian Kerr. 'We tell the Free Derry story, and a huge part of that story is Bloody Sunday. You can't understand Bloody Sunday without putting it in context by presenting this community's history. That way, people can find out how and why it all developed the way it did. The whole point is to stimulate discussion.'

'The reaction has been fantastic, locally and internationally. It's telling the story in the way we want it told, what really happened rather than the media version of events.' Adrian is hopeful that Phase Two will be completed to coincide with Derry's City of Culture year, 2013.

'The museum is vital in telling the story of the campaign – it's like the final legacy – a central repository. Two of the museum's three employees lost brothers on Bloody Sunday, this shows exactly where the museum comes from and where it will remain.'

Recognising four decades of tireless journalism highlighting the issue of Bloody Sunday, campaigner and chair of the Bloody Sunday Trust, Eamonn McCann, was awarded two prestigious media awards. At the Guardian/Private Eye Paul Foot Awards in November 2010, he received a Special Lifetime Campaign Award. The following year, he received a human rights reporting award at the Amnesty International Media Awards, in recognition of his contribution to the public's awareness and understanding of human rights issues. Receiving his award, McCann paid tribute to the families of the Bloody Sunday victims. 'This award belongs to them', he said.

Lawyer Patricia Coyle also paid credit to Eamonn McCann for his steadfast commitment. 'Eamonn McCann was critical to that campaign, he never let the subject of Bloody Sunday lay still,' said Patricia. 'Even his monitoring of Saville is something which, I am sure, will become historically very important.'

With Saville's report complete, the Director of Public Prosecutions in Northern Ireland (DPP) and Crown Prosecution Service (CPS) in London are evaluating a potential case for soldiers' prosecutions for Bloody Sunday and for perjury before the Saville inquiry. For families, it is another waiting game.

Mickey Bridge still wants the military brought to book. 'It's still in my head and I can't shake it off – I don't want to see them walking free. I don't give a monkey's if they spend one day in jail – but I do want them put before a court. Then it will be over. After all, there's a man somewhere out there who killed at least four people – and he's walking around with a medal for his bravery. Where else in the world would that happen?'

Mickey McKinney agrees. 'Other relatives are content with the declaration of innocence, but I have a responsibility to my brother to seek justice and I feel it is not fulfilled yet.'

'The people who needed justice most are all dead and buried,' Kevin McDaid reflects. 'Only one parent was left by the time the report was finished. I saw what my mother and father went through, it was soul destroying to see over the years. They never had a life after Bloody Sunday; they just survived from day to day. You never saw my mother enjoying herself. It just wasn't fair that they weren't here when we finally got answers. Never in a million years did I think it would take this long.

'I think it's unfair that no other cases will get an inquiry as big as ours. There is a guilt complex there. There are dozens of families, in Derry alone who will never see justice for the death of their loved ones and I really think that these families should get together and seek justice collectively. We had people marching all over the world for our cause, and I fear that other cases won't get the same support, but maybe they could if they came together. . . .'

Martin McGuinness acknowledges the importance placed on Lord Saville's report by the people of Derry. 'The issue of Bloody Sunday has been a running sore in this city for over thirty-five years. It was something that had to be healed, and if the families are, in the main, satisfied with the outcome, then the people of Derry are satisfied.

'From my perspective, the heroes in all of this are the families and all those who were killed and injured on Bloody Sunday. The way the families rose to the challenge, and achieved all they did, is an immense credit to them,' McGuinness added.

Damian Donaghy believes it was all worthwhile. 'It was a long road, but it was worth it in the end. I would urge anyone to campaign if they were innocent – no matter where they are in the world – you have to stand up for justice.'

Olive Bonner agrees. 'I don't care who you are – Catholic, Protestant, Falls Road, Shankill Road, if you think your loved one was murdered you have a right to go and fight for justice for them. If other people see our campaign, they might say, "The Bloody Sunday crowd did it, and that was after forty years," and they would try themselves.'

Frances Gillespie is immensely glad the campaigners kept at it. 'You have to try, regardless of who you are, or what your religion is. You can't just sit back and talk about it.'

Don Mullan feels pride for the families and hopes they can now get on with their lives unencumbered. 'It has been a long struggle and it is an enduring legacy,' he says.

'I was very honoured and fortunate to be welcomed by them, and I genuinely believe that this is one of the greatest campaigns that any group of families any-where in the world has done. They changed history. They are a shining example of perseverance and their story should educate and inspire.'

Patricia Coyle, who now runs her own practice, HarteCoyleCollins, in Belfast is proud of her involvement in the campaign. 'As a native of Derry and a young lawyer, this case was a unique opportunity the like of which I will never experience again. For me, this remains the most important case I have ever worked on. It was an honour to work with the clients and campaigners and to make a contribution to the collective effort that was required to right the wrong.'

In Summer 2011, Lawrence McElhinney, father of Kevin and the last surviv-ing parent of Bloody Sunday, passed away peacefully at home a week short of his eighty-seventh birthday, after a brief battle with cancer. His passing was widely reported in Ireland, with tributes pouring in from politicians and citizens alike. Eamonn McCann described Mr McElhinney as 'the last of a heroic generation.'

Some months after Mr McElhinney's death, his daughters Jean Hegarty and

Roslyn Doyle discovered some interesting papers while sorting through his belongings. A handful of bank slips and documents suggested that the first generation affected by Bloody Sunday, the parents, and perhaps wives of those killed, had been active as a group – the Bloody Sunday Memorial Maintenance Fund – from at least 1976 until 1982. The discovery amazed Jean – she had no idea that their parents had been active more than sixteen years before the official justice campaign got underway. Nor, it seems, did anyone else. Roslyn, however, vaguely recalled some kind of group and that she had just passed her driving test and often taken her father to various families' houses. The primary aim of the early group was no doubt to fund and maintain the Bloody Sunday Memorial on Rossville Street, unveiled by Bridget Bond on 26 January 1974.

The healing power of the truth has been evident to many since 15 June 2010. 'Since the truth came out I can sleep easier in my bed at night,' Alana Burke says. 'Bloody Sunday is something that was imprinted in my head and will never go away, but that day in June should be a beacon for people all over the world who are struggling for justice, human rights and independence. Look what we came through – take heart from this and try.'

Eamonn McCann reflects on the successes of the campaign. 'It's kind of unusual for any campaign to be able to sit back and say, "we won". To win such acclaim and on the global scale we did, makes the time and work invested all worthwhile. I'm delighted to have been part of it. It's certainly one of the best things I've ever done in my life.

'Nothing mattered, as far as the families were concerned, as long as they won their loved one's innocence. In the process, however, they have become emblematic of the need for people to persist in campaigning for truth and justice. In the end, that might be the legacy of the Bloody Sunday Justice Campaign, the extent to which it enables people elsewhere faced with impossible odds to look at the Bloody Sunday campaign and say of their own campaign "Let's keep on – this might just fucking work."'

John Kelly says: 'Over the years, we've met with five secretaries of state, three Taoisigh, and been in touch with three different prime ministers. We got there in the end. We took them all on and we won. How we did it, I've no idea!'

Gerry Duddy reflects John's sentiments. 'People told us from the start that we were mad, but if we hadn't been mad, we would never have got where we are today. If we had listened to everyone around us, we would have cleared off years ago.'

'We moved a mountain,' says Mickey McKinney of the campaign's efforts. 'To sum it all up in one word – determination.'